POLITICAL AFFECT

CARY WOLFE, SERIES EDITOR

POLITICAL AFFECT

Connecting the Social and the Somatic

John Protevi

posthumanities 7

University of Minnesota Press
Minneapolis
London

See page 233 for information on previously published material reprinted in this book.

Published by the University of Minnesota Press
111 Third Avenue South, Suite 290
Minneapolis, MN 55401-2520
http://www.upress.umn.edu

Library of Congress Cataloging-in-Publication Data
Protevi, John
 Political affect : connecting the social and the somatic / John Protevi.
    p.   cm. — (Posthumanities ; 7)
Includes bibliographical references and index.
ISBN 978-0-8166-6509-9 (hc : alk. paper) — ISBN 978-0-8166-6510-5
(pbk. : alk. paper)
1. Political science—Philosophy. I. Title.
JA71.P77 2009
320.01—dc22   2009015506

Printed in the United States of America on acid-free paper
The University of Minnesota is an equal-opportunity educator and employer.

15 14 13 12 11 10 09   10 9 8 7 6 5 4 3 2 1

POLITICAL AFFECT

Connecting the Social and the Somatic

John Protevi

posthumanities **7**

 University of Minnesota Press
Minneapolis
London

See page 233 for information on previously published material reprinted in this book.

Published by the University of Minnesota Press
111 Third Avenue South, Suite 290
Minneapolis, MN 55401-2520
http://www.upress.umn.edu

Library of Congress Cataloging-in-Publication Data
Protevi, John
 Political affect : connecting the social and the somatic / John Protevi.
    p.   cm. — (Posthumanities ; 7)
Includes bibliographical references and index.
ISBN 978-0-8166-6509-9 (hc : alk. paper) — ISBN 978-0-8166-6510-5 (pbk. : alk. paper)
1. Political science—Philosophy. I. Title.
JA71.P77 2009
320.01—dc22   2009015506

Printed in the United States of America on acid-free paper
The University of Minnesota is an equal-opportunity educator and employer.

15 14 13 12 11 10 09   10 9 8 7 6 5 4 3 2 1

Contents

Preface

THIS BOOK complements my *Political Physics: Deleuze, Derrida, and the Body Politic* (2001). There, I used the notion of self-organization of material systems common in complexity theory, as well as the critique of hylomorphism that Deleuze and Guattari develop related to that notion, as a reading grid for certain episodes in the history of Western philosophy. To provide a focus for that book, I developed a concept of the "body politic" to mark the intersection of the social and the somatic and used it in order to contrast Derrida and Deleuze on basic epistemological and ontological issues. Whereas *Political Physics* was primarily concerned with tracing the effects of that concept in reading the philosophical texts of others, here in *Political Affect* I pluralize the notion to that of "bodies politic," and add to it several others ("political physiology" among them), with an eye toward using them in detailed case studies of the ways in which politics, psychology, and physiology intersect in socially embedded and somatically embodied affective cognition.

The notions of bodies politic and political physiology I develop here reflect a shift in contemporary philosophy, one I explored in *Political Physics:* the turn to a new, nonmechanistic materialism. As I argue at some length in that book, attaining the neomaterialist standpoint of Deleuze requires that we turn away from a postphenomenological stance in which the real is only a retrojected effect of entering signifying systems, a brute force that cannot be articulated but can appear only as a disturbance to a signifying field or to a consciousness. The rejection of that model of "force and signification" is complemented by the articulation of a Deleuzian neomaterialism that does not begin with consciousness (even a fragmented and internally hollowed-out consciousness) but which accounts for consciousness and for signification on the basis of a nonmechanistic and nondeterministic materialism underlying historically variable subjectification and signification practices. Such a neomaterialism allows for a productive engagement with contemporary scientific findings and, most important, for a productive engagement with political practice, as I argued with Mark Bonta in *Deleuze and Geophilosophy* (2004). This book attempts to cash in on some of that promise.

I have learned from many discussions on these issues with Manola Antonioli, Miguel de Beistegui, Chris Blakely, Rosi Braidotti, Andy Clark, Jon Cogburn, Amy Cohen, Claire Colebrook, William Connolly, Dan Conway, Manuel DeLanda, Ros Diprose, Rich Doyle, Kevin Elliot, Fred Evans, Peter Hallward, Mark Hansen, Eugene Holland, Len Lawlor, John Marks, Todd May, Philippe Mengue, John Mullarkey, Jeff Nealon, Paul Patton, Dan Selcer, Dan Smith, Charley Stivale, Alberto Toscano, Alistair Welchman, Bertrand Westphal, and James Williams.

I am grateful to the organizers and audience members at conferences and departmental talks at which I presented various versions of these ideas: at Birkbeck, Cologne, Edinburgh, Dundee, Duquesne, Limoges, Memphis, Penn State, the Society for Literature, Science, and the Arts (SLSA), the Society for Phenomenology and Existential Philosophy (SPEP), Staffordshire, Texas Tech, Trent (Ontario), Paris VIII, Vanderbilt, and Villanova. In writing this book I benefited from a summer research stipend from Louisiana State University's Council on Research; I am grateful for the extended study this grant allowed.

I am not a scientist or even a philosopher with much technical training in science, so I am very grateful that many people with those characteristics—among them, Alistair Welchman, Chuck Dyke, Ravi Rau, Phil Adams, and Vince LiCata—would help me with great patience and prompt replies. I thank them for their assistance and, as is the custom (and a good custom it is), resolve them of any blame for the clumsiness that remains.

I thank my research assistants, especially Ryanson Ku, Thomas Brasdefer, and Jane Richardson, and the anonymous reviewers of the manuscript, who provided many exceptionally penetrating comments. Roger Pippin was an excellent collaborator for part of what became chapter 6. The book was considerably improved by the comments of Cary Wolfe, series editor of Posthumanities, and Doug Armato, director of the University of Minnesota Press. More than that, it would not have been possible at all without their initiative.

Finally, along with my colleagues at Louisiana State University, I thank all my students who listened to what must have sometimes seemed mere rants as these thoughts came to me in fits and starts. I especially thank Robert Rose, who some time ago became a friend and colleague as well as a student.

Introduction

IN THE MOST GENERAL TERMS, this book investigates the imbrications of the social and the somatic: how our bodies, minds, and social settings are intricately and intimately linked. I do this by bringing together concepts from science, philosophy, and politics. I call this perspective "political physiology" to indicate not only this mix of intellectual resources but also in order to indicate that subjectivity is sometimes bypassed in favor of a direct linkage of the social and the somatic. For instance, we see a direct linkage in politically triggered basic emotions, such as rage and panic, and in direct political/medical control of physiological processes—an intense form of biopower, to borrow Foucault's term. I do not neglect the subjective level, however. In addition to treating instances in which the subject is bypassed, my treatment of affective cognition in social contexts also challenges both the exclusion of affect from cognition and the individualism of most treatments of the subject, insisting that subjectivity be studied both in its embodied affectivity and in terms of the distribution of affective cognitive traits in a population.

A central strand in the philosophy of mind has built up a picture of cognition as the emotionless capture and processing of information, that is, as representation. Today, however, some of the most interesting work in the field focuses on the role of emotion in cognition and/or challenges the notion of representation as the key factor in our knowing the world. It thereby challenges what we can call the "rational cognitive subject." But even these two challenging schools—affective neuroscience and the embodied-embedded mind, respectively—tend to presuppose an adult subject that is supposedly not marked in its development by social practices, such as gendering, that influence affective cognition. As there are many different gendering practices—as well as an indeterminate number of other kinds of practices influencing affective cognition—I propose that we need to turn to population thinking to describe the development and distribution of cognitively and affectively important traits in a population as a remedy to this abstract adult subject. In other words, to do philosophy of mind properly, we need to study the multiple ways in which subjects develop as a result of different social practices.

In pursuing this line of thought I develop three basic concepts—bodies politic, political cognition, and political affect—to examine the interlocking of the social and the somatic. The concept of bodies politic is meant to capture the emergent—that is, the embodied/embedded/extended—character of subjectivity, or in other words, the way the production, bypassing, and surpassing of subjectivity is found in the interactions of somatic and social systems. In bodies politic, the inherent relations of freedom and constraint, of individual and group, of subordination and hierarchy, make these systems amenable to political analysis; the regulation of material flows performed by these systems makes them objects of physiological study; and the triggering of qualitatively different feelings by those material flows, as well as the subtle negotiations of dynamic coupling of social emotions, makes them the object of psychological study. These networks of bodies politic are knitted together by the interlocking of processes that link the patterns, thresholds, and triggers of the behavior of the component bodies to the patterns, thresholds, and triggers of the behavior of the emergent superordinate (and sometimes transversal) bodies.

My analysis posits three compositional scales of bodies politic—personal, group, and civic—as well as three temporal scales—short-term, mid-term, and long-term. Borrowing concepts from Deleuze's ontology, which I will explain in chapter 1, on all these compositional and temporal scales, we see events as the resolution of the differential relations that structure a dynamic bio-social-political-economic field. These processes are crudely analogous to crystallization in a metastable supersaturated solution, with the important proviso that with bodies politic we are dealing with heterogeneous biological and social components. On the personal scale of political physiology, for example, we see the formation of a somatic body politic: the patterns and triggers of bodily action and reaction. On the group compositional scale, we see short-term events of concrete social perception and action, forming evental bodies politic, or, perhaps less barbarically named, social encounters. Finally, on the largest scale of political physiology, we see the formation of a body politic in the classical sense, what we will call a civic body politic: the patterns and triggers of institutional action.

We must be clear at the outset that these compositional and temporal scales are only analytical categories and that all concrete bodies politic operate by the imbrications of all scales. In principle and in fact, all bio-social-political events enfold all levels of political physiology, as a concrete encounter occurs in a short-term social context between embodied subjects formed by long-term social and developmental processes encoded in social custom and (today) increasingly regulated directly and indirectly by processes of governmentality and biopower. More precisely, since context is too static, a bio-social-political event, like all the emergent functional structures of political physiology, is the resolution of the differential relations of a dynamic field, in this case, one operating at multiple levels: civic, somatic, and group. (Once again, we see here the limits of the crystallization analogy: crystals form in homogeneous solutions, while political encounters coalesce in heterogeneous environments.)

I develop these concepts from a variety of scientific and philosophical sources, of which I provide a sketch in chapter 1. Because I draw on so many fields, this is by necessity a synthetic and at times a speculative book, not a definitive one. I am trying to construct a plausible account that gives the outlines for and provides some examples of the field of affective cognition in bodies politic. In order to do so in a book of reasonable length, I cannot provide detailed arguments on many subpoints. Thus, in several places I select a certain position from among many, but I do not defend it against its specialist critics. This is both the better part of valor (no one person can be a specialist in all these fields) and a necessity to keep the narrative going. I do try in the notes to refer to the main issues at stake. With all these lines at work, I hope this book will appeal to philosophers trained in either the continental or the analytic tradition. To do that I need to explain the jargon and common references of each field in ways that threaten to bore the experts and alienate the novices. I can only ask for patience and open-mindedness from my readers to help me navigate this strait.

The book has three parts, which correspond to the theoretical and practical study of politically shaped and triggered affective cognition. As a bridge, I discuss the implicit political theology of some instantiations in the history of philosophy of concepts of the organism.

Part I, "A Concept of Bodies Politic," begins in chapter 1 with a survey of the scientific and philosophical works that enable me to develop my basic concepts. I show how we are led to rethink the dominant picture of the rational cognitive subject by advances in a number of fields: dynamical systems modeling, what is commonly called "complexity theory"; the ontology of Gilles Deleuze and Félix Guattari; the autonomous systems theory proposed by Humberto Maturana and Francisco Varela; developmental systems theory (DST), a new development in biological thought; new research on human emotion; and the situated cognition school in cognitive science. Together, these advances allow us to situate subjectivity in a network of natural and social processes and practices. We thus are led below the subject to neurological and physiological processes that at least condition subjectivity, if not void it altogether in extreme cases; here, in some of the findings of the embodied mind school, we see the basis for a careful discourse on human nature grounded in such basic emotional patterns as rage, fear, and protoempathic identification. We are also led above the subject in considering the way we are embedded in social practices that inform the thresholds and triggers at which those basic emotions come into play. Finally, we are also led alongside the subject to phenomena of teamwork and technological supplementation of subjectivity (the extended mind thesis).

In chapter 2, I put all the resources examined in chapter 1 together in laying out the interrelations of our three basic concepts of bodies politic, political cognition, and political affect. The following formula captures their interaction: politically shaped and triggered affective cognition is the sense-making of bodies politic. The concept of bodies politic is meant to capture the emergent—that is, the embodied and the embedded—character of subjectivity: the production, bypassing, and surpassing of subjectivity in the imbrications of somatic and social systems. Individual bodies politic are cognitive agents that actively make sense of situations: they constitute significations by establishing value for themselves, and they adopt an orientation or direction of action. This cognition is co-constituted with affective openness to that situation; affect is concretely the imbrication of the social and the somatic, as our bodies change in relation to the changing situations in which they find themselves. I trace the relations among compositional and temporal scales of bodies politic, insisting that we overcome the tendency toward individualist thinking and embrace population thinking about the effects of multiple subjectification practices, so that subjectivity is studied in terms of the distribution of affective cognitive traits in a population.

Part II, "Bodies Politic as Organisms," has two chapters as well. Chapter 3 looks at Aristotle and Kant from the point of view of Deleuze and Guattari's notion of the organism as a body politic locked into imposed stereotyped patterns of politically shaped and triggered affective cognition produced by and in turn reproducing centralized and hierarchical social systems. In the mainstream of Western philosophy, the unity and teleologically ordered finality of nature as a whole and the organism as a microcosm of that unified whole have often been patterned on divine perfection and/or been brought about by God's plan. Deleuze and Guattari indicate the theo-bio-political register with their phrase the "organism is the judgment of God." In pursuing this reading, we must keep in mind that the organism in Deleuze and Guattari's sense is a hierarchically ordered body, a body whose organs are constrained to work for the benefit of the organism as an integrative and emergent whole that functions politically in the proper way, as determined by its role in a hierarchical social system. "Organism" is thus not a strictly biological term, but a term of political physiology, indicating the patterning of a somatic biological system by a hierarchical social system.

Chapter 4 examines Deleuze and Guattari's own treatment of the rigidly patterned organism and its counterpart, the "body without organs," which allows experimentation with patterns of bodily order. I provide readers with a guide to Deleuze and Guattari's somewhat bewildering terminology in order to clarify how the political genesis of capitalist subjectivity shown in *Anti-Oedipus* is placed into a naturalistic philosophy of great depth and breadth in *A Thousand Plateaus*. It was Deleuze and Guattari's work that led me to formulate the main concepts of the present work, and a detailed reading of their own conceptual formulations in the fields of political physiology and bodies politic will, I hope, show some of the roots, and hence untapped potentials, of this line of thought.

In Part III, "Love, Rage, and Fear," I examine three case studies of contemporary instances of politically shaped and triggered affective cognition as concrete imbrications of the social, the physiological, and the psychological. Again, it is vital to remember that although all compositional and temporal scales are active in all concrete cases, we can nevertheless identify one as most intense in each case. Thus, I examine the Terri Schiavo case in terms of the personal scale, the Columbine High School case in terms of the group scale, and the case of Hurricane Katrina in terms of the civic scale. Although I will develop a different emotional focus in each case (love in Schiavo, rage in Columbine, and fear in Katrina), to provide continuity across the analyses I concentrate on empathy as an important instance of affective cognition. Empathy—sometimes called, at least in its basic form, "emotional contagion," that is, an immediate emotional link between embodied beings—is biologically widespread, both in primates and in humans. Although such a protoempathic identification capacity is widespread, it needs to develop and hence needs the right genetic background and social environment, and it is therefore not present in all. Furthermore, even if present, it is most easily triggered by those in the in-group; its extension to others is thus fairly fragile and can be overridden by such social factors as political indoctrination and military training, which manipulate thresholds for rage and fear. Therefore, protoempathic identification is an aspect of political physiology, and as such, it is biological, yet susceptible to political manipulation.

In chapter 5, I examine how political institutions directly invest the organic life of Terri Schiavo without regard to consciousness or subjectivity, rendering it a simultaneously undead and obscenely mediatized body. By a horrible twist operating at the personal scale, Terri Schiavo's parents are trapped in a pseudoempathy triggered by phenomena of faciality; their love then conflicts with the love that Terri had for them and for her husband and that led her to express her wish not to receive tubal feeding. In chapter 6, I examine how the killers in the Columbine High School massacre maintain a cold rage, initiating the act of killing yet staying in enough control to carry out their plans. Here we see the scale of group dynamics in which protoempathic identification is overcome by quasi-military training, a freelance experiment in political physiology on the part of the killers. Finally, in chapter 7, I look at how a racialized fear contributed to the delay in government rescue efforts in Hurricane Katrina until sufficient military force could confront thousands of black people in New Orleans; the government's racialized fear flew in the face of the massive empathy of ordinary citizens, a communal solidarity that led them to rescue their friends, neighbors, and strangers until they were forced to stop by government order.

Figure 1 expresses these relations among the case studies. To reiterate the essential point: all the compositional and temporal scales are involved in each of the case studies, but in each case a particular scale achieves a point of highest intensity. Although a punctual event occurs in all three cases (the cardiac crisis of Terri Schiavo, the attack by Dylan Klebold and Eric Harris at Columbine, the storm and flood of Katrina), it comes largely without warning in the Schiavo case; in addition, the developmental/training and geosocial historical timescales assume an importance in the other cases that is relatively muted in the Schiavo case. This intensity can be different in different cases. In chapter 2 for example, we will analyze a case, relayed in an article by Francisco Varela, in which the compositionally per-

composition	personal	group	civic
body politic	somatic	transverse	governmental
highest intensity	Schiavo	Columbine	Katrina
relation to subject	below: subpersonal module	alongside: biotechnical assemblage	above: sociopolitical system
timescale	punctual event	habit/training	geosocial history
emotional focus	love	rage	fear
technical focus	medical/legal	military	geography

Figure 1. Relation of the compositional scale of bodies politic to various factors

sonal scale is most intensely marked by a mid-term developmental temporal scale, and the group compositional scale is marked temporally by a punctual event. Thus, we see the utility of the concept of *kairos*, or singular event, that gives us a heterogeneous time: some events are regular or ordinary, whereas others are singular, marking turning points in a system's history.

Part I   A Concept of Bodies Politic

Chapter 1   **Above, Below, and Alongside**
the Subject

THE INDIVIDUAL AS RATIONAL COGNITIVE SUBJECT is a deep-seated presupposition of many strands of philosophy. In this picture, the subject gathers sensory information in order to learn about the features of the world; processes that information into representations of those features;[1] calculates the best course of action in the world given the relation of those represented features of the world and the desires it has (whether the subject is thought to be able to change those desires through rational deliberation or not); and then commands its body and related instruments to best realize those desires given the features of the world it has represented to itself. We thus see cognition placed between perception and action in what Susan Hurley memorably called "the classical sandwich model of the mind" (Hurley 1998, 401). For many philosophers, the rational cognitive subject is what we are, or at least what we should become: it is the epistemological standard by which our judgments are measured and the ethical goal for which we should reach, for we are enjoined to act the way rational subjects would act were they to be in our situation.

On the other hand, for many other philosophers—of more or less leftist political orientation—this notion of the subject is at best ahistorical and apolitical, an arid abstraction from concrete life and at worst a sham, a tool for use in political oppression: "We're rational, you're emotional, so just shut up and do as we say." We can say that these philosophers go above the subject, locating it in a social field that at least constrains the field of its action but is often thought to more strongly constitute that subject through multiple and sometimes conflicting subjectification practices. To be more precise, as we will insist in chapter 2, above the subjective level we find a social field, itself multiple, which through its practices constitutes a field or population of subjects with varied affective and cognitive traits.

But it is not just politically active philosophers who call the rational cognitive subject into question. Recent approaches in cognitive science have squarely called into question the cognitivism of this picture of the subject and, to a lesser extent, its individualism. Philosophers have taken up these critiques of the individual cognitive subject in what they call variously the study of "embodied," "embedded," "extended," "enactive," and "affective" cognition; as a group, these philosophers can be said to pursue studies of 4EA cognition. Many of these critiques go below the subject to automatic, subpersonal, embodied cognitive and affective mechanisms. Many of these analyses, especially in studies of (socially) embedded and (technologically) extended cognition, also go alongside the subject to the immediately surrounding social and technical milieu or assemblage (this passage to the assemblage is what we will call transverse emergence). But, and this will be an important topic for us in chapter 2, the partisans of embedded and extended cognition rarely if ever thematize the social fields that structure and benefit from subjectification practices; that is to say, they rarely if ever submit to political analysis the fields within which different cognitive practices are developed, so I do not count them as going above the subject.

Bringing together the political and the 4EA critiques of the subject here, in *Political Affect*, I go above, below, and alongside the subject in examining politically shaped and triggered affective cognition: above to the social, below to the somatic, and alongside to the assemblage. In this endeavor I develop three basic concepts—bodies politic, political cognition, and political affect—to examine the interlocking of the social and the somatic; these imbrications sometimes, in the short term, bypass the subject and always, in the long term, constitute it. I develop my concepts from a variety of scientific and philosophical sources, each of which I will discuss later in this chapter: (1) the notion of emergence drawn from philosophical reflection on the scientific practices of dynamical systems modeling, what is commonly called complexity theory; (2) the ontology of Deleuze and Guattari; (3) the concept of autonomous systems proposed by the Chilean biologists and philosophers Humberto Maturana and Francisco Varela; (4) the eco-social take on biology known as developmental systems theory (DST); (5) a hybrid theory of emotion drawn from a variety of psychological and neurobiological approaches, with a particular focus on protoempathic identification or "emotional contagion"; and (6) the 4EA cognition school of philosophical work in cognitive science.

Complexity Theory

We have rich resources in complexity theory for overcoming individualism, especially the concepts of emergence and entrainment.[2] We should first note that working scientists do not use the term "complexity theory"; instead, they talk in terms of the mathematics used in modeling nonlinear dynamical systems. However, "complexity theory" does have some history of popular use, and it is considerably shorter to use than a more fully descriptive phrase. But its real utility for us is that it enables us to distinguish two fields within nonlinear dynamics: chaos theory and complexity theory. Chaos theory treats the growth of unpredictable behavior from simple rules in deterministic nonlinear dynamical systems, while complexity theory treats the emergence of relatively simple functional structures from complex interchanges of the component parts of a system. In other words, chaos theory moves from simple to complex while complexity theory moves from complex to simple.[3]

To explain how complexity theory studies the emergence of functional structures, we need to understand three sets of linked concepts: (1) in the system being modeled—range of behavior, fluctuation, patterns, and thresholds; (2) in the dynamical model—phase space, trajectory, attractors, and bifurcators; and (3) in the mathematics used to construct the model—manifold, function, and singularity. A phase space is an imaginary space with as many dimensions as "interesting" variables of a system; the choice of variables obviously depends on the interests of the modeler. The phase space model is constructed using a manifold, an n-dimensional mathematical object. The manifold qua phase space represents the range of behavior open to the system. At any one point, the global condition of a system can be represented by a point in phase space with as many values as dimensions or degrees of freedom. If you track the system across time, you can see the point trace a trajectory through the manifold/phase space, a trajectory representing the behavior of the system.

For some systems, you can solve the equation that governs the function represented by that trajectory; for other systems, you simply run a computer simulation of the model and see what happens. Often these simulations will show trajectories following a particular configuration. These shapes of trajectories are called attractors and represent patterns of behavior of the real system. There are various kinds of attractors: point (for stable or steady-state systems), loop (for oscillating systems), and strange or fractal (for turbulent or chaotic systems). Here we must make an important distinction: chaos—in the sense of chaos theory or complexity theory—is not the ancient cosmogony sense of chaos, which is now called a random system, one whose model produces no attractors. On the contrary, the models of what are now called chaotic systems do have attractors, albeit fractal ones. Although the behavior of chaotic systems is unpredictable in quantitative detail, it is sometimes predictable in the long run or qualitatively via the examination of the layout of attractors in the model.

The areas of phase space surrounding attractors—representing normal behavior of the system in one or another of its behavior patterns—are called basins of attraction. The behavior patterns described by attractors are, in highly complex (biological and social) systems, formed by the action of negative feedback mechanisms;[4] these are to be contrasted to positive feedback loops, which instead of returning a system to a homeostatic set point, set up runaway growth or decline, which often pushes the system to adopt another behavior pattern. Positive feedback loops are thus represented by bifurcators, which model the points at which systems jump from one pattern of behavior to another: that is, in model terms, they move from one basin of attraction to another. Positive feedback loops can also in some cases nudge a system to produce new behavior patterns, which would be represented by a new layout of attractors.

The layout of attractors and bifurcators in the phase space, which describes the layout of the patterns of behavior of the system, is defined by the layout of singularities, which are mathematical objects that define the topological structure of the manifold; a singularity is a point where the graph of the function changes direction as it reaches local minima or maxima or, more dramatically, where the slope of the tangent to the graph of the function becomes zero or infinite. A singularity in the manifold indicates a bifurcator in the phase space model, which in turn represents a threshold where the real system changes qualitatively. A singularity is not an attractor, but the distribution of singularities defines where attractors are found by indicating the limits of basins of attraction.[5]

When systems are poised at the edges of one of their behavior patterns (when they can't quite "make up their minds"), we find a zone of sensitivity in which minimal fluctuations—those that would otherwise be swallowed up by the negative feedback loops whose operation defines normal functioning of a system following one of its patterns of behavior—can now push the system to a new pattern or perhaps even to develop new behavior patterns. In modeling zones of sensitivity or crisis situations, we find fractal borders between basins of attraction, so that any move, no matter how small and no matter what direction, might—or might not—trigger the move to another basin of attraction or even to the creation of a new attractor layout. The most conservative explanation is that such systems are merely unpredictable rather than undetermined. In other words, "chance" is here just an epistemological term for the limits of our prediction; it is not ontologically grounded in the sense of allowing the system to escape from deterministic laws.

As we have said, what keeps complex bio-social systems inside a behavior pattern—represented by the trajectories inhabiting a basin of attraction—is the operation of negative feedback loops that respond to system changes below a certain threshold of recuperation by quickly returning the system to its pattern. These changes can be either endogenous fluctuations or responses to external events. Quickly recuperating systems are called stable. With regard to normal functioning, fluctuations or external events are mere perturbations to be corrected for in a stable system. Changes of a certain magnitude—beyond the recuperative power of the negative feedback loops or homeostatic mechanisms—will push the system past a threshold, perhaps to another pattern in its fixed repertoire or perhaps into a death zone, where there are no patterns but only static or chaos. Thus, some stable systems are brittle: they can be broken and die; some systems are resilient: a trigger that provokes a response that overwhelms its stereotyped defensive patterns and pushes the system beyond the thresholds of its comfort zones will result not in death but in the creation of new attractors representing new behaviors. We can call this learning, although of course there is a sense that the old system has died and the new one has been reborn.[6] (All sorts of questions of personal identity could be raised here.) Sometimes this creation of new patterns for a particular system repeats patterns typical of systems of its kind; we call this normative development. Sometimes, however, this change of patterns is truly creation: we can call this "developmental plasticity" (West-Eberhard 2003), or "diachronic" emergence (Morowitz 2002).

Emergence

To understand the production of interlocking bodies politic, we have to understand the phenomenon of emergence, the appearance of self-organizing systematic focus achieved by constraining the action of the components making up the system.[7] While the concept of emergence plays a crucial role in debates in philosophical reflection on science as a whole (the question of reductionism), as well as in the fields of biology (the status of the organism),[8] social science (the practical subject), and cognitive science (the cognitive subject), I will not deal at length with those debates in this book.[9] Instead, I will examine how the concept of emergence implicit in the philosophy of Deleuze and that of Deleuze and Guattari[10] can provide a vocabulary to frame my discussion of bodies politic, political cognition, and political affect. I define emergence as the (diachronic) construction of functional structures in complex systems that achieve a (synchronic) focus of systematic behavior as they constrain the behavior of individual components. "Synchronic" should be taken to mean "on a fast temporal scale," while "diachronic" should be taken to mean "on a slow temporal scale." The terms "fast" and "slow" are here relative to the characteristic temporal patterns of the systems under study; "synchronic" thus refers to the real-time performance of the system, while "diachronic" refers to the development of the system. Synchronically arising or developmentally appearing patterns are said to emerge when a system's feedback loops constrain the behavior of its parts so that a systematic focus of behavior becomes possible. In this way, the whole is greater than the sum of the parts.

Emergence is the contrary of mechanism; reductionists believe the latter to be the fundamental case. According to the reductionists, the behavior of the whole can be accounted for on the basis of the aggregated behavior of the parts, leaving no unexplained remainder. Reductionists in the social sciences are thus at least methodological and sometimes ontological individualists: they deny the efficacy or even the reality of positing collective entities such as social groups as anything more than collections of individuals. The debate between emergentists and reductionists is long-standing, extensive, and complex; we cannot hope to enter its details, but will content ourselves with adopting an emergentist perspective on pragmatic grounds. That is, we will try to see how adopting emergence enables us to construct our concept of political physiology and thereby to illuminate our case studies.

Emergentists have proposed as examples of emergent behavior phenomena that range from the physical to the social; the list of candidates includes lasers, chemical oscillators (Belousov-Zhabotinsky reactions), biological homeostasis (the ability of organisms to regulate their internal milieus), neurological firing (resonant cell assemblies), and social cooperation, as in military units or sports teams (although social groups will probably never be successfully modeled due to their forbidding complexity). Social groups can be either hierarchically stacked or dispersed in networks; the important point is to see that the real emergent effects of social groups belie both ontological and methodological individualism. Furthermore, even in hierarchies the physiological, subjective, and social are not just stacked on top of each other, but can be linked together in entrainment, the assumption of a common frequency, that is, the falling into step of previously independent systems. Entrainment is common in biological (J. Scott Turner 2000), interpersonal (Hendriks-Jansen 1996), social (McNeill 1995), and ecosocial systems (Haila and Dyke 2006); of most importance to us, entrainment in systems containing subjective/neurological components is arguably mediated by "mirror neurons" (Gallese 2001; Decety and Lamm 2006), which are thought by some to underlie empathy and are thus key mechanisms for linking the social and somatic in political affective cognition. (We will return to this point in more detail later in the chapter.)

The notion of emergence has the potential to help us rethink the "structure versus agency" or "freedom versus determinism" impasse that has beset much social science. Instead of being stuck with the all or nothing of free-atomic individuals and organic-determining societies, we can think below and above the subject: below to the myriad physiological and psychological processes whose interaction constitutes the subject, and above to the intermediate level of myriad social groups and networks whose emergent effects are real enough, but whose resonance and dissonance, whose coalescence and dissolution, never add up to a unitary, organic "social whole."[11] In this way, we avoid the microcosm/macrocosm analogy of somatic organism and organic social whole, what we will analyze in chapters 3 and 4 as "the judgment of God."

The concept of emergence entails reciprocal or circular causality. Upward causality is the emergence of systematic focused capacities (the parts of a system function in such a way as to provide for capacities of the system that the individual parts do not possess), and downward causality is the constraint on the behavior of component parts that enables systematic capacities (the whole exerts an influence on the parts that now have a reduced field of action).[12] Enormous mischief is created when downward causality is conceived as a type of efficient causality, that is, as localized interaction of individuated bodies, for system-level interactions can never meet the criteria of localization and individuation demanded by the notion of efficient causality when it comes to the relation of the system to its component parts. This is simply because when viewed from below, from the perspective of their component parts, systems are merely patterns of interaction of those components; this does not mean that systems are not themselves localized and individuated with regard to other systems.

Part of the difficulty in the controversies over circular causation is a widespread misunderstanding of efficient and final causes in Aristotle *Physics* 2.3, where, notoriously, Aristotle uses the poietic model of statue construction alongside a discussion of the biological phenomenon of development.[13] What we have come to call the efficient cause is the commanding origin of motion or development, in Aristotle's examples, the art of sculpting, the adviser to the ruler, or the father of a child. Even in the case of the sculpture, it is the art of sculpting that counts (*Physics* 2.3.195a8), not the hammer blows of the sculptor; it is not billiard ball causality, but the *archē metabolēs*, the foundational directing principle of the change (194b30, 195a20). The material cause, that from which the development occurs, offers only constraints; it does not positively contribute to the perfection of the final product. The best it can do is faithfully carry the form imposed by the efficient cause; at worst, the self-assertion of material inputs cause departures from type, in a certain sense perhaps even monstrosities, the "first step" toward which is the female (*Generation of Animals* 4.3.767b8).

The formal cause is the essential properties of the thing to be, and the final cause is the perfect state of development or end state of motion (*Physics* 2.3.194b32, 195a22). While the sculptor might have something in mind to guide his work, we need not impute purpose or intention to biological development. The final cause or end state channels development, but the infant does not consciously intend to grow into an adult. It is this notion of channeling toward an end state that is the key to understanding systematic constraint and focused behavior in synchronic emergent functional structures. We can even say that, strictly speaking, synchronic emergence is a misnomer, for there is always a coming into being of functional structures, even on a fast, real-time, temporal scale. All instances of emergence, fast or slow, can be conceptualized as a system being drawn toward a final cause in the sense of a channeling toward an end state; this channeling can be modeled by the approach of a trajectory to an attractor within a basin of attraction.

We can distinguish one other form of emergence in addition to synchronic emergence as reciprocal causality and diachronic emergence as the coming into being of novel functional structures. The third form is transverse emergence, the coming into being of assemblages formed from biological, social, and technical components. Transverse emergence can be analyzed either synchronically or diachronically. This third form of emergence will be of particular importance in our investigation of bodies politic, political cognition, and political affect.[14]

Deleuzian Ontology: The Virtual, Intensive, and Actual

In a series of very interesting works, Manuel DeLanda (1991, 1997, 2002) claims that Deleuze establishes the ontology of a world able to yield the results forthcoming in complexity theory.[15] In order to do so, DeLanda reconstructs Deleuze's ontology so that Deleuze's thermodynamic register is compatible with what is now known as complexity theory.

In *Difference and Repetition*, Deleuze works within a thermodynamic register to articulate a threefold ontological difference in which the intensive serves as a mediating register between the virtual and the actual. The virtual is a purely differential field, composed of differential elements, differential relations, and singularities. The actual is the set of stable substances endowed with sets of extensive properties and locked into stereotypical behavior patterns. The intensive is first encountered as the actual knocked off its tracks. Intensive processes are triggered by differences between a system and its environment such that the resultant matter/energy flow moves systems toward thresholds where their behavior patterns might change. Such a change of behavior patterns—not merely a change to a different behavior within an established pattern—is what Deleuze calls a "deterritorialization," a "line of flight," or a "becoming."

The virtual realm is not an undifferentiated chaos, but is articulated by "Ideas" or "multiplicities" that serve as regional ontologies, laying out the many ways in which a society, a language, an animal, and so forth, can exist. An Idea is a set of differential elements, differential relations, and singularities. Ideas structure the intensive processes that give rise to the behavior patterns of systems, and they mark the thresholds at which systems change behavior patterns. In a word, the virtual is the transformation matrix for systems. Systems are determinate solutions to the problem that lays out the manifold options for incarnating bodies of that nature. As we have seen, singularities are turning points of systems; they are remarkable points as opposed to ordinary ones. They present us with a naturalized notion of the term *kairos*, or special event, and necessitate a notion of heterogeneous time: what Deleuze will call Aion to distinguish it from the Chronos of homogeneous time. This mathematical sense of singularity should be distinguished from the logical sense of singularity in which the unique is distinguished from the generic. We can combine them by saying that a mathematical singularity indicates a threshold whereby a logically unique or singular system changes behavior patterns.

The self-differentiating process by which Ideas spread throughout the virtual, as the possible ways of being of different formations become more complex, is named differentiation by Deleuze, in contrast to differenciation, which names the process of actualization: for example, the incarnation of the Idea of a society in one particular actually existing society.[16] The series of singularities in an Idea are arranged in inclusive disjunctions, so that they are compossible, even those that when actualized would be incompossible, that would preclude each other. Thus actualization or differenciation is the construction of exclusive disjunctions, the selection of a series of singularities whose actualization precludes the simultaneous actualization of others, which would then have the modal status of the (virtual) road not taken.

While the virtual/actual distinction is primary in *Difference and Repetition,* in *A Thousand Plateaus,* Deleuze and Guattari hold that the virtual and actual are only limits or end points of tendencies; all that exists are systems displaying intensive properties that asymptotically tend toward one end point or the other. In other words, high-intensity systems tend toward virtual fluidity, and low-intensity systems tend toward actual fixity. The virtue of DeLanda's *Intensive Science and Virtual Philosophy* (2002) is to articulate this thermodynamic register with contemporary complexity theory. As we have seen, complexity theory models material systems using the techniques of nonlinear dynamics, which by means of showing the topological features of manifolds (the distribution of singularities) affecting a series of trajectories in a phase space, reveals the patterns (shown by attractors in the models), thresholds (bifurcators in the models), and the necessary intensity of triggers (events that move systems to a threshold activating a pattern) of these systems. By showing the spontaneous appearance of indicators of patterns and thresholds in the models of the behavior of complex systems, complexity theory enables us to think of material systems in terms of their powers of immanent self-organization and creative transformation.

In DeLanda's reconstruction of Deleuze, the distinction of virtual and actual is a modal distinction, indicating the difference between long-term tendencies and momentary states of systems. Virtual Ideas provide for the tendencies or patterns of behavior represented as attractors in phase space portraits of systems; other structures of the virtual realm are bifurcators, represented by singularities, which indicate the borders of basins of attraction, that is, the thresholds at which systems change patterns of behavior and sensitive zones, those areas between basins of attraction. Actual systems are disturbed or driven to their thresholds or sensitive zones by intensive differences, provoking qualitative change in their behavior patterns, while virtual multiplicities account for the structure of these morphogenetic processes. Throughout, the antiessentialism of Deleuze comes forth, as the focus is on the structures of the process of production of substances rather than on the properties of those substances, once formed.

Diachronic emergence, or creativity in the production of new patterns and thresholds of behavior, is what Deleuze will call an "event," which is not to be confused with a mere switch between already established patterns or with the trigger, or external event, that pushes the system past a threshold and produces the switch. The Deleuzian event, also known as counteractualization, repatterns a system. The key to the interpretation of Deleuze in DeLanda 2002 is that the virtual is the realm of patterns and thresholds: in other words, Ideas structure the intensive morphogenetic processes that produce actual systems and their behaviors. A behavior pattern, or a threshold at which a behavior pattern is triggered, needs to be ontologically distinguished (or modally distinguished) from behavior, just as singularities are distinguished from ordinary points on the graph of the function.[17] Thus, patterns and thresholds are virtual whereas behaviors are actual. An event, in creating new patterns and thresholds, restructures the virtual.

To sum up this all-too-brief sketch of Deleuze's ontology, we find the three basic categories are patterns, processes, and thresholds: actual states or habitual patterns of behavior, intensive processes producing those states or patterns, and virtual singularities marking the thresholds at which processes producing states or patterns shift. Deleuze expresses this threefold ontology in a formula: beneath the actual (any one state of a system) we find impersonal individuations (that is, intensive morphogenetic processes that produce system states), and beneath these we find preindividual singularities (that is, the key elements in virtual fields, marking system thresholds that structure the intensive morphogenetic processes).

Some examples will help us see the interest and power of this ontology. Take a sports match and freeze the action to arrive at the actual. The state of the players in the game would yield extensive properties (they are so many meters apart, the ball is at XY coordinates relative to the goal, etc.).

But that state was arrived at via concrete moves, which are intensive processes in which certain thresholds can be attained (when the player with the ball gets close to the goal, the condition of the game changes qualitatively, as also happens with certain goal differences, etc.). In other words, a move in a game is an impersonal individuation that yields a temporary shape of the game, a determinate relation of differential forces. Finally, the sport—of which the match is an actualization—is an Idea, a set of differential relations with singularities as its borders, that is, places where you can either change the internal configuration of the sport by the addition of a new technique or change to another sport by changing the relations of possible moves. (If, in addition to being able to kick the [soccer] ball, you are able to pick it up with your hands but pass it only backward, you have rugby; allow the forward pass as well as the lateral and the kick, and you have American football.)[18]

For a second example, you could take adult fixed-personality structures as actual, socialization practices as intensive processes or impersonal individuations that produce personality (in conjunction with the endogenous potentials of the child subjected to the practices) and the Idea of society as a virtual differential field (the set of relations of practices) with preindividual singularities as turning points for the production of one society or another.

In a third example, the virtual would be the nervous system state space, a set of differential relations of possible firing patterns whose possible layouts are marked off by pre-individual singularities. In more detail, we can see the embodied and embedded nervous system as a pre-individual virtual field: (1) a set of differential elements (reciprocally determined functions—in other words, neural function is networked: there is no such thing as the function of "a" neuron; some argue the same for higher-level cognitive processes, that they emerge from global brain activity and hence cannot be understood in isolation); (2) with differential relations (linked rates of change of firing patterns); and (3) marked by singularities (critical points determining turning points between firing patterns). The dynamics of the system as it unrolls in time are intensive processes or impersonal individuations, as attractor layouts coalesce and disappear when singular thresholds are passed. Learning, then, is the development of a repertoire of stable and recurrent firing patterns, and any one decision is an actualization, a selection from the virtual repertoire (the coalescing of a singular firing pattern); this is modeled by the fall into a particular basin of attraction from the attractor layout "proposed" by system dynamics. Counteractualization is the reshuffling of potentials for firing patterns, not merely the move from one firing pattern to another.

Two implications of these notions need to be noted. First, it may be possible to improve the ontology Deleuze has established, but I do think it will serve as a constraint on future ontologies in that future ontologies must account for the features of the world accounted for by Deleuze's ontology. Second, although Deleuze is a realist, he is not an essentialist. He is a realist with regard to what he calls the virtual, which means that he doesn't believe surveying the properties of substances to identify essences as a finite set of necessary and sufficient conditions for membership in a category is a fruitful way of doing philosophy. Rather, for Deleuze, we should look to the virtual to see the structures of production processes instead of looking to the properties of products to identify essences. Two of DeLanda's favorite examples to illustrate this point are the soap bubble and the salt crystal. Focusing on the geometric properties of their actual, final, produced form would have you gathering soap bubbles with other spheres and salt crystals with other cubes, but focusing on the intensive morphogenetic processes of their production would lead you to the topological properties of their phase space models, and there you would discover they both display point attractors. Thus soap bubbles and salt crystals belong together in the "machinic phylum" (Deleuze and Guattari 1987, 406) of processes searching for minimal free energy (DeLanda 2002, 15).

Once we have clarified these points, we are in a position to appreciate five main benefits to the DeLandean approach of reading Deleuze as providing the ontology of a world of complex dynamic systems. (1) It provides common ground for a discussion among analytic and continental philosophers concerning the philosophical implication of the widespread scientific use of nonlinear dynamical modeling, especially in an area of special interest to philosophers, brain studies.[19] (2) It provides for a critique of hylomorphism, the notion that matter is chaotic or passive and so in need of rescue (by means of the laws of God, or a transcendental subject, or the scientific project) to provide it with order or novelty.[20] (3) We can thus avoid the issue of reduction to physics, the science whose laws predict the behavior of matter at its simplest.[21] (4) Furthermore, by modeling the negative and positive feedback mechanisms characteristic of complex systems, complexity theory thereby enables us to ground the concept of emergence in the effects of such mechanisms (Silberstein and McGeever 1999, 197). (5) Finally, we are able to dispense with the false problems that arise in trying to think of the downward causality of emergence in terms of efficient causality by showing that the constraints of a pattern, described by an attractor, are not a case of efficient causality, which relies upon localized and individuated agents, but instead need to be thought of as a "quasi-cause."[22]

Varela: Sense Making in Autonomous Systems

Bodies politic, although embedded in a co-constituted ecosocial environment, are still bodies: they have an individuation, a self-reference. To reflect their individuation, we can say that they are "autonomous systems."

To understand this last term, we need to turn to Francisco Varela, whose work is a monumental achievement in twentieth-century biological and bio-philosophical thought. After his early collaboration in neocybernetics with Humberto Maturana (autopoiesis), Varela made fundamental contributions to a wide range of fields, among them immunology (network theory), Artificial Life (cellular automata), cognitive science and philosophy of mind ("enaction" and "neurophenomenology"), neuroscience (resonant neural assemblies and large-scale integration), and East-West dialogue (the Mind and Life conferences). In doing so, Varela influenced many important collaborators and interlocutors, as well as formed a generation of excellent students and touched the lives of many with the intensity of his mind and the strength of his spirit (Rudrauf et al. 2003).

For Maturana and Varela, autonomous systems have sufficient internal complexity and feedback that coupling with their environment triggers internally directed action. This means that only those external environmental differences capable of being sensed and made sense of by an autonomous system can be said to exist for that system, can be said to make up the world of that system (Maturana and Varela 1980, 119). The positing of a causal relation between external and internal events is possible only from the perspective of an observer, a system that itself must be capable of sensing and making sense of such events in *its* environment (81).

To understand the embodied nature of bodies politic, we have to see the biological basis of the judgments "good" and "bad."[23] This basic value polarity is well noted in affective neuroscience and is in fact grounded in basic organic capacities for affective cognition. Witness the single-celled organism's ability to make sense. "Sense" has, perhaps fittingly, a threefold definition: sensibility, signification, and direction. (There is an archaic use of the English word "sense" meaning "direction," as in "the sense of the river." This sense is still present in French, as in, among other uses, the expression *sens unique* for "one-way street.")[24] A single-celled organism can sense food gradients (it possesses sensibility as openness to the environment), can make sense of this difference in terms of its own needs (it can establish the signification good or bad), and can turn itself in the right sense for addressing its needs (it orients itself in the right direction of movement). This fundamental biological property of sense-making or affective cognition is one reason why the Cartesian distinction of mental and material has no purchase in discussions of sense-making. There is no mental property (in the sense of full-blown reflective consciousness) attributable to the single-celled organism, but since there is spontaneous and autonomous sense-making, there is no purely material realm in these organisms either. Affective cognition in humans is simply a development of this basic biological capacity of sense-making.[25]

Autonomous systems, attractor formation, reciprocal or circular causality, and diachronic emergence play major roles in two treatments that are important for our theory of sense-making or affective cognition in bodies politic. The traditional complaint about materialist theories is that they cannot account for human action, or better, that they cannot account for the feeling of freedom we have; if materialism implies mechanistic determinism, then that feeling of freedom is illusory. The solution to this problem is to critique the presupposition of mechanistic determinism upon which it relies and substitute the notion of the brain-body-environment assemblage (the body politic in our terms) as a complex dynamical system capable of intentional action.

We find support for this move in Walter Freeman, who offers a dynamic systems account of the neurological basis of intentional behavior (Freeman 2000a, 2000b), and in Alicia Juarrero, who uses the concept of dynamic systems to intervene in philosophical debates about decisions and intentional action (Juarrero 1999). The basic notion in their accounts is that nervous system activity is a dynamic system with massive internal feedback phenomena, thus constituting an autonomous system in Varela's terminology. Neural firing patterns, blending sensory input with internal system messages, emerge from a chaotic background in which subliminal patterns compete with each other for dominance. Once it has emerged victorious from this chaotic competition and established itself, what Varela 1995 calls a "resonant cell assembly" (RCA) forms a determinate pattern of brain activity that can be modeled as a basin of attraction. Over time, the repetition of a number of such patterns provides a virtually available response repertoire.

In these theories, intentions are seen as grounded in neural patterns. The autonomous nervous system constrains the path of future firings as long as the pattern or RCA lasts. (Some intentions entail long strings of firing patterns, yielding coherent complex behavior, as in the intention to play a game of basketball.) Sensory input continually feeds into the system along the way, either reinforcing the settling into a pattern or shocking it out of a pattern into a chaotic zone in which other patterns strive to emerge. Decisions are precisely the brain's falling into one pattern or another, a falling that is modeled as the settling into a basin of attraction that will constrain neural firing in a pattern. There is no linear causal chain of input, processing, and output. Instead there is continual looping as sensory information feeds into an ongoing dynamic system, altering or reinforcing pattern formation; in model terms, the trajectory of the system weaves its way in and out of a continually changing attractor landscape whose layout depends upon both the recent and the remote past of the nervous system.

Developmental Systems Theory: Embodied and Embedded Biology

In recognizing the embodied individuality of bodies politic, we shouldn't overemphasize their autonomy (that way lies the "organism as judgment of God," as we will see in chapters 3 and 4), but we must also recognize their embeddedness. By the same token, we cannot think of embedded bodies politic as mere input/output machines passively patterned by their environment (that way lies a discredited social constructivism) or passively programmed by their genes (an equally discredited genetic determinism). To prevent us from thinking of embedded bodies politic in terms of such passive and mechanical devices patterned by transcendent forces, we turn to two schools of thought in contemporary critical biology: developmental systems theory (DST), taken from the writings of Richard Lewontin (2002), Susan Oyama (2000), Paul Griffiths and Russell Gray (1997, 2001, 2004, 2005), and others, and the developmental evolutionary biology of Mary Jane West-Eberhard (2003). With the help of this new critical biology, we can see the body politic as biologically open to its cultural embedding. We thus see another instance of a move in contemporary critical science away from a transcendent source of order—that is, away from a hylomorphic schema—toward an immanent, distributed system of self-organization, a move whose implications for certain classical positions in the history of philosophy I analyzed in Protevi 2001.

DST is primarily a reaction to genetic determinism or reductionism. In discussing these topics, we have to remember that the model of them I'm presenting here is indeed a straw man for biologists, but unfortunately (and for many social-political reasons), it has become—and remains—the standard popular view in mainstream media and in the minds of most educated but not specialized people (Keller 1996, 2000). In other words, it may be that the crude ideas presented here never existed in the writings of real biologists, as opposed to being popular misconceptions right from the start, just as, for example, nothing like "postmodernism" as some scary nihilism about the impossibility of meaning or reference ever existed except as a misunderstanding right from the start.

In any event, genetic determinism is an ontological thesis proposing that genes are the sole source of order of (that is, they determine) physiological and developmental processes, beginning with protein synthesis and extending upward to organic, systemic, and organismic processes. No one has ever upheld such an absolute position if by that one means epigenetic conditions have no influence whatsoever, that developmental and physiological processes are determined the way a stone is determined to fall by gravity. The real target of critique by DST thinkers is the idea that there are two classes of developmental resources, genetic and epigenetic, and that genes provide the information or blueprint or plan or program, such that the epigenetic resources are the materials or background upon which and/or in which genes act (Oyama 2000; Griffiths and Gray 2001, 2004). The real question of so-called genetic determinism, then, is the locus of control rather than absolute determination.

Genetic reductionism is an epistemological issue. It's my impression that many practicing biologists think of reductionism as asking this question: Can the portion of physiology and development due to genetic control be considered separately from the portion due to epigenetic influences?[26] The DST response to this question is known as the "parity thesis" (Oyama 2000; Griffiths and Gray 2001, 2004), which rests upon the idea that there is a distributed system with both genetic and epigenetic factors (e.g., at least cell conditions and relative cell position) that controls gene expression and protein synthesis. It's a mistake, however, to attribute portions of control to components of that system, such that one could isolate the portion of genetic control. That would be analogous to saying that prisoners are partially under the control of the guards, when it would be better to say they are under the control of the prison system in which guards play a role (alongside architectural, technological, and administrative components). In the view of Griffiths and Gray, the undeniably empirical differences in the roles played by DNA and by non-DNA factors do not support the metaphysical decision to create two classes of developmental resources or the additional move to posit genes as the locus of control and epigenetic factors as background, as matter to be molded by the information supposedly carried in genes (Griffiths and Gray 2001, 2004).

A second key notion for DST thinkers is "niche-construction." Rather than seeing evolution as the adaptation of organisms to independently changing environments (the organism thus being reactive), DST follows Richard Lewontin (2002) and others in focusing on the way organisms actively shape the environment in which they and their offspring will live. They thus play a role in selecting which environmental factors are most important for them and their offspring. Evolution should be seen not simply as the change in gene frequency (a mere bookkeeping perspective) but as the change in organism-environment systems, the organism in its constructed niche (Griffiths and Gray 2005).

Allied with niche-construction, a third key notion of DST is that the life cycle should be considered the unit of development and evolution. For DST adherents, the developmental system considered in an evolutionary perspective is the widest possible extension of developmental resources that are reliably present (or better, re-created) across generations. The life cycle considered in an evolutionary perspective is the series of events caused by this developmental matrix that recurs in each generation (Griffiths and Gray 1997, 2001, 2004). (The evolutionary perspective on developmental system and life cycle is thus different from the individual perspective, where events need not recur: a singular event might play a crucial role in the development of any one individual, but unless it reliably recurs, it will not have a role in evolution; DST thus avoids the specter of Lamarckism.) In their evolutionary thinking, DST thinkers thus extend the notion of epigenetic inheritance from the intranuclear factors of chromatin markings to the cytoplasmic environment of the egg (an extension many mainstream biologists have come to accept) and beyond to intra-organismic and even (most controversially) to extrasomatic factors, that is, to the relevant, constructed, features of the physical and social environments (for example, normal [i.e., species-typical] brain development in humans needs language exposure in critical sensitive windows) (Griffiths and Gray 1997, 2001, 2004; Jablonka and Lamb 2005).

Such a maximal extension of the developmental system raises the methodological hackles of many biologists, as it seems suspiciously holistic:

Sure, they might say, we can see how in principle it's the entire universe that contributes to the precise details of individual development, but that's no way to run a science. Where are the principles by which you identify the dependent and independent variables necessary for good experimental design? First, comes the DST reply, we must distinguish between individual development, which includes singular events, and population-centered development, with its reliably recurrent features, which is the evolutionary perspective (Griffiths and Gray 1997, 475). Second, with regard to the selection of variables for experimental design from the infinitely complex causal web impinging on any phenomenon, there are no such principles, a DST biologist might reply, but that doesn't mean we can't provisionally and self-critically design experiments that isolate one or another factor, as long as we realize that such experimental design is an abstraction for a particular purpose from the concrete reality of nature.

Furthermore, the reply might continue, in doing so, we're not doing anything different from any self-critical scientist who wishes to avoid the trap whereby one's methodology unconsciously becomes one's metaphysics (480). In other words, standard scientific practice requires the isolation of factors to establish a relation of dependent and independent variables. But the production of such a linear relation of dependent and independent variables almost always requires an intervention into a nonlinear system (i.e., one with complex feedback loops) that in effect creates an artificially simplified system of study. The development and transmission of such scientific practice is a monumental cultural achievement; all one can ask is that one realizes that the creation of the simple system to be studied is just that, a creation or abstraction from concrete complex reality.

These methodological reflections remain among the most controversial in contemporary philosophy of science and are intimately tied in to the notion of dynamical systems theory we discussed previously (i.e., that linearity is the special case of generalized nonlinearity). It would take us too far afield to explore fully all the implications of these debates, but we can see them as well in the background of the notions of developmental plasticity and environmental co-constitution found in West-Eberhard 2003. That the development of organisms is plastic and co-constituted with its environment means that it is not the simple working out of a genetic program. Rather, development involves a range of response capacities depending on the developing system's exposure to different environmental factors, just as those responses feed back to change the environment in niche-construction. Thus the notion of developmental plasticity displaces gene-centric notions of programmed development just as organism-environment co-constitution displaces notions of gene-centric natural selection in favor of a notion of multiple levels of selection.

We cannot enter the details of the controversy surrounding the notion of multiple levels of selection here (Jablonka and Lamb 2005), but it seems a most interesting way of thinking of evolution would be to think of the "modular sub-units" involved in phenotypic plasticity proposed by West-Eberhard 2003 (above the gene, but below the level of the organism) along with the notion of the reliable repetition of co-constructed organism-environment niches or life cycles (including parental and social environments, thus above the level of the organism) proposed by DST. This would take us below and above the level of the organism—below to the embodied unconscious physiology and above to ecosocial embeddedness—just as the study of politically shaped and triggered affective cognition takes us below and above the level of the subject. While we cannot enter the details of the relation of developmental evolutionary biology (West-Eberhard's term, which she prefers to the usual "evolutionary developmental biology," or "evo-devo") and DST (see Robert, Hall, and Olson 2001; Griffiths and Gray 2005), we can at least note that the key notion of DST is that the unit of selection in evolution is the life cycle of the organism in its ecosocial embeddedness; in other words, DST's notion of the life cycle is also a thought of the assemblage, a biological complement to the embeddedness of situated cognition (Griffiths and Stotz 2000).[27]

As we have noted, my approach in investigating the subjective aspect of political affect in terms of subjectification practices is not hylomorphic or pure social constructivist. As we will see in chapter 4, I accept that the infant is not a pure blooming, buzzing confusion, with no way to register somatic boundaries, but has an innate body schema enabling self-other differentiation (Gallagher 2005), just as I accept that normal development entails the emergence of certain "innate cognitive models" involving "moral intuitions," or a gut feeling of what is right or wrong (Haidt 2001; Hauser 2006). The acceptance of certain innate features need not underplay the political when we remember the emphasis critical biology places on the life cycle, developmental plasticity, and environmental co-constitution. When we follow these thinkers and replace "innate" with "reliably produced given certain environmental factors," we have room to analyze differential patterns in societies that bring forth important differences from common endowments. We can then say in analogy with these critical biological points that the development of a body politic is not simply the working out of a disciplinary program. In other words, we do not genetically inherit a self, though a self-other distinction based on a body schema reliably develops early given the standard sort of intrauterine and neonatal environment (Gallagher 2005); we don't genetically inherit a subject, but we do inherit the potential to develop a subject when it is called forth by cultural practices. The various types of subject called forth (the distribution of cognitive and affective patterns, thresholds, and triggers in a given population) are analyzed in the study of politically shaped and triggered affective cognition.

A Hybrid Theory of Emotions

The interdisciplinary study of emotion has undergone a renaissance in the last two decades. In particular, the neuroscientific study of emotion has exploded onto the intellectual scene, changing our understanding of emotion, cognition, and consciousness. Although no single name has caught on for this interdisciplinary field, we could propose "affective science" as an analogy with "cognitive science" or perhaps better—to indicate the plurality of disciplines involved—"the affective sciences," just as we sometimes see "the cognitive sciences."

Among the many fields involved in the affective sciences, affective neuroscience studies the neurobiological processes underlying the production of the physiological changes and, more speculatively, the phenomenological experience of various emotions (Damasio 1994, 1999, 2003; LeDoux 1996; Panksepp 1998). A subfield of affective neuroscience is the cognitive neuroscience of emotion (Lane and Nadel 2000), which attempts to find the neurological correlates of appraisals or evaluative judgments that identify the content of emotions, that is, the "actual or imagined state of affairs in the world that corresponds to that emotion" (Griffiths 2004, 144). Cognitive psychologists have proposed numerous typologies of emotion and have posited various mental operations of appraisal. Among the many other scientists in fields involved in the affective sciences are anthropologists, who study the cultural range of emotional performance, and developmental psychologists, who study the development of emotional capacities in infants and children.[28] In debating the merits of particular theories of emotion in affective and cognitive neuroscience, as well as those of cognitive psychological theories, philosophers now interrogate the epistemological and ontological status of emotion (Griffiths 1997; Hatzimoysis 2003; Solomon 2004; Prinz 2004); they also are rethinking empathy and social cognition (Thompson 2001; Stueber 2006; Ratcliffe 2007) as well as moral judgment (Greene and Haidt 2002; Greene 2003; Hauser 2006). We should take particular note of recent essays (Griffiths and Scarantino 2009; Colombetti and Thompson 2007) that propose to study emotions in terms of the "embodied-embedded" and "enactive" schools, respectively.

In constructing a theory of emotion from the current state of the affective sciences that will be useful for our investigation of politically shaped and triggered affective cognition, we present what is perforce an extremely condensed schematic treatment. We begin with a distinction between basic emotions (all lists of basic emotions include at least anger and fear, upon which we focus; in extreme cases these operate as "affect programs"—that is, fast-acting, preprogrammed, and automatic behavior modules)[29] and the higher, or cognitive emotions, such as guilt, shame, jealousy, and so on. These are slower to develop, involve judgments as to states of affairs, and offer opportunities for conscious control of behavior, if not control of feeling.

We now need to recognize two debates within the affective sciences. The first dispute is whether there are universal emotions found in all cultures, or whether there are only superficial similarities between ranges of culture-specific emotions, a social constructivist position.[30] Upholders of universalist positions in this debate sometimes call upon evolutionary psychology, which maintains that all or at least most emotions are modular inheritances, adaptations generated by evolutionary selection pressures (Griffiths 1997). In the second dispute, psychologists debate the relative merits of a thesis upholding the "primacy of affect," in which the focus is on the way emotions influence cognition, and a thesis upholding an "appraisal" theory, in which the focus is on the way cognitive evaluations of the world trigger emotions (for summaries, see Prinz 2004 and Lewis 2005).

Putting dynamical systems modeling and DST together enables us to resolve the universalist versus social constructivist controversy. We can accommodate universal patterns of basic emotions, which although not genetically determined, do reliably develop from our shared genetic makeup, given minimally shared developmental contexts, such as some form of providing nutrition and care. I think we can satisfy the social constructivists, however, by noting that the thresholds and triggers of these basic emotional patterns develop during the singular contacts of unique somatic endowments and complex socialization practices, as do the patterns, thresholds, and triggers of higher emotions. These socialization practices instill "emotion scripts" that indicate culturally specific forms of acceptable performance of emotions; the interface of somatic and social here forms an emergent system, with emotion scripts constraining somatic performance, which has to be developmentally shaped to sustain appropriate script performance (Parkinson et al. 2005).

The psychological debate about the primacy of affect or appraisal can also be resolved using the perspectives we have previously discussed. For instance, Marc Lewis and Walter Freeman, a developmental psychologist and a neuroscientist, respectively, have each used dynamic systems approaches to show that emotion and cognition must be thought of as co-emergent, as components of "emotional interpretation episodes," to use Lewis's terminology (Lewis 2005; Freeman 2000b). Instead of a linear process of input, evaluation, and output, they propose a continuous cycle in which sensory information triggers modifications in the nervous system, conceived as an autonomous system. Since the system is always already affectively primed, the primacy of affect thesis can be accommodated, as the world is made sense of according to the values of the system at the time (X or Y feature of the world might be valued as good or bad at any one time, depending on the internal state of the system). But as emotional episodes develop, higher-level feedback from cognitive appraisals can accelerate or halt the nascent RCA, a development that can be modeled as the formation of an attractor layout—in Deleuzian terms, an intensive process producing a selection from the virtual repertoire of the system—and the falling into or out of any one temporarily dominant basin of attraction—in Deleuzian terms, actualization as the selection of one line of differenciation. Thus emotion and cognition are partners in an ongoing series of emergent processes.[31]

The upshot of this recent work in the affective sciences is that cognition and affectless rational calculation performed on representations can no longer be identified. Affective science thus reinforces the position of the situated action or embodied-extended school that cognition can no longer solely be seen as simply the processing of representations, but must be seen primarily as the real-time direction of an organism's action in the world, with representation used only in certain circumstances and with affect an important component of such direction. While cognition as direction of situated action is often nonrepresentational, even when it uses what Wheeler 2005 calls "action-oriented" representations, it is both affective *and* cognitive, with, if anything, an emphasis to be placed on the unconscious affective evaluations that precede and color representations and the calculations performed thereupon (Bargh and Chartrand 1999).

While cognition as situated action is affectively tinged, the early stages of affective cognition episodes are subcortical and, in a certain sense, precognitive. For example, some episodes of fear are triggered by impulses along nerve pathways on a "low road" to the amygdala that affectively primes our reaction before any nerve signals on the "high road" have even reached the cortex where cognitive (qua situated action) evaluation of the event later occurs (evaluating the escape/attack affordances the world offers), an evaluation that is colored by the already activated affective dynamic (LeDoux 1996). (This somewhat linear presentation of the triggering of a specific fear incident has to be seen as simply a heuristic device for talking about a qualitative shift in the ongoing dynamics of the living being as autonomous system.) The new picture that emerges from this work is that emotion is no longer the enemy of cognition, but its necessary partner (Damasio 1994); the affective aspects of the way we navigate our world (indeed, the way we co-constitute our world, picking out what is important to us [Varela and Depraz 2000]) are essential and not simply a regrettable animal heritage we should do our best to overcome.

In thinking about the mechanisms by which affect operates, I adopt for the most part Antonio Damasio's somatic theory of emotion (1994, 1999, 2003).[32] Briefly put, Damasio says that emotions writ large (extending the emotions proper to include pleasure and pain behaviors and the drives and motivations)[33] are revelatory states of the body; they reveal the "state of life within the entire organism" (2003, 6). Emotions are corporeal reactions of the organism to the world, aimed not simply at neutrality but at "well-being," so as "to create the most beneficial situation for its own self-preservation and efficient functioning" (35). Damasio distinguishes background emotions (moods), basic emotions (e.g., panic, rage, disgust), and social emotions (e.g., shame, guilt, pride) (43–45). While intense episodes of basic emotions can best be seen in terms of "affect programs"—that is, automated responses to environmental triggers—social emotions aim at reestablishing group dynamics, and so are not predetermined; they are best conceived as dynamic "negotiations" with others, in the words of Griffiths and Scarantino (2009).[34]

"Feeling," for Damasio, is the consciousness of affect; feelings "translate the ongoing life state in the language of the mind" (85). This "translation" image is somewhat unfortunate, as it implies a temporally extended information processing procedure; more precisely, for Damasio, feelings are "perceptions" of the body state based in the brain's "body maps" (85).[35] What Damasio calls "core consciousness" is "the feeling of what happens":

a feeling of the body state together with an image of the object triggering the change in the body state (1999, 16). Beyond such first-level consciousness is reflective self-consciousness, which is mediated by memory: we have to remember that "I am the one going through this experience, just like I went through those other experiences."

We can concretize our discussion with the notion of empathy, which we will trace in each of our case studies. Its most basic component is what is known as "emotional contagion," or a shared affective state: you feel what another person is feeling (Stueber 2006). We will refer to this as "protoempathic identification." In recent philosophy, empathy is involved in the controversies surrounding "Theory of Mind," our ability to attribute mental states to others. As explanations for the widely shared capacity for empathy, we first find simulation theory, which in its most rigorous formulation posits the idea that perception of others triggers a separate internal modeling that enables the attribution of affective cognitive states to them (Ratcliffe 2007). Simulation theories are thus a "first-person" standpoint; the discovery of human "mirror neurons" (which fire when we observe a goal-oriented action) gave a great boost to simulation theory (Gallese and Goldman 1998). The most current scholarship (Decety and Lamm 2006) here does not rely on action-oriented mirror neurons (as Gallese thought in his "shared manifold" article of 2001), but on what Gallese, Keysers, and Rizzolatti 2004 call "viscero-motor centers." An important set of findings are those of Singer et al. 2004, in which "empathy for pain" is correlated with increased activity of the anterior insula and the anterior cingulate cortex, which map the viscera.

A second approach to empathy comes from phenomenological accounts, which find the simulation theory approach still too representational and appeal to a field of directly felt corporeal expressivity or "primary embodied intersubjectivity" grounding our "pragmatic interaction" with others (Gallagher 2005, 223; see also Thompson 2001). These phenomenological accounts are therefore a "second-person" standpoint. Thus, for Gallagher, simulation theories align with fully cognitive inferences or "Theory Theory" models ("third-person" standpoints in which perception of others leads to inferences as to the affective cognitive states to be attributed to them) as special cases "unable to capture the full range of second-person interactions." Empathy for the second-person phenomenologists is grounded in a primary corporeal intersubjectivity in which body expressions of the other are immediately felt as meaningful: "In most intersubjective situations we have a direct understanding of another person's intentions because their intentions are explicitly expressed in their embodied actions, and mirrored in our own capabilities for action" (Gallagher 2005, 224; see also Ratcliffe 2007). The phenomenological approach finds support in the widespread recognition of humanity through the sight of the face. Face recognition is one of the earliest infant capacities (Hendriks-Jansen 1996, 252–77; see also Stern 1985, and Gallagher 2005). As we will see again in chapter 6, many battlefield accounts show how the face of the enemy has profound inhibitory effects; the blindfold on the victim of a firing squad enables the shooters by breaking eye contact between victim and executioners (Grossman 1996, 225).

The Embodied-Embedded Subject

Going above, below, and alongside the subject in studying bodies politic does not entail ignoring the subject, though we must dispense with a purely cognitivist subject. Fortunately, we now have rich resources for overcoming cognitivism. In a way that produces a bit of terminological tension, the first of these resources for overcoming cognitivism is the "embodied-embedded" school commenting on and seeking to contribute to cognitive science. It is now commonplace to talk of three approaches to human cognition: the computationalist, the connectionist, and the embodied-embedded. The first two approaches still dominate the field, though the third is gaining adherents. The first two schools use the representational and cognitivist notion of the subject described earlier, though the computationalists describe cognition as the rule-bound manipulation of discrete symbols, and the connectionists describe it in terms of the distributed properties of neural networks.

Using notions drawn from a variety of sources—phenomenology, in particular the work of Husserl, Heidegger, and Merleau-Ponty; phenomenological critiques of computationalist and connectionist work by Hubert Dreyfus (1992); robotics, in particular the work of Rodney Brooks; and dynamical systems theory—the adherents of the embodied-embedded school define cognition as the direction of the situated action of an organism in its world (Varela, Thompson, and Rosch 1991; Clark 1997, 2003; Wheeler 2005; Thompson 2007). Because much of this direction is accomplished in nonrepresentational ways—the precise relation of representational to nonrepresentational forms of the direction of situated action is the matter of much debate, as is the relation between pure or theoretical representation and "action-oriented" representation—we can see that the very term "cognitive science" is under pressure, at least if we do not pay careful attention to the redefinition of cognition by the embodied-embedded school away from a total reliance on calculation performed on representations.

While the embodied-embedded approach does help us overcome cognitivism, it has not yet come to grips with the individualism that binds it to the other schools of cognitive science. Now, it is true that the "distributed cognition" proposed by the embodied-embedded school can accommodate a unit of cognition in which several people play a role, as when it adopts Edwin Hutchins's celebrated example of the cognitive cooperation of a ship's crew (Hutchins 1995).[36] Each sailor, embedded in a technosocial assemblage—some working with charts, others with boiler room gauges, etc.—works with his comrades so that a distributed intelligent guidance of the ship emerges from their coordinated but decentralized cooperation. While this synchronic emergence from a decentralized network is an important concept to retain, the distributed cognition school has not examined the political context for the diachronic emergence of each crew member's affective cognition skill set: the ability to remain cool under pressure while still getting pumped up in times of crisis and the simple ability to get along well with others are just some of the affective traits necessary for successful distributed cognition. In other words, insofar as the embodied-embedded school strives for a model of mind that is biologically (evolutionarily and developmentally) "plausible" (Clark 1997), it incorporates population thinking (that is, thinking in terms of the distribution of traits in a population rather than in terms of an ideal type) in speaking of the phylogenetic and ontogenetic production of "the" human subject, but it has not yet incorporated population thinking into its understanding of the political context of the development of affective cognition capacities in a population of subjects.

To understand fully the complex interplay of "brain, body, and environment," as the slogan of the embodied-embedded school goes, we have to understand the diachronic, not just the synchronic, social environment. That means we have to study populations of subjects and the way access to skills training and cultural resources is differentially regulated along political lines.[37] Lacking a population perspective on the development of affective cognition capacities, the abstraction of the embodied-embedded school impoverishes its notion of "cultural scaffolding" by relegating the cultural to a storehouse of heuristic aids for an abstract problem solver who just happens to be endowed with certain affective cognition capacities qua the ability to interact successfully with the people and cultural resources to which it just happens to have access. Positing an abstract subject neglects the way in which culture is the very process of the construction of bodies politic, so that access to certain cultural resources and to the training necessary to acquire certain forms of affective cognitive capacities—once again, not simply technical training for cognitive capacities in a restricted sense but also the training necessary for acquiring positive and empowering emotional patterns, thresholds, and triggers—is distributed along lines analyzable by political categories.

As an example of the sort of abstract, apolitical subject posited by the embodied-embedded mind school, let me cite a passage from Clark 2003. A fascinating work brimming with insights, Clark's book links together DST biology, interactive technology, and cognitive heuristics embedded in cultural scaffolding, but Clark still doesn't think in terms of the politics of subject production, positing instead a homogeneous subject, "us humans." Clark writes: "A more realistic vision depicts us humans as, by nature, products of a complex and heterogeneous developmental matrix in which culture, technology and biology are pretty well inextricably intermingled. It is a mistake to posit a biologically fixed 'human nature' with a simple wrap-around of tools and culture; the tools and culture are indeed as much determiners of our nature as products of it. Ours are (by nature) unusually plastic and opportunistic brains whose biological proper functioning has always involved the recruitment and exploitation of nonbiological props and scaffolds" (86). This is all true, as far as it goes. But it needs to go further to examine the political practices that regulate access to those "nonbiological props and scaffolds" and thereby regulates subject production.

It could be said that I am being too harsh and should merely propose the population study of the production of subjectivities as a next step, rather than as the making up of a gap left in the study of cognition. After all, one could object, you cannot really blame people interested in cognitive science for looking for the abstract principles of cognition and leaving the empirical study of actually existing subjectivities to psychologists. Here we see a sort of replay of how the embodied-embedded mind school critiqued functionalists. For functionalists, the abstract principles of cognition were the important thing, and neurology need not be consulted, as it provided merely the "implementation details" of mind, the "hardware" to which cognitive "software" was indifferent. The embodied mind school, however, insisted that biology was relevant to the study of mind, so that whatever cognitive software was proposed could not be indifferent to its "wetware" instantiation. Here the question is the level of concretion required of philosophers.

While we can leave individual differences to therapists, can philosophers really leave the gender differences produced by contemporary subjectification practices aside? If all concrete subjectivities are gendered—or at least have developed via gendering practices and have to navigate a world where gender matters—can we be satisfied with abstract principles of cognition that ignore gender effects? Is it enough to criticize computationalism and connectionism in the name of an embodied subject and not realize that bodies are gendered, and that such gendering changes the sphere of bodily competence within which objects appear, as detailed in Iris Marion Young's famous critique of Merleau-Ponty, "Throwing Like a Girl" (Young 2005)? We can only broach these questions here.[38]

Subjectification Practices and De-subjectivizing Effects

To be complete, the study of bodies politic must preserve room for the psychological. Our perspective is materialist, but not eliminative; it does not think of the psychological register as a mistake or as a mark of temporary and regrettable ignorance that can one day be eliminated as scientific progress is made and we can identify brain states and mind states. Thinking the subject in terms of affective cognition, situating the development of subjectivity in its historically variable political context, is not being "against" the subject. Nor does it celebrate the alleged "death of the subject" thought to be the outcome of thinkers like Deleuze and Foucault. What these thinkers really do is enable us to speak about subjectivity as an emergent capacity of bodies when they are placed in the appropriate subjectification practices. To situate our perspective in the terms of continental philosophy, the corporeal focus of our approach is poststructuralist, in that it focused on the differential structures underlying the historical formation of embodied subjects rather than on universal unconscious structures of language or kinship or mythological systems. It is also postphenomenological in that it focuses on the gaps and shortfalls of consciousness produced by automatic, unconscious affective processes, rather than tracing experience back to transcendental structures grounded in a transcendental subjectivity or an intersubjective community.

The focus on subjectification practices might not help us with pinning down the concept of experience, the "hard problem" of consciousness (Chalmers 1995), but my question here is not that of consciousness per se, but the role of consciousness in what we might call the political economy of consciousness. To be more precise, I focus on personal subjectivity —that is, reflective self-consciousness ("extended consciousness" in the scheme laid out in Damasio 1999)—rather than "sentience" (Thompson 2007) or "basic consciousness" (Damasio 1999). Even in a blind rage, the body-agent is sentient, but it is de-subjectivized. Although political affect is especially visible in specific cases of politically triggered de-subjectivizing emotions, such as rage and panic, as well as in the development of patterns of emotional life, we can also see it in other ways in which a body is patterned by the social system into which it is acculturated. Two references to contemporary French philosophy are germane to this latter sense of political affect. One is to Bourdieu's notion of "habitus," by which he means the embodied capacities or skills for participating in social life one develops in the course of social development;[39] the other is to what Foucault calls "biopower," or the social management of biological processes. Although Foucault also discusses how individualizing subjectivities can direct biopower practices,[40] in the Schiavo case study (chapter 5), I focus on how certain aspects of biopower in end-of-life issues skip the subjective level and directly intertwine the social and the somatic, just as in the cases of the political triggering of de-subjectivizing basic emotions.

Chapter 2 Bodies Politic

THE THREE BASIC CONCEPTS of this book are bodies politic, political cognition, and political affect. They are brought together in the following formula: politically shaped and triggered affective cognition is the sense-making of bodies politic. In chapter 1 I reviewed the theoretical sources of these concepts. Here I define them and work out their interrelations.

Preliminary Remarks

The concept of bodies politic is meant to capture the emergent—that is, the embodied and embedded—character of subjectivity: the production, bypassing, and surpassing of subjectivity in the imbrications of somatic and social systems. Individual bodies politic are cognitive agents that actively make sense of situations: they constitute significations by establishing value for themselves, and they adopt an orientation or direction of action. This cognition is co-constituted with affective openness to that situation; affect is concretely the imbrication of the social and somatic, tracking the ways our bodies change in relation to the changing situations in which they find themselves.

Although the concrete reality of politically shaped and triggered affective cognition links affect and cognition, we can isolate the concept of political cognition. While there is an established field studying social cognition, I prefer the term "political cognition," since bodies politic make sense of situations using political categories, and the habits of using those categories develop as the result of subjectification practices amenable to political analysis.[1] The mid-level categories (Rosch 1978; Varela, Thompson, and Rosch 1991) with which we make sense of social situations—race, class, gender, and other political categories—are precisely the categories with which we must analyze the development of subjects who use those categories. In other words, you have to develop the capacity to see that way.[2]

Although many philosophers will admit a notion of subject engaged in self-other relations, few appreciate that these are abstract notions that miss the concrete nature of political cognition in which, for instance, gender and race are immediately perceived.[3]

I do not wish to be doctrinaire about the distinction between "social" and "political," however. The terms have enough overlap that I sometimes use the term "sociopolitical," or sometimes simply "social," for reasons of euphony, as in the subtitle of the book. Furthermore, in my notion of political cognition, I do not limit the term "political" to states and formal institutions, since bodies politic are formed within any human group in which reciprocal causality operates, that is, when emergent effects exert a constraining and enabling effect on the internal rhythms and external connections of individuals just as the dynamic interaction of the individuals so patterned constrain and enable the functions of the group. If others wish to say that human relations outside formal state institutional structures are social, and not political, I do not wish to spend too much energy on the terminological distinction.

It is worth a few more words, however, so I should note that despite this extension beyond formal institutions, I have two further reasons for retaining the term "political" as opposed to the term "social" in the notion of political cognition. First, the relation of the political and the social is a matter of dispute. In *The Human Condition,* Arendt names the "social" as the introduction into governance of biological concern for the population; for her, this "biopower" (to use Foucault's term) is the end of politics as agonistic/cooperative action in favor of politics as the direction of the population (Arendt 1998). Other thinkers, however, reject Arendt's restriction of the political to the ancient Greek model of public action among citizen equals. For them, social categories such as gender and race need to be made the object of explicit political practice rather than remain as the hidden domestic or "eco-nomic" basis for the freedom of the few who are able to direct the polis.[4] Second, while the state is not an exclusive focus, I do pay special attention to two roles of the state as basic problems of politically shaped and triggered affective cognition: in chapter 5, on the Schiavo case, we look at what Foucault would call the biopower control exerted in end-of-life issues; in chapter 6 on Columbine and in chapter 7 on Katrina, I examine the control of violent behavior on the part of the agents of the forces of order of the state. Despite this attention paid to the state, I do not want to minimize the importance of thinking the myriad relations of bodies politic in the contemporary world found when states engage with nonstate actors, especially international corporations, quasi-governmental agencies (WTO, IMF, World Bank), NGOs, and, of course, the many guerrilla, insurgent, and insurrectionist groups involved in fourth-generation warfare.[5]

When we turn from the sociopolitically embedded to the embodied or individuated somatic aspect of bodies politic—that is, to the notion of political physiology—I have a similarly loose sense of the physiological. In other words, I do not limit the physiological to homeostatic mechanisms (e.g., temperature regulation, digestion, metabolism, and the like), but mean it to include reflex, neuronal, and hormonal activity in the preconscious affective response to events when connections with things and others are made or broken.

In acknowledging that collective political categories are those by which individual bodies politic cognize situations, we come upon the notion of political affect. In order to make sense of the world by establishing significance and assuming an orientation, we must first be open to the world, to things, and to others. We must be able to be affected by the world in sensibility, the first meaning of "sense." This openness to the world is both synchronic and diachronic, as seen in our ability to imitate and to learn, the means by which we develop and change. By always developing in concrete situations that shape us, our openness is not absolute, but patterned; singular, yet socialized. We see this patterned openness in three temporal scales: short-term, in emotional episodes; mid-term, in moods; and long-term, in personality (Lewis 2000). The affective response patterns of bodies politic, which are triggered by sensation and play a key role in on-the-spot political cognition, are conditioned by our moods and personalities, which are themselves formed by the repetition of episodes of affective cognition. Although cognitive sense-making constitutes and reproduces bodies politic by the patterns of its action, this action is itself patterned by virtue of the sociopolitical and historical embeddedness of bodies politic. In other words, the differential relations of our autonomous reactions and their approving or disapproving reception by others form patterns of acculturation by which we are gendered and racialized as well as attuned to gender, race, and other politically relevant categories. Put yet another way, we make our worlds in making sense of situations, but we do so only on the basis of the world in which we find ourselves.

Thus, in the notion of political affect I stress the historically and socially embedded aspect of affective cognition. But this embeddedness is not determinism. There is no gainsaying the singular nature of autonomous systems; an infant is not a tabula rasa but contributes to the patterning in which it is formed. And once formed—or better, at any one point in the ongoing formation of our personality—there is almost always the potential for changing affective cognitive patterns, even if this often entails a long and intense sociocorporeal practice (that is, one involving other bodies politic) in which individuals place themselves (or are placed) in situations wherein they deal with what is given by their personal history in and through changing the sociocorporeal relations in which they find themselves.[6] Bodies politic thus must not be seen as mechanical in the sense of a determinist, behaviorist, or disciplinary stimulus-response system (even though certain intense training situations might have this as the limit case to be aimed at), but must be seen in terms of developmentally plastic and co-constituted patterns, thresholds, and triggers that include the subjective level. In other words, while some of the responses of systems to their triggers are stereotyped and expected (and thus "successful" with regard to the aims of a disciplinary program), others are creative and novel. This means that no disciplinary program, even in closed institutions, can ever be completely successful. In Foucault's terms, there is always resistance; in Deleuze and Guattari's terms, there is always a line of flight.

Several points are important here. (1) For Foucault, discipline is a means to intensify power relations. Power is action on the action of others, attempting to render their behavior patterns predictable. All socialization is a form of power, but "power" carries no hint of moral opprobrium; to define freedom or justice as the absence of power relations is nonsensical for Foucault, for it would substitute mere chaos for sociality. (2) While the classical forms of discipline work only in institutional settings, we can more loosely describe disciplinary forms of training in extra-institutional settings. But if even the most complete institutions cannot guarantee complete disciplinary success in producing stereotyped and predictable behavior patterns, then the ability to produce such responses in more open settings is all the more limited. (3) Domination, torture, the physical control of bodies are not forms of power for Foucault; power requires the interaction of free subjects. (4) Deleuze and Guattari put the line of flight first, with power chasing after, while for Foucault, power and resistance are co-constitutive. Thus even while many behavior patterns are stereotyped, bodies develop new patterns of behavior. They also develop thresholds at which those patterns are activated, and they develop sensitivity to triggers in the world. Triggering is not mechanical, but dynamic—that is, intensive and context-dependent: in different contexts, the "same" trigger may or may not push a body to the threshold of behavior activation, depending on the recent dynamic history of the body. Furthermore, the links of bodies politic are of different types: meshworks and hierarchies, to use the terms of DeLanda 1997, or consistencies and strata, to use the terms of Deleuze and Guattari 1987. The first of these pairs of terms means systems that preserve the heterogeneity of components, while the second means systems that produce or select homogeneous components.

Personal, Group, and Civic Bodies Politic

With these preliminary distinctions in mind, let us note again that bodies politic are embodied, with individuated physiological and psychological somatic dimensions, and they are embedded in multiple and overlapping sociopolitical relations with other bodies politic, relations that are themselves also physiological and psychological. We can thus distinguish compositional and temporal scales for bodies politic. Compositionally, we can distinguish first- and second-order bodies politic. First-order bodies politic are at the personal scale, whereas second-order bodies politic can be at either the group or the civic scale. Temporally, we can distinguish the short-term or punctual event scale, the mid-term or habit/training/developmental scale, and the long-term or historical scale. It must be remembered, however, that these scales are analytical rather than concrete; all concrete bodies politic are imbrications of all compositional and temporal scales.

An individual, then, is a first-order body politic, at once social and somatic, embedded and embodied, connected and individuated, in both physiological and psychological dimensions. This is the microlevel of compositional analysis, the personal. When viewed synchronically (that is, on a relatively short timescale), a first-order body politic is a dynamic physiological system that regulates its material and energetic flows as they enter, circulate within, and leave the socially embedded yet individuated body to take part in the economy of higher-order bodies politic at the group and civic scales. These dynamic physiological patterns can be modeled as basins of attraction in the phase space of the body (as regions of its virtual), and they are experienced as background affects, as sharp or diffuse feelings of well-being, unease, or any of a variety of intermediate states. Neural events on the fast/personal scale are the formation of resonant cell assemblies, or RCAs. Viewed diachronically (that is, on a relatively slow mid-term/habituation or long-term/developmental timescale), the patterns of this physiological flow regulation coalesce through childhood, change at critical points entering and leaving puberty, and often settle down into stable habits during adulthood. In other words, system patterns gradually crystallize or actualize as intensive processes disrupt previous patterns; this can be modeled as the construction of new attractor layouts and is experienced as being out of touch with your new body (the gawkiness of adolescents).

Psychologically, the first-order or personal body politic engages in affective cognition, making sense of the situations in which its somatic life is lived in sociopolitical embeddedness. This making sense is profoundly embodied; the body subject opens a sphere of competence within which things show up as affordances, as opportunities for engagement, and other people show up as occasions for social interaction, as invitations, repulsions, or a neutral live and let live. In most synchronic episodes a quite precisely limited virtual repertoire of affective cognitive response is available (a limitation of all that the body could do, modeled as a regularly recurring attractor layout) and efficacious (although we can at any time be overwhelmed by events that seem senseless to us and that scramble our sense-making codes). Diachronically, however, we can see changes at critical points as intensive processes disrupt actual sets of habits; this can be modeled as the production of new attractor layouts and is experienced as psychic turmoil or exciting novelty. During childhood, such transitions in affective cognition are well mapped by developmental psychologists, while even in adulthood, traumatic events or flashes of insight can profoundly rearrange our habitual ways of making sense, that is, rearrange the virtual repertoire, modeled as the production of new attractor layouts.

A second-order body politic is composed of individuals who themselves are first-order bodies politic. Here we find the interaction of the personal with the group compositional scale, where encounters can be one-off occurrences or can be patterned and customary or even institutionalized (and thus operate at the border of group and civic). A second-order body politic is at minimum a couple, but it can be larger; a second-order body politic has itself somatic and social aspects in both physiological and psychological dimensions.

A second-order body politic has a physiology, as it regulates material flows (1) among its members (the first-order bodies politic as the components of its body) and (2) between itself (its soma as marked by its functional border) and its milieu. For example, a second-order body politic might regulate the production, distribution, and consumption of food and drink: think of the way a family kitchen is a distribution node for affectively charged material flows. This regulation of group system dynamics can be seen as construction of a virtual repertoire, modeled as the production of an attractor layout and affectively experienced as the background affect or mood of the group. A second-order body politic can also be studied psychologically, as it regulates intersomatic affective cognition, the emotional and meaningful interchanges (1) among its members and (2) between their collective affective cognition and that of other bodies politic, at either personal, group, or civic compositional scales. In other words, groups have characteristic ways—a limited virtual repertoire—of making sense of what happens, on the basis of which decisions take place as actualizations or selections from that repertoire. These decisions can be seen as channeling toward an end state, modeled as the approach to an attractor in the group's state space, and experienced as a spontaneous agreement in which the collective subject makes up its mind: "All of a sudden it dawned on all of us that this is what we had to do."[7] In terms of its temporal scales, a short-term event for a second-order body politic is an encounter of first-order bodies politic. In the mid-term, we see repeated patterns of such encounters or subjectification practices, and in the long-term, we see the becoming custom of such practices, their deep social embedding.

First- and second-order bodies politic are linked in what Deleuze calls mutual presupposition, or what I called in chapter 1 synchronic emergence. That is, a social group, a second-order body politic, is composed of somatically individuated and socially connected members, or first-order (personal) bodies politic; the behavior capacities of these first-order bodies politic—the potentials for connection that provide the physiological and psychological dimensions of the first-order body politic—are patterned by the social group to which they belong; and it is this very patterning of first-order connections that allows the functioning of the social group, the physiology and psychology of the second-order body. When the encounters that make up second-order bodies politic move beyond the customary to become institutionalized, we reach the political compositional scale, or civic bodies politic. In terms of its temporal scales, a short-term event might be as dramatic as a revolution or as mundane as the encounter of a government agent with a first- or second-order body politic. Mid-term, we see repeated patterns of such encounters in daily administration, while long-term we see institutionalization of these patterns. These relations are expressed in Figure 2.

This is no hidden social contract theory; I am not claiming that first-order bodies politic temporally precede second-order bodies politic, nor am I claiming that social groups came together at some historically dated time

compositional			
		personal	group	civic
temporal	short-term	RCA	encounter	revolution
	mid-term	habituation	subjectification	administration
	long-term	development	custom	institutionalization

Figure 2. Temporal and compositional scales of bodies politic

to form political bodies. The concept of mutual presupposition (or mutual causality, as some theorists of emergence might say) belies this misconception. A further safeguard against such linear temporality can be gained by considering our next point, the necessity of population thinking, which brings along with it the notions of generational reproduction as the concrete site of the imbrications of social and somatic.

Population Thinking: The Multiplicity of Bodies Politic

Our treatment so far has been too simple. We have assumed an abstract body politic, "the" body politic. To think bodies politic, to think the plural being of humans, our sociality, we have to think in the manner of population biologists; we do so by tracking the distribution of body competences as determined by differential access to developmental resources, rather than by tracking the distribution of genes or traits. Let us take the example of gender and advance the claim that the development of physiological and psychological patterns in first-order bodies politic is shaped by sociopolitical gendering practices. (In other words, the personal and group compositional scales are only analytic categories; the reality is a concrete imbrication, the process of social patterning of individual bodies.) Access to training in affective and cognitive coping skills, and hence the development of those skills, is differentially distributed with regard to the categories of masculine and feminine. Feminized and masculinized bodies politic have different spheres of competence: a flat tire can appear as a mildly irritating challenge or as an insurmountable problem, a subway entrance as the enticing gateway to the city or as an anxiety-producing danger. As we noted in chapter 1, Iris Marion Young's "Throwing Like a Girl" (2005) is the classic piece in discussing the restricted body competence of the feminized body-subject. Young's critique is aimed at Merleau-Ponty, in which the assured competence of the presumably neutral or

nongendered body subject hides a masculinist presupposition (see also Butler 1989).

But this is still too simple. It does no good to replace a single abstract subject, "the" body politic, with two abstractions, "the" feminized and "the"
masculinized body politic. We need to think in terms of a range of gendering practices that are distributed in a society at various sites (family, school,
church, media, playground, sports field) with variable goals, intensities,
and efficacies. These multiply situated gendering practices resonate or
clash with each other and with myriad other socializing practices (racial-
izing, classing, religionizing, nationalizing, neighborhoodizing ["that's
the way we roll"]). In other words, we have to think of a complex virtual
field of these differential practices, a complex phase space for the production of bodies politic, with shifting attractor layouts as the subjectification
practices—intensive morphogenetic processes, to use DeLanda's terminology—clash or resonate with each other. But even this is still too simple, as
these gendering practices also enter into complex feedback relations with
the singular body makeup of the people involved; these corporeal constitu-
tions are themselves regionalized slices of the virtual, modeled with a phase
space of what that body can do, its own habitual yet variable patterns of
attractor layouts. These complex dynamics cannot be analyzed into a relation of independent and dependent variables, no matter how powerful the
regression analysis one attempts in order to isolate their effects. There is no
one magic element that enables us to find the key to gender.

We can take Schore 1994 as an example of the troubles one finds in
neglecting the population study of concrete bodies and positing a binary
sex-gender system. Schore's book helps us see that political physiology, as
the openness of bodies politic to direct interaction of the social and the
somatic, is grounded in infantile development. Schore's major point is that
"the mother's [*sic*—but this is not the important point] external regulation
of the infant's developing yet still immature emotional system during particular critical periods may represent the essential factor that influences the
experience-dependent growth of brain areas prospectively involved in self-
regulation" (31–32). In other words, emotional control migrates from the
dyadic caregiver-infant relation to the developing child. This social patterning of affect is directly physical: "I have proposed that maternally regulated
high intensity stimulation provided in synchronized, face-to-face affective interactions induces physiological alterations that directly influence
the imprinting of corticolimbic areas of the infant's postnatally maturing

nervous system" (135). So far, so good. Schore's biosocial perspective, reliant upon intersections of the social and somatic, supports our notion of bodies politic, and it is compatible with a dynamic systems analysis, which he himself provides in Schore 2000. But when he discusses gendering, he relies upon a binary model, first of sex steroids and then of their effects on the brain, linked with a biological determinism: "I contend that the sexual dimorphism of this corticolimbic structure is responsible for various documented gender differences in affect, cognition, and behavior" (1994, 261).

The problem with Schore's approach is that it neglects population thinking. On a population basis, we do not find a simple bimodal distribution of relations among hormones corresponding to a binary sex-gender system. Anne Fausto-Sterling's memorable study *Sexing the Body* (2000) demonstrates how hormone relations vary considerably within sexes, which are themselves abstractions from a distribution of concrete singular bodies, a good number of which are examples of intersexuality. This means that the study of bodies politic has to be done on a population basis. The object of our study is made up of concrete distributions of singular developmental systems, which arise from the differential relations of gendering and other subjectification practices intersecting populations of bodies with genetic diversity and with developmental plasticity. Bodies politic form their patterns in complex interactions of multiple and overlapping, resonating and clashing, dynamic systems, both social and somatic.

A few caveats are important at this point: there are third- and fourth-order bodies politic; for instance, the body politic of a nation is composed of multiple levels of subordinate collective (second-order and above) bodies politic. There are also multiple overlaps of bodies politic, as first-order bodies politic can belong to many different second-order (and higher) bodies politic, which creates resonance or dissonance at the various levels. And bodies politic can interact transversally with other bodies politic of different orders. Also, the physiological and psychological patterns of bodies politic need not be rigidly fixed; the creative development or developmental plasticity of bodies politic means that the creation of new patterns is an essential element in their life. Finally, and most important, we should note that the synchronic form of mutual presupposition of first- and second-order bodies politic appears only with adults who are set in their ways; this mutual presupposition or synchronic emergence is produced by diachronic processes of acculturation of infants and children, and it is reinforced or mutates according to the relations of repetitive and experimental practices present in the group.

Aknto
Depelteau's critique of
Luhmann's autopoesis?

Varela's Warning against the Notion of an Autopoietic Social System

In thinking about bodies politic, we must think of them as dynamic systems, but we must not have a rigid homeostatic notion, as in functionalist sociology.[8] In a late interview, Varela gives his reasons for resisting an extension of autopoiesis to the social:

> It is a question on which I have reflected for a long time and hesitated very much. But I have finally come to the conclusion that all extension of biological models to the social level is to be avoided. I am absolutely against all extensions of autopoiesis, and also against the move to think [of] society according to models of emergence, even though, in a certain sense, you are not wrong in thinking things like that, but it is an extremely delicate passage. I refuse to apply autopoiesis to the social plane. That might surprise you, but I do so for political reasons. History has shown that biological holism is very interesting and has produced great things, but it has always had its dark side, a black side, each time it has allowed itself to be applied to a social model. There are always slippages toward fascism, toward authoritarian impositions, eugenics, and so on. (Varela 2002; my translation)

What is the key to the "extremely delicate passage" necessary to think of social emergence while avoiding the "dark side" of the slide into fascism? First, we should note the complete rejection of autopoietic social notions, while the notion of social emergence is less strongly condemned. I argue that the difference lies in Varela's conception of autopoiesis as synchronically emergent, which locks out the sort of diachronic emergence we need in understanding the development of bodies politic. If one could think of the formation of second-order bodies politic using dynamic systems conceptuality (even if we will never be able to model rigorously such hugely complex systems), if one could see them as resolutions of a dynamic differential field, then we would at least have the possibility of an "extremely delicate passage" in thinking of political change. But without that possibility of novel production, modeled by dynamic systems, then autopoietic social systems, once formed and mature, construct a world only in their own image and, when locked in conflict with another such system, cannot ascend to an "observer" status that would see them both as parts of a larger social system. Instead, the two conflicting systems are locked in fratricidal combat, producing a torn civic body politic, producing civil war.

Let us turn here to "Reflections on the Chilean Civil War" (Varela 1979) for some historical detail about Varela's worries about the political misuse of "biological holism," a misapplication of autopoiesis in considering the formation of higher-order bodies politic. The stakes are the highest possible for Varela in this deeply personal and emotional piece: "Epistemology does matter. As far as I'm concerned, that civil war was caused by a wrong epistemology. It cost my friends their lives, their torture, and the same for 80,000 or so people unknown to me" (19). Varela's analysis is conducted in terms of epistemology, which we can interpret in terms of the synchronic sense-making of produced subjectivities. This epistemological analysis can be converted to our dynamic corporeal perspective by focusing on the developmental processes, the corporeal subjectivizing practices that produced the characteristic sense-making patterns of the subjects he considers. Varela shows that Chile had become polarized into two separate worlds without communication, two autonomous systems with no sense-making overlap, no means of mutual recognition.

Varela recounts his moment of insight when he overcame that polarization: "polarity wasn't anymore this or that side, but something that we had collectively constructed"; political worlds, previously autonomous, had to be considered merely "fragments that constituted this whole" (18; see also Varela 1976, 63). The fragment/whole terminology still seems to us synchronic; Varela is analyzing the deadly effects of civil war as epistemological conflict rather than providing an ontogenetic analysis of how the civil war developed. The problem, of course, is establishing the observer position that can appreciate this larger whole encompassing the mutually blind autonomous systems. Varela finds this position in Buddhist practice, with its necessity of stressing the "connection between the world view, political action and personal transformation" (Varela 1979, 19). To avoid the fratricidal polarization of competing autonomous systems, adopting positions of relativistic fallibility is the key to the construction of a political world: "We must incorporate in the enactment, in the projecting out of our world views, at the same time the sense in which that projection is only one perspective, that it is a relative frame, that it must contain a way to undo itself" (19). But the adoption of such reflexive flexibility or relativistic fallibility is not an act of will; it is a learned affective cognition skill, available only to those bodies politic that develop via socializing practices that enable the enacting of this comportment. When already formed systems without this capacity collide we find only mutual misunderstanding, or perhaps more precisely, the production of what Lyotard calls a differend, a dispute in which the complaint of one side cannot be made sense of, cannot be recognized, by the other. The result, all too often, is the miserable violence Varela describes.

Political Physiology and Political Feeling

Although I work with Deleuze's dynamic materialist ontology, I want to preserve the utility of psychological description, so as a rough approximation, we can say that political affect has both objective and subjective aspects, which I will name "political physiology" and "political feeling," respectively.[9] Political physiology involves the direct interaction of the social and the somatic, skipping the subjective level, while political feeling is the conscious, subjective registration of that interaction. Political physiology is accessible only in a third-person, objective standpoint, while political feeling is accessible only in a first-person, subjective standpoint.

We cannot forget the second-person standpoint, however. Bodies politic are not just embodied; they are also sociopolitically and historically embedded. In appreciating embeddedness, the second-person relation is primary, for the patterning of bodies politic develops from what is often termed a "primary intersubjectivity" (as I explain in chapter 5, I prefer to call this a "primary corporeal inter-ipseity" to indicate that body-selves precede subjects) in the caregiver-infant relation. As we have seen, the synchronous emergence of mature embodied-embedded political affective cognition—the mutual presupposition of embodied patterned connections that allow group functions—only develops diachronically from an acculturation process in which the embedded aspect is privileged (though not absolutely) over the embodied aspect. As we will see, the infant is not a tabula rasa; in other words, political affect is not a form of social constructivism—but after an initial complexification in childhood and adolescence, maturation, most often concluded in early adulthood, is a progressive rigidifying, a limitation of potential as patterns become more entrenched. There are positive and negative aspects here: we need order in our lives, we must have a personality, but we have to beware of the tendency toward fixation, especially when we are being forced into stereotyped roles that make possible the regulation and reproduction of unjust social dynamics (as we will see, the correlation of rigid bodily organization and hierarchical social organization is what Deleuze and Guattari call the "organism").

The two aspects of political affect, political physiology and political feeling, are often linked, but not always. For instance, tissue damage is an objective phenomenon that is at first registered unconsciously, triggering reflexes, and then shows up as the conscious sensation of pain. Pain is thus the subjective registration of objective states of body damage. Instances of tissue damage count as instances of political physiology when the damage results as the direct interaction of social and somatic: in crime, war, or starvation. Here again, the second-person relation is possible: simply being in the presence of severely traumatized people can itself be traumatizing, leaving both physiological and psychological traces popularly known as compassion fatigue (Rothschild and Reid 2006). As we will see in chapter 5, however, brain damage can eliminate the possibility of the feeling of pain, so all that is left when tissue is damaged are reflex movements. We will say that there is a self in these cases, a body-agent engaged in self-preserving reflex movements, but not a subject, even though a tragic illusion of intersubjectivity can be produced in observers. Similarly, the motivational dispositions or appetites can be seen as the subjective aspect of the body's objective relation to homeostasis, so that regulating body processes addressing a lack or a surplus is felt as eagerness or repugnance for an object. Again, brain damage can eliminate the possibility of the feelings of hunger and thirst, no matter the state of the body (Panksepp 1998). Finally, conscious social emotions are the subjective aspect, the political feeling side, of an objective process of regulating social system dynamics, the political physiology of the second-order body politic.[10]

A key element in our consideration of political affect is the triggering of affect programs such as rage and panic. These are both de-subjectivizing and decontextualizing, and they follow a continuum with limit cases of the individuated and the collective poles of the body politic. In approaching the individuated limit, drastic cases of rage and panic cause the subject to drop out (as in a blind rage) or be reduced to a helpless spectator (as in a freezing or fleeing panic). In these drastic episodes of basic emotions, an affect program is triggered that effectively de-subjectivizes the body. The body is left as a self-preserving agent capable of emergency action, but this is a body-agent without a self-conscious subject. The body agent in a full-blown rage or panic is sentient but has no reflective consciousness. In approaching the individuated limit, just as the subject is evacuated in favor of a body-agent, the social embeddedness aspect shrinks into tunnel vision so that any dialogue with others ceases and the body only confronts an object, tightly focusing on a single element of the situation, its rage- or fear-provoking element, which polarizes the world into attack and retreat directions (Scarry 1985).

In approaching the limit case of pure collectivity of the body politic, we see the same de-subjectivation and decontextualization in mob affects, collective rage and panic. Through processes of positive and negative feedback promulgating emotional contagion, individuals are entrained in an enraged or panicked collective agent without individuated self-consciousnesses or consideration of the social context. The world of social relations drops away, and all that remains is a collective agent with a tight focus on the objects of rage or panic. What focuses, as in the cases approaching the individuated limit, are the de-subjectivated bodies: I don't believe it is useful to talk about a mob subject as opposed to a mob agent (Canetti 1984; Wilson 2004).

Guardedly taking up a computer metaphor, we can say that when automated affect programs of blind rage or freezing panic are triggered in certain situations, they run the system using the body as hardware, but without subjective/conscious control, without a user interface. This pallid computer metaphor is much less compelling than the mythic images of the ancient Greeks: rage as possession by Ares, or panic as possession by Pan. When it comes to drastic episodes of political affect, we'll never surpass the gut-wrenching phenomenological descriptions of Homer. We are particularly interested in these limit cases of de-subjectivizing and decontextualizing when considering political affect because even though rage states are effective for allowing violent acts on the part of single somatic units or mob agents, they pose significant control problems for the forces of order wielded by political institutions. Modern armies are not mobs, nor are they collections of individual berserkers. To use ancient Greek analogies, they are neither a rabble of camp followers nor a fragile coalition of Homeric champions. Rather, they are a disciplined unit, even if they rarely assume the massed-wall position of the phalanx, dispersing instead in decentralized, open tactical formations tasked with open-ended objectives, what are sometimes called swarming tactics.[11] This is an important issue for us because one of the key problems of political affect is the control of violent behavior on the part of the forces of order of a political institution: not just suppressing the extra-institutional uses of violence but also reliably triggering—and controlling, once triggered—violent behavior in the bodies politic of the military and law enforcement.

Pause

Let me pause and give a brief example of research in social psychology that recognizes the embodied and embedded dimensions of political affect in bodies politic as we have encountered them so far. Nisbett and Cohen (1996) go below and above the subject in studying this topic. They go below the subject (political physiology of the first-order body politic) to examine physiological response, demonstrating that white males of the southern United States have markedly greater outputs of cortisol and testosterone in response to insults than a control group of northern white males (44–45). They go above the subject to examine social policy forms (the political physiology and psychology of the second-order body politic, regulating material and affective flows), showing that southern states have looser gun control laws, more-lenient laws regarding the use of violence in defense of self and property, and more-lenient practices regarding use of violence for social control (domestic violence, corporal punishment in schools, and capital punishment) (57–73). They also offer in passing some speculation as to the role played by slavery in the South in constructing these bodies politic in which social institutions and somatic affect are intertwined and mutually reinforcing in diachronically developing and intensifying mutual reinforcement—what complexity theorists call dynamic coupling.

Even if the notion of political affect is underappreciated among philosophers, as I believe it to be, it is not so among other academics, for whom the notion is not strange in the least. For instance, Richerson and Boyd (2005), in discussing Nisbett and Cohen's work, don't blink an eye in writing: "An insult that has trivial effects in a Northerner sets off a cascade of physiological changes in a southern male that prepare him to harm the insulter and cope with the likelihood that the insulter is prepared to retaliate violently. This example is merely one strand in a skein of connections that enmesh culturally acquired information in other aspects of human biology" (4). Although I would prefer a complex notion of developmentally plastic and environmentally co-constituted corporeal patterns, thresholds, and triggers to that of "information," it is the term "enmesh" that is the key to the thought of political affect contained in this last sentence.

Political Affect and Bodies Politic

At this point we need to examine the connection between the use of "affect" in affective neuroscience and in Deleuze. The key here is to appreciate the ecosocial embeddedness of affect. Affect indicates that living bodies (we will see in chapters 3 and 4 why I prefer this term to "organism") do not negotiate their worlds solely—or even for the most part—by representing to themselves the features of the world, but by feeling what they can and cannot do in a particular situation.[12] The primary contact with another being in the world is a feeling of what the encounter of the two bodies would be like; in the cases that interest us, this means what the assemblage or second-order body politic to be formed would be like (the mechanism for this felt imaginal encounter is what Damasio calls the as-if loop producing a somatic marker). There are multiple possibilities here. The encounter can (1) enhance the power of one of the bodies and decrease that of the other (in eating or in enslavement), (2) decrease both (in a mutually destructive encounter), or (3) increase both (in a mutually empowering encounter, what Deleuze and Guattari call a consistent assemblage). Many short- and long-term temporal modulations are possible, of course: conversations take many twists and turns; a dispute about sports allegiances can end up in maudlin toasts at the bar; or more seriously, slaves can overthrow their masters, enemies can become friends, love affairs can go sour, and so on.

Deleuze and Guattari follow Spinoza, defining affect as a body's ability to act and to be acted upon: what it can do and what it can undergo. Affect has two registers. First, it is being affected, that is, undergoing the somatic change caused by encounter with an object; this aspect of affect can also be called "affection," as the composition or mixture of bodies, or more precisely the change produced in the affected body by the action of the affecting body in an encounter (roughly speaking, political physiology or the objective aspect of political affect). Second, affect is the felt change in power of the body, the increase or decrease in perfection, felt as sadness or joy (roughly speaking, political feeling or the subjective aspect of political affect).[13] For Deleuze and Guattari, affect is thus physiological and psychological at once. Deleuze and Guattari operationalize the complex notion of affect as the ability of bodies to form assemblages with other bodies, to form what dynamical systems theory would call emergent functional structures that conserve the heterogeneity of their components. In this notion of assemblage as emergent functional structure (namely, a dispersed system that enables focused behavior at the system level as it constrains component action), we find parallels with the situated cognition work on scaffolding, which maintains that cognition operates in loops among brain, body, and produced environment (Clark 2003). In noting this parallel, we should likewise note that Deleuze emphasizes the affective dimension of assemblages, while the embodied-embedded school focuses on cognition. We follow Deleuze's lead in this book and focus on the affective, but we should remember that both affect and cognition are aspects of a single process, affective cognition, as the directed action of a living being in its world.

Note, however, that Deleuze and Guattari, while acknowledging the feeling aspect of affect, place feeling as the subjective appropriation of affect. Just as for them pleasure is the subjective appropriation of joy, feeling is the subject's appropriation of physiological-emotional changes of the body, the recognition that "this is me feeling this way." Deleuze and Guattari's point about affect's extension beyond subjective feeling dovetails with our analysis of extreme cases of rage and panic as triggering an evacuation of the subject as automatic responses take over; as we have put it, drastic episodes of rage and fear are de-subjectivizing. Thus the agent of an action undertaken in a rage or panic state is the embodied affect program acting independently of the subject. Here we see affect freed from subjective feeling. There can be no complaints about eliminating the first-person perspective in studying these episodes of political affect because there is no first-person operative in these cases. Agency and subjectivity are split; affect extends beyond feeling; the body does something, is the agent for an action, in the absence of a subject. We will explore this in more detail in chapter 6, on the Columbine killers.

Affect is inherently political: bodies are part of an ecosocial matrix of other bodies, affecting them and being affected by them; affect is part of the basic constitution of bodies politic. In thinking of the political aspect, the difference between the first (dominating) and third (mutually empowering) sense of power is obviously important. It is reflected in the French language in the distinction between *pouvoir* and *puissance*. (Antonio Negri's work on Spinoza, and his later collaboration with Michael Hardt, turns precisely on this distinction; see Negri 1991; Hardt and Negri 2000, 2004.) We will have to exaggerate differences for clarity, and we need to remember that everyday French usage does not draw such clear distinctions. Nonetheless, we can say that *pouvoir* is transcendent power: it comes from above. It is hylomorphic, imposing form on the chaotic or passive material of the mob. In its most extreme manifestation, it is fascistic: it is expressed not simply as the desire to rule, but more insidiously as the longing for the strong leader to rescue us from the chaos into which our bodies politic have descended. *Puissance*, on the other hand, is immanent self-organization. It is the power of direct democracy, of people working together to generate the structures of their social life.

The difference between *pouvoir* and *puissance* allows us to nuance the notion of joyous and sad affect with the notions of active and passive power. Consider the paradigm case of fascist joy. The Nazis at the Nuremberg rallies were filled with joyous affect, but this joy of being swept up into an emergent body politic was passive. The Nazis were stratified; their joy was triggered by the presence of a transcendent figure manipulating symbols—flags and faces—and by the imposition of a rhythm or a forced entrainment—marches and salutes and songs. Upon leaving the rally, they had no autonomous power *(puissance)* to make mutually empowering connections. In fact, they could only feel sad at being isolated, removed from the thrilling presence of the leader.[14] They had become members of a society of the spectacle, to use Guy Debord's term: their relations with others were mediated by the third term of the spectacle the others had attended (the in-group) or had not attended (the out-group).

Political affect then includes an ethical standard: Does the encounter produce active joyous affect? Does it increase the *puissance* of the bodies, that is, does it enable them to form new and mutually empowering encounters outside the original encounter?

Political Affective Cognition

We are now in a position to flesh out our formula: affective cognition is the sense-making of bodies politic. We must first recall that sense has three aspects: sensibility, signification, and direction. Sense-making is threefold as well: bodies politic are open to the world, able to be affected in sensibility; they establish significance as value for the body; and they establish a direction for action. Let us take each of these in turn.

Sensibility is the openness to the world, our ability to sense aspects of situations. We propose that the world is structured by Deleuze's threefold ontology of virtual, intensive, and actual. The actuality of a situation is composed of extensive properties, sensed as objects recognized by habitual categories. The intensity of the situation is composed of tendencies, sensed as approaches to switch points, as anticipation of triggers to thresholds. Intensity is felt both positively and negatively, as inviting or repelling, or even as simply strange, as in the sensation of being off-kilter, when things do not make the sense they ordinarily do. Our ordinary language reflects the bipolarity of such affect: "Don't make me go there," we say, in wanting to avoid escalation of conflict, or "Just a little more, that's what we need to get things going around here," when the situation is about to hit a desired threshold. The virtuality of situations is their phase space of patterns and thresholds that structure morphogenetic processes. The virtual is sensed in our feeling for the genesis and future of situations: our intuition of how we got here and of what could happen next, if we go past one or the other of these looming thresholds or if we stay below the threshold, "on this side" of an irrevocable change. We all know that once past certain thresholds, new futures unfold: some angry or hateful words once uttered can't be taken back, or, positively, you just know that once you say "I love you," things will never be the same.

Signification or value production, the second aspect of sense-making, is an intensive process. It is the feeling of the change in the body as it comes in contact with a sensed object, the feeling that this encounter is good or bad or indifferent to you, in as fine-grained a way as is called for. It can operate in real time, telling you what is happening now, and it can also proceed by as-if loops, producing somatic markers that let you feel what it would be like to live through this or that scenario. Such signification can be modeled at the formation of attractor layouts, which represent the potential reactions of the living being to its situation.

Alva Noë's notion of the virtual content of perception can help us here in understanding the intensive aspect of sense-making as value production (Noë 2004). Noë posits a differential relation between movement and perception so that the content of perceptual experience is virtual.[15] Thus some content is present *as available* (66–67). In other words, you experience an object as something whose appearance would vary in precise ways as you move in relation to it (117). This means that some perceptual detail is present *as accessible*; furthermore, "experiential presence is virtual *all the way in*. Experience is fractal and dense" (216). Noë continues in this vein: "Qualities are available in experience as possibilities, as potentialities, but not as completed givens. Experience is a dynamic process of navigating the pathways of these possibilities. Experience depends on the skills needed to make one's way" (217). The ground of perceptual experience is embodied sensorimotor skills; because of this embodied ground, "What we experience outstrips what is represented in consciousness" (217). Borrowing Gibson's term, Noë claims that objects in the world are perceived as "affordances": "to perceive is (among other things) to learn how the environment structures one's possibilities for movement and so it is, thereby, to experience possibilities of movement and action afforded by the environment" (105).

We can give a Deleuzian reading to Noë's notion: to conceive of perceptual content as virtual means that concrete perception happens as the resolution of a differential field, an Idea or multiplicity. The differential elements are movement and perceptual presence or appearance, the differential relations are those between these two elements, and the singularities are thrown out in those relations as thresholds where qualitative perceptual change occurs (e.g., move too close to a pointillist painting and all you see are color dots, no longer forms) (Smith 1996). I propose using our Deleuzian take on Noë's account as a model of political affective cognition as sense-making, that is, as the perception of social affordances. When we make sense of a situation, we determine the potentials in this encounter for making assemblages. This sense-making has different temporal scales: it is often an extended process of dynamic exchange/negotiation, but it can also arrive as a flash of insight, a feeling of what is possible. This feeling can be a definite reading of the situation ("This stinks!" or "This is for me!"), but it can also sometimes be just a vague feeling of good or bad possibilities ("I don't know, I can't quite put my finger on it, but just maybe . . ."). Neurologically, intensive sense-making happens via Damasio's somatic markers generated by as-if loops, which tell us what it would feel like to live through such and such a scenario.[16]

Now, if we want to use Noë's notion of virtual perceptual content to help us think of sense-making, we cannot stick with the physical/visual vocabulary of a differential relation between movement and appearance. The differential relation in the sense-making of bodies politic is that between potentials for becomings or assemblage formations, which vary as the members of the encounter make a move in the social game, moves in which someone offers, commands, cajoles, persuades, pleads, and so on. The possible moves of a situation are the moves allowed by the social grammar and syntax. (A syntax is at work here in social situations: the order of moves is somewhat prescribed; some moves just cannot come after other moves.) Such grammar and syntax are not propositional rules, of course, but are embodied competences.[17] These possible moves are themselves taken up in relations of change: what Deleuze and Guattari call deterritorialization (leading to what would be unexpected, because changing the allowable patterns of the game) and reterritorialization (settling back into an old game, or setting forth the potentials of the new game) (Massumi 2002, 71–80).

Affect exists in and as this variation; it is the intensive as opening up access to the virtual, to the differential field, Idea, or multiplicity of the situation. As Brian Massumi puts it: "Affect is *the virtual as point of view*, provided the visual metaphor is used guardedly" (35; italics in original). Affect is the change in the relation of bodies politic: the change in the first-order body politic in the encounter with another body politic. Insofar as it is felt, it is a feeling of the body in relation, and the feeling of how the present feeling might vary in relation to what might happen next in a variety of futures. Affect, then, is a resolution of a complex differential field, relating changes in bodies politic or, more precisely, the changes in the relations among changing first- and second-order bodies politic.

In some cases, situations are well in hand, and affects collapse into emotions having something of a representative function: they show us how things actually are and how they will evolve. But this is emotion as subjective capture of affect. In some other cases, the situation exceeds our ability to make sense of it; affect extends beyond the body's ability to emotionally represent the situation; we are overwhelmed and thrown off-kilter. Here we are at the limit of faculty of sensibility: these situations cannot be sensed from an actualized point of view of recognition and common sense ("it makes no sense"), but can only be felt—that is, "sensed"—as pointing to a differential field beyond normal sense-making as recognition, as conceptual-emotional capture and processing. In other words, an intensive encounter outside normal/actual affective cognition habits (modeled as a move outside the basin of attraction, or better, outside the normal attractor layout as habitual response capacities) provides access to the virtual. This access is experienced as a strange feeling, a feeling of being out of step with your normal habits; in this strangeness lies the potential to open an adaptive response as a creative event proposing a new attractor layout, giving new options to the system.

Finally, and quite simply, adopting a direction for action is actualization, the selection of a path from among the options laid out by signification. Such a decision is modeled as the falling into a basin of attraction. At this point it is necessary to address the question of intentional action. The thought of bodies politic is materialist, but not mechanistic; we want to account for the production of subjectivities via subjectification practices, but we do not wish to deny the reality of subjective action. Now, it is no doubt true, as the situated cognition people remind us, that many of our actions are habitual and skilled and hence proceed without need for conscious control: our training has allowed a second nature so that consciousness is freed to plan ahead without having to direct all the details of an action. (Here the sports register is most clear: a skilled tennis player is thinking about what will happen in the next few strokes, not attending to weight shift, hip movement, arm extension, etc.) Nonetheless, there are cases where a deliberate, conscious decision is made that directs an overall plan (even if one does not decide consciously to shift one's weight in striking a tennis ball, one does indeed decide to play a tennis match).

Now, if one adopts a linear causality (input, processing, output) framework and concentrates on a very short temporal scale of simple muscular action, then it seems free will is compromised, or at least rendered problematic, by some neuroscientific results. Libet 2004 summarizes a celebrated series of experiments that show that brain processes necessary for muscular activation (the readiness potential) begin some 350 milliseconds before subjects are aware of their intention to move their arms. It seems that the true cause of action lies in unconscious neural processes and that subjective consciousness merely registers the results of these processes; consciousness is thus epiphenomenal with regard to such action. Extending the results of these experiments can tempt some thinkers to render consciousness a completely superfluous observer in all contexts.

Two sources enable us to call this picture into question. Freeman 2000a shows how the notion of circular causality drawn from dynamic systems modeling enables us to see consciousness as a dynamic operator, as an emergent functional structure operating in the "dynamic architecture of brain state space" (136). Freeman puts consciousness in a nested hierarchy of emergent processes, extending "both below the level of the neuron, in the chemistry of synaptic membranes and the readout of the genome during learning, and above the global state of the hemispheres, to include self-awareness and the environment, especially the social encounters by which individual brains assimilate meaning" (136). Conscious decisions must be seen on the timescale appropriate to intentional action, which is longer than that of readiness potentials and is involved in the ongoing life of the human as an autonomous system, with its continuous history of feedback between intention and results, built up into habitual patterns of response capacities.

Gallagher 2005 picks up on Freeman's analysis at the phenomenological level. Gallagher shows that the timescale appropriate to the analysis of intentional action is that of the act as a whole informed by consciousness, not the millisecond scale of neural processes (238–39). Focusing on the presence of feedback loops in living beings, Gallagher argues that "feedback loops that involve conscious deliberation require an extended duration equivalent to a specious present—that is, a duration that is stretched out over at least several seconds, and is experienced as such" (239; see also Varela 1999). Following Freeman and Gallagher, we can say that a dynamic systems approach to situated cognition enables us to think of the actualization phase of sense-making—the adoption of a direction for action—

as sometimes encompassing deliberate intention without compromising our commitment to a materialist and naturalistic take on the embodied-embedded nature of bodies politic.

To sum up, then, sense-making in all its aspects—sensibility, signification, direction—occurs in concrete encounters of bodies politic, which unfold in a social context between embodied subjects formed by that context. More precisely—since "context" is too static—a sense-making encounter, like all the emergent functional structures of bodies politic, is the resolution of a dynamic differential field operating at multiple levels and different time-scales: first- and second-order bodies politic arranged in transversal assemblages or concrete situations, acting in real time with response capacities that have crystallized over developmental timescales.

In "Reflections on the Chilean Civil War," Varela provides an example of mid-level categories in concrete social perception and affect (1979, 18): "I remember very well that the soldier, whom I saw machine-gunning the other fellow who was running down the street, was probably a 19-year old boy from somewhere in the South. A typical face of the people of the South. . . . I could see in his face what I had never seen, a strange combination of fear and power." Varela's reminiscence rings true to concrete social perception. He did not see a neutral subject, an other; he saw a Southern Chilean boy of nineteen, a concrete person who is marked as to gender, age, and race (or at least ethnicity). In that marking, and in the perception of a new affective state on the soldier boy's face, that "strange combination of fear and power," we engage all temporal and compositional scales of bodies politic: the historically long and compositionally civic body politic torn apart in civil war; the temporally mid-term and compositionally personal scale of the development of the repertoire of behavioral modules, as the boy is marked by this affective combination, this "strange combination of fear and power"; and the temporally fast and compositionally group scale of political encounter, an episode of affective cognition on Varela's part in which he is affected by the arising of this event, the "becoming" of this assemblage or momentary transversal emergence: street, gun, soldier, shooting, running, dying, observing. He is affected by it, he makes sense of it, but in a way that exceeds his normal perceptual habits: "I could see in his face what I had never seen." This emergent structure functions, it works in the world it enacts: it leaves its mark on Varela's brain-body memory system (LeDoux 1996, 179–224) as well as, sadly, on the body of the machine-gunned victim.

We are challenged here: can we develop a thought of political affective cognition to enable us to understand this haunting scene as the resolution of a differential field, as the feeling of what is happening in the relations among civic, somatic, and transverse bodies politic, as an event in which a civil war is concretized in the encounter among somatic bodies politic—the victim, the soldier, and the observer?

Part II **Bodies Politic as Organisms**

Chapter 3   **The Organism in Aristotle and Kant**

THE NEXT TWO CHAPTERS of this book examine some aspects of the notion of bodies politic in the history of philosophy. As my guiding thread, I use Deleuze and Guattari's enigmatic saying in *A Thousand Plateaus*, the organism is "the judgment of God." They indicate by this phrase the way in which major Western philosophers have held that God's perfection is the model for the self-ordering of the ideal, politically attuned human organism.[1] This long-standing notion, which we analyze in Aristotle, Kant, and finally Deleuze and Guattari, is the principal way in which the history of philosophy has thought of bodies politic. In order to clear the way for our own reading of the imbrications of the social and the somatic, we need to confront this archetype. In other words, in the organism as the judgment of God, we see a theo-bio-politics that is the projection of a hierarchically ordered body politic onto a divine natural order.

Here I show how the concept of such a theo-bio-political production can be found in Aristotle and Kant. We must keep in mind that "organism" in Deleuze and Guattari's sense is a hierarchically ordered body, a body whose organs are constrained to work for the benefit of the organism as an integrative and emergent whole that functions politically in the proper way, as determined by its role in a hierarchical social system. "Organism" is thus not a strictly biological term, but a term that indicates the patterning of a somatic biological system by a hierarchical social system.

The Organism as Judgment of God

In the mainstream of Western philosophy, the unity and teleologically ordered finality of nature as a whole and the organism as a microcosm of that unified whole have often been thought to be patterned on divine perfection and/or to have been brought about by God's plan. Deleuze and Guattari capture this theo-bio-politics by saying the organism is the "judgment of

God" (Deleuze and Guattari 1987, 158–59). In this chapter I examine this notion as exemplified in Aristotle and Kant.

First, though, we must address the question, Why focus on Aristotle and Kant? Why not Plato and Hegel? Or any other pair of great canonical figures whose linkage of theology, biology, and politics was equally thoughtful and influential? Precisely because the very arbitrariness of the pairing will display the cohesiveness of the theo-bio-political structure expressed by the concept of the organism as the judgment of God and thus the utility of Deleuze and Guattari's insightful formulation of it. I cannot explore it here, but I am confident that a reading of the *Timaeus* and the *Encyclopedia* could demonstrate that, for Plato and Hegel as well, the organism is the judgment of God (Protevi 2001). Showing that two philosophers as disparate in time, method, and cultural presuppositions as Aristotle and Kant share a profound similarity in the way God provides the model of the organism should reveal the repetition of that structure in a way that a single point of reference—say, Aristotle alone—would not.

The concept of the organism as the judgment of God could have come only from the bold syncretism of Deleuze and Guattari, who gleefully bring the rantings of Artaud to bear on the deepest questions of Western philosophy. To understand how the organism is the judgment of God for Aristotle and Kant (implicitly) and for Deleuze and Guattari (explicitly), we must unearth how theology, biology, and politics interact in their philosophies. In a word, we must think of nature as the production of bodies politic. But nature is conceived differently in the three thinkers, and thus so will God be, for the question of God is inextricably linked to the question of nature.

For Aristotle, nature is unidirectional: it is oriented to the best, to foundational principled self-direction or *autarcheia.*[2] Deviation from this natural striving for self-direction is unnatural: it is monstrosity, femininity, slavishness. Thus for Aristotle, *ho theos,* the god, the most perfectly realized instance of self-direction, is the prime mover of cosmic locomotion and its lesser analogue, species reproduction, and it is also the model for organismic unity. For Kant, nature is the field in which mechanism and purposiveness must be reconciled via the thought of God as moral author of the world whom we must presuppose to understand (1) the self-organizing unity of part and whole in nature and in the organism, and (2) reason's rule of the inclinations, which constitutes the human moral agent.

For Deleuze and Guattari, nature is the abstract machine of stratification and destratification. There is a bivalent, or double, directionality to Deleuzoguattarian nature, toward unity and toward dispersion, toward capture and toward escape, toward stratification and toward the line of flight. On the other hand, for Deleuze and Guattari, God is a lobster, the double-pincered abstract machine of natural stratification, and thus part, but only part, of nature. It is precisely this restriction of God to a part of nature that constitutes Deleuze and Guattari's break with the tradition represented here by Aristotle and Kant and that enables their critical stance toward the theo-bio-politics of the organism as judgment of God.

The most important questions are at stake in the question of nature as the interchange of theology, biology, and politics. Are both natural theology and theologically modeled nature hidden forms of politics that are then projected outward and said to form the conditions for that which is in fact the sole material reality? Does Aristotle project the ideal of the adult citizen male onto a nature—onto a biology and theology—that he will then claim justifies his political decision to favor the interests of adult citizen males? Is mechanistic nature for Kant the projection of alienating modern industrial production, and political and moral freedom as self-determining organic unity, a reactive bourgeois fantasy?

A good case can be made for this sort of projective analysis, but this dialogue would be fruitlessly unending, as every projective analysis can be met with a sneering rebuke for its idealism or relativism, and in its place a realist/objectivist ontology can be proffered that would put politics second to the natural reality upon which it is modeled. This structure holds not just for premodern theistic ontologies but also for the modern claims of a biological reality founded on sociobiologistic calculations as to payoffs in gene frequency in a population as returns on investments in reproductive strategies, a sort of genetic stock market governed by an adaptationist invisible hand (McKinnon 2006). Capitalism would simply be the social expression of this natural process, which would then be doubled back onto nature by theorists who call for self-entrepreneurship extending to the management of genetic capital.[3] On another level, however, investigating just how this interchange of theology, biology, and politics in nature has been thought of prepares us for our later case studies, which bring us to the heart of our study in which the concept of complex dynamic systems enables us to think of the intersection of political and somatic systems: sometimes at the full subjective level of affective cognition, sometimes in a direct interaction of social and somatic.

Before we begin our analyses of Aristotle and Kant, we must first tackle the question of discourse, the question of the *logos* underlying this natural intersection of theology, biology, and politics in the organism as judgment of God. For Aristotle and for Kant, the key to the conceptual interchange in the term "nature" is analogy. For Aristotle, nature is the universal pull to realizing the good as the internal *telos* of things, so that the unidirectional orientations to self-direction in theology, biology, and politics are analogous to one another. For Kant, owing to the limits imposed on knowledge by the critical system, natural organisms pose questions that can, in lieu of an unthinkable thought of living matter, only be answered by the presupposition of God as moral author operating on a remote analogy with our own purposive causality.

Aristotle

Scholarship on Aristotle's biological writings has enjoyed a golden age in the last thirty years or so; in the process, those writings have been rescued from those who would denigrate them as a confused grab bag of empirical observation and fantastic gullibility (among others, see Preus 1975; Gotthelf 1985; Pellegrin 1986; Gotthelf and Lennox 1987; and Lennox 2001). Many if not all of these recent scholars insist on the unity of Aristotle's thought, which in their eyes extends to the interchange between the natural science writings and the logical/metaphysical writings. Pierre Pellegrin writes: "There is no line of demarcation between Aristotle's logico-metaphysical work and the biological corpus" (1987, 313). Aryeh Kosman, a leading Aristotelian scholar, is particularly clear on the need to see a field of bio-ontology: "Animals, in Aristotle's view, are paradigm instances of substance. We may wonder whether Aristotle began with that conviction and shaped his ontology in light of it, or arrived at it as a result of what his ontology revealed the nature of substance to be" (1987, 303).

I would like to extend this implicit recognition of a field of bio-ontology to examine Aristotle's ethical/political thought and its relation both to biology and to the highest point of first philosophy, theology. Kosman writes in another brilliant article: "The answers to logical, metaphysical and ethical questions have their common origin in his [Aristotle's] view of individual substances acting out their identity in the world" (1969, 62).[4] We must think through the reasons why Aristotle will say that *autarcheia* characterizes both the adult citizen male and the prime mover. The perfection of *autarcheia* or foundational principled self-direction thus unifies theo-bio-political thought.

As the theology of *Metaphysics*, Lambda 7–9, teaches us, the highest being is pure activity, pure being-at-work, *energeia*.[5] This work or function, *ergon*, has nothing of externally directed labor about it; it is purely self-directed and purely self-oriented, insight into insight, *hē noēsis noēsos noēsis* (*Metaphysics* 12.9.1074b34).[6] In fact, the very activity of insight is itself life, *hē gar nou energeia zōē* (12.7.1072b27), and furthermore, this purely immanent activity of insight into insight is a life of pure constant pleasure (1072b24–26). The god who eternally and continually enjoys such a life is the highest substance, *ousia;* it is not merely unified, but simple (1072a32). Aristotelian ontology is thus grounded in a divine biology that is immanent, noetic, and hedonic.

At this point we should note that Richard Norman leads the contemporary campaign of those who refuse to see divine thought as some sort of narcissistic self-contemplation, instead locating the identity of thought and its object in theoretical intuition or, as he puts it, "pure abstract thought" (1969, 66). Norman further posits the identity of active intellect in divine and human theoretical intuition, the latter being actualized only in intermittent flashes. He is criticized for this latter claim in Wedin 1988 (especially 229–45), which emphasizes the essentially representational and imagistic nature of human thought, and is defended in Bradshaw 2001, a fine article that provides comprehensive references and is noteworthy as well for arguing for the efficient and not simply final causality of the prime mover. (In doing so, Bradshaw examines a fascinating episode of political ontology in Aristotle—which we unfortunately cannot deal with here— the comparison of the god to a general as an example of a transcendent ordering principle, and to the members of a household as an example of immanent order, at *Metaphysics* 12.10.1075a11–25.) We will adopt the Norman-Bradshaw position on the identity of human and divine theoretical intuition, but we cannot engage the details of these arguments in this context, as the aim of this section is not to contribute to the millennia of scholarship on the fine points of Aristotelian epistemology, theology, and ontology but simply to establish what it would be like to extend the field of inquiry to establish the outlines of the field of bodies politic in Aristotle as the interchange of ontology, theology, biology, *and* politics. That the identity-thesis for human and divine theoretical intuition is plausible and well represented in the secondary literature should be enough to sanction its use in that endeavor.

We learn from the *Metaphysics* 12.7 passage that the god serves as the erotic spur of cosmic locomotion and biological reproduction; the god moves others, as does the object of eros: *kinei hōs erōmenon* (1072b3). Stars desire the simplicity of the life of the god, but they can only move in circles, the perfect motion. As such, they must settle for mere unity rather than simplicity, as they contain a matter susceptible of locomotion. Divine life is the prime mover, erotically provoking the circles of stellar locomotion and species generation, which mimetically supplement, in their motion and generation, the unreachable constancy of divine life (*De Anima* 2.4.415a25–b7; *Metaphysics* 9.8.1050b28). Sublunar life is here revealed as an erotic mimesis inspired by divine immanent noetic pleasure.

While stellar circular locomotion is the closest approximation to the life of the divine, sublunar biological generation is also circular, after a fashion.[7] The closed circle, that curious pleonasm, is indeed the very medium of Aristotle's thought of generation, the encircling of life. For Aristotle, generation is a change, and all change is ecstatic, moving "from this to that," *ek tinos eis ti* (*Physics* 5.1.225a1). But in generation, the ecstasy is recaptured in the passage of form from father to child, the circle of the species. James Lennox puts it well: "The best possible state of affairs for organisms, given that each of them cannot exist eternally, is that each of them be a member of an everlasting, continuous series of organisms which are the same in form if not in number" (2001, 137). *On the Generation of Animals* portrays generation as immanent change within the protective borders of the circle of the species, oriented to the ideal case in which the superior male principle, working in the spermatic motions of the father that victoriously overcome the motions inherent in the maternal material on which it works, provokes the appearance of the same form in a father-resembling male child: "If the generative residue in the menstrual fluids is properly concocted, the movement imparted by the male will make the form of the embryo in the likeness of itself" (4.3.767b15–17). The detour of the mother's matter does not break; it only provides the circumference, the circle, of the species. Within the circle, change is tamed, kept within the bounds of form. When Aristotle says "from humans come humans" (*Physics* 2.1.193b8; *Metaphysics* 7.7.1032a25, 12.3.1070a29), the orienting ideal case, the closing of the circle in father-resembling male children, must always be kept in mind. But with ideal patriarchal repetition comes the necessary supplement of feminine teratology: if the repetition of masculine form is the ideal, then femininity is the first step to monstrosity, though it is a necessary deviation (*Generation of Animals* 4.3.767b7–11).

With this masculinist orientation, the immanence of circular species generation is reflected in the motif of change being attributed to a thing of the same name (*Metaphysics* 12.3.1070a5) or the same form (7.7.1032a24). So there is no leaving the shelter of form in proper generation, and immanence is preserved in the paternal-filial passage. This teleological semenology of animal generation is literally a patri-archy, since the father, the one responsible for form and finality, is also the efficient cause, the foundational principled source of the change, the *arche metaboles* (*Physics* 2.3.194b30; 195a20). The formal identity of father and child recuperates the exteriority of generation via numerical material/maternal difference. Thus the divinely inspired erotic mimesis in sublunar generation reveals that form dominates repetition in the circular reproduction of the species, which is governed by a patriarchal semenology regulating the maternal material provided by the supplement of feminine teratology.

The basic concepts of ontology, which are coupled in first philosophy with the theology we have just sketched, depend upon a prephilosophical intuition that men and higher animals are substances, *ousiai*. The search for *ousia* in the great central books of the *Metaphysics* is the search for a schema that will reveal the substantiality of those things our prephilosophical intuition has named as *ousiai*. Now, "substance" is a misnomer for *ousia*. An *ousia* is a thing, but also the "thinghood" of the thing, *to ti estin kai tode ti* (*Metaphysics* 7.1.1028a12).

First subject, then matter, and, with difficulty, form are disposed of as candidates for *ousia*. Matter is the unlimited, the indeterminate, *hyle*. Form, *morphe* or *eidos*, is limit, *peras*. Formation is selection from a pool of potentials, cutting off some functions while selecting others. Here we see that eidetic selection, guided by erotic imitation of divinely perfect life, entails hylomorphic limitation. The stumbling block in the identification of *ousia* is always the question of the individuation of *ousia*. Matter is indeterminate; form is general. Both are analytic concepts extracted from the hylomorphic composite, to which the search for substantiality now turns.

In examining this third candidate, questions remain as to the ground of the vertical unity of the hylomorph and the horizontal unity of generation. Hylomorphism, the imposition of form on matter, must be supplemented by the functionalizing of potential, *dynamis*, in a unity wholly devoted to an activity, *energeia*. After the travails of the ousiology, the successful candidate for substantiality is activity: *hoste phaneron hoti he ousia kai to eidos energeia estin* (9.8.1050b1). Activity is not motion; it is self-directed; it has therefore a telos immanent to itself, as does practice (praxis), as opposed to production *(poiesis)*, which has an external telos. Practice is done for its own sake. For Aristotle, the good man is not courageous for the sake of reputation, and he builds a house for the sake of shelter. *Ousia* is not static; it is active and powerful, the ability to rule over parts, to form a unity of heterogeneous materials. Substance is not stasis, nor is it motion; it is self-directed activity. In the pursuit of the model of divine life, energetic dynamism entails ruling unification.

The soul, *psuchē*, is the principle of energetic unity in sublunar living beings, although bodily fatigue prevents it from being pure activity. Rather, it is *hexis*, the capability of a body to perform its characteristic functions (*De Anima* 2.1.412a27).[8] With the soul as principle of integration, the body becomes unified, a single instrument dedicated to living the life—that is, performing the life functions that define the being of the animal—that establishes it as a member of its kind, *panta gar ta physika sōmata tēs psychēs organa* (2.4.415b18). Kosman puts it well: "An animal's body is . . . essentially an organ or instrument . . . an organ . . . is just an entity whose essential nature is to be telic, an entity whose being is to be for the sake of that activity of which it is the organ" (1987, 379).

Now, any formation of a unity is always that of ruler/ruled, and the unification of the animal body under the rule of soul is masterly rather than political, economic rather than civic (*Politics* 1.5.1254a30). The biopolitical register, the thought of the body politic, is never more clearly articulated than in the Aristotelian demand that the energetic organization of the emergent organism, the obedience of the body as instrument of the soul, entails somatic enslavement.

When it comes to a human being, what is it that is to be enslaved? What must be organized to serve the purpose for which the soul rules the body? The *ergon* of humans, our particular activity, is living the life in which the emergent whole, whose integrative principle is *psuchē*, or soul, works with excellent reason, or logos (*Nicomachean Ethics* 1.7.1098a13–16). If the human body is to be an organ or instrument for the soul working with logos, it must be prepared so that its potential to be so organized is selected and cultivated. (In our terms, its virtual phase space must be patterned by the production of a limited repertoire of habitual response capacities, that is, the regular production of certain attractor layouts.) Such preparation of the body consists of correct ethical training (*orthē paideia*, 2.3.1104b13), which develops the virtues focused on the emotions and the appetites, both of which involve pleasure and pain (1104b8, 1104b27); ethical training thus involves training the embodied soul by judicious application of pleasure and pain, not simply by giving rules to the theoretical soul (Burnyeat 1980).

Aristotle offers two conflicting analyses of pleasure. In the *Rhetoric*, pleasure is the movement of the soul accompanying homeostatic regulation, the unifying principle qua nutritive soul bringing the body back into balance, while pain is the movement into disharmony (*Rhetoric* 1.11.1369b33). In the *Nicomachean Ethics*, however, pleasure is not a movement but that which comes to supervene on an activity (10.4.1174b32). This discrepancy points to the difference between types of pleasure. The homeostatic account is relevant only for bodily pleasures associated with food and drink (10.3.1173b5–15); it does not cover the intellectual pleasures, or even many sensory and psychological pleasures (b15–21). With regard to the emotions *(pathē)*, we should note that they are feelings that change men so as to affect their judgment; they are accompanied by pain or pleasure (*Rhetoric* 2.1.1378a20). The emotions are affections of the embodied soul, not the theoretical soul: "It seems that all the affections of soul involve a body—passion, gentleness, fear, pity, courage, joy, loving, and hating; in all these there is a concurrent affection of the body" (*De Anima* 1.1.403a16–18).[9] Reflecting the embodiment of soul—that is, the way in which the soul is the unifying principle *of* the body—the duality in the analysis of the emotions is methodological rather than content driven; emotions can be interpreted in either a physiological or a dialectical manner. For example, anger can be seen as either boiling blood or the desire to return pain for pain (*De Anima* 403a30–b1).

Correct ethical training means the embodied soul must be attuned, at first through the judicious application of pleasure and pain in corporeal training and later, once the proper training has taken hold, through discussion (*Nicomachean Ethics* 10.9.1179b25). When nature, habit, and discussion have come together, the good man is capable of moral intuitions that align with those of the culture, as expressed in the intuitions of previous generations of good men, for what is decent is the common concern of good men regarding action toward others (6.12.1143a31).

What are moral intuitions? It is not simply a matter of having controlled appetites; ethical excellence is not simply the psychic control of the corporeal. The intuitive faculty of the soul is understanding, *nous*, which can be both practical and theoretical; *nous* involves the perception, the immediate seeing *(aisthesis)* of particulars (1143b5). The undemonstrated practical intuition of properly trained people, their immediate grasp of the right course of action, is the standard in ethics, for experience has given them the eye with which to see correctly (1143b14). While intuition is a faculty of the soul, developing practical intuition is a matter of the body politic. Although it may look like simply natural development (1143b6), the development of practical intuition depends on embodied political experience, the enmeshing of the social and the somatic, for the quality of practical *nous* achieved by the body politic is appropriate to one's age (1143b8).

The attainment of correct intuition, the correct grasp of the particulars that reveals what is right and wrong, is at the root of ethical choice *(prohairesis)*, which is both appetitive and rational, a deliberative desire, *orexis bouletikē* (6.2.1139a22). In excellent choice, then, reason (logos) and desire are aligned, with reason revealing the true and desire pursuing the correct (1139a23). The human being is moved, therefore, not by thought alone (1139a35) but by practical choice, which is a desirous understanding or a thoughtful desire *(orexis dianoētikē)* (1139b4–5). The composite nature of the origin of human practical action is essential, for without it, we would have no control of the appetites; we would simply be moved by the objects of desire (3.1.1109b9–15). This means properly trained and mature human beings move themselves: the good person exhibits *autarcheia*, or foundational principled self-direction (Furley 1980).

Aligned with the duality of ethical choice, desire, and intellect, there are two ways to go wrong here: an excess of appetite or a weakness of intellect. Regarding appetite, the desire for the pleasant, the weak-willed person (those with *akrasia*, or "incontinence") intellectually knows what is right, but powerful emotions *(pathē)*, such as gut reactions *(thumos;* e.g., anger) and sexual appetites, disturb the body (7.3.1147a16); in such cases, feeling (pathos) overpowers the weak-willed person's desire to do what intuition tells him is right (7.7.1150b20–21).[10] Regarding problems with intellect, we must distinguish those with the potential to achieve self-direction and those without that potential. The bad man ("intemperate" is a rather weak term) presumably could have developed a proper understanding of practice, but never did, so that he is "persuaded" to pursue perverse or excessive pleasure (7.8.1151a12). On the other hand, slaves lack decision-making ability, while in women it is not strong enough to rule the appetites and in (male) children it is incomplete (*Politics* 1.3.1260a10).

Aristotelian ethical education thus entails the subjectification practices that result in the formation of bodies politic, that is, the selection and consolidation of self-directing traits. The ethicopolitical formation of citizen male children is a process of pedagogic corporeal masculinization, the selection and reinforcement of the right quality of the faculties of the embodied soul with the capacity to withstand the powerful changes to the body that overwhelm the weak-willed person.

We can pause for a moment to consider that the body politic or the patterning of human corporeality by the subjectification practices found in a political context is the key to Aristotle's distrust of the pathetic appeal. In the *Rhetoric*, Aristotle clearly prefers the logical appeal, grudgingly accepts the ethical appeal, and can barely disguise his disdain for the pathetic appeal, even though he describes at great length its emotional bases. We can say that the pathetic appeal aims to move people, aims to divert their bodily flows and hence manipulate their tastes and desires. Now, the more homogeneous the society, the more predictable the emotional response to political triggers, the more predictable the political affect. But in even the most homogeneous society, the channeling of these emotional responses is tricky business; the situation in a multicultural society with transverse and perverse corporeal subjectification practices (i.e., those that render people unpredictable) is even more precarious. Thus, rhetoric is doubly dangerous: even in the best case it moves people by relying on the predictable responses of well-trained solid citizens in a homogeneous society; in the worst case it inflames the multiple flows of unpredictable passions generated in a multicultural society and so enhances social strife. Rhetoric's very existence, then, is a scandal: it exposes the embodied and imitative nature of the political animal, its condition of political affect—that is, precisely that which disrupts the transcendent vision of the intellect, which, as we will see at the end of our discussion, is the most full expression of the organism as the judgment of God.

The political context of embodied ethical training is our next topic. Politics is the science of arranging the city so the citizens can live well; the well-ordered city is also an expression of political physiology, for its being is natural, organic: it is not a mere aggregate of parts but an essential bringing together of components (*Politics* 7.8.1328a22; see also Ferguson 1985). In forming such a natural unity, the character of the citizens is the most important task of the legislator (*Politics* 8.1.1337a10). He must form the bodies of the male children of citizens so they can reproduce the model of their fathers as organized or instrumentalized bodies, allowing their lives to be self-directed emergent wholes displaying excellent reason.

We are finally in a position to see the full contours of Aristotle's thought of bodies politic as social and somatic, as embodied and embedded. In the *Nicomachean Ethics*, everything is gathered under the end state or complete state of flourishing, the telos of *eudaimonia*, which is aimed at by the three main types of lives: pleasure, honor, or theory (*Nicomachean Ethics* 1.4.1095b17). Logos-ruled activities of the soul (1.7.1098a17–20) are the works or functions proper to man (1098a1). Flourishing is an activity *(energeia)* (10.5.1176b1), and our proper activity is found in bringing the most honorable of the logos-ruled functions of the soul to bear: wisdom *(sophia)* (6.12.1144a5), which is excellence of the vision *(theoria)* of the principles *(archai)* of the highest beings (10.6.1177a18). Now the most self-directed of all citizens is the theoretician (10.7.1177a28), and politics is the necessary supplement to safeguard the production of the leisure necessary for theory.

We should pause to note that the relation of the life of theory to human flourishing is a key point in scholarship on the *Nicomachean Ethics.* As with the question of the identity of human and divine in theoretical insight, we cannot enter the details of the many contributions to this issue. The question is (1) whether theory only contributes to flourishing or (2) whether it alone constitutes flourishing or (3) whether it is simply the best sort of flourishing, so that the life of honor is a type of flourishing but not as good as that of theory. If the last is the case, then the life of honor, in a political context, is either a sacrifice some make so that the city can support others who will devote themselves to theory, or it is a temporary duty that philosophers take on once in a while in order to safeguard the leisure necessary to their theorizing, thus compromising their chance for the fullest possible flourishing in order to retain some measure of it. Kraut 1989 and 1999 uphold the position I adopt here, that theory is the best life, with politics a necessary supplement. Ackrill 1999 will uphold the contrary, inclusive, position (i.e., that theory contributes to flourishing).

We see now that affective cognition, the result of our embodied and embedded nature, is a compromise with necessity for Aristotle. It is our natural condition that must be overcome when possible. The body politic is something we have to put up with; the best we can do is to live in a polis that grants us leisure, or *scholē*. Leisure is necessary because the body is the other within our composite nature, which is made up of body *(soma)* and soul *(psuchē)*. At 7.14.1154b22 we read that "our nature *[phusis]* is not simple, but there is in us something else *[heteron]*, in virtue of which we are destructible." This other within us is *ponēros* (1154b31): not "wicked," but "beset by toil," "sweaty," or "hard-working" (1154b8; physiologists tell us that *zōa* are always *ponēi:* living things are always working, always tossing and turning, always stressed). Although the most self-directed of all humans, the theoretician needs a leisured body. Such a leisured body is not one that lies about—as a slavish notion would have it—but is rather a fit and healthy body, an organic or instrumentalized body achieved via a balance of exercise, food, and rest (10.8.1178b35).

The entire argument in the tenth book of the *Ethics* about the proper definition of *eudaimonia* depends on the logical separation of the properly divine pleasure of theory from the base pleasures of the body, which are called childish or trifling *(paidaia)*. We can read at 10.8.1178a23 that "the flourishing *[eudaimonia]* of the nous is separate." What separates the noble from the base is the separation of the controlling element from the controlled: the happiest man is the theoretical, who is said especially to have *autarcheia* (10.6.1177a28), who is self-ordering, independent; on the other hand, the slave, the base one, is susceptible to change from outside, is controlled by another. The leisured body of the theoretician is organized so that it can become effaced before the object of *nous*, its enslaved appetites complacent and quiet, allowing for those precious flashes of theoretical intuition.

In these flashes of active intellect, the identity of divine and human thought is actualized; the philosopher, benefiting from the properly ordered city, is the one who most often and most fully actualizes this identity. Bradshaw clearly enunciates the identity thesis: "It is true that God, being wholly in act, is identical with intellect thus active, but so is human intellect when and to the extent that it achieves perfect realization" (2001, 13). The model of a foundational, principled, self-directed being whose life is immanent pleasurable theory is the god. Kosman comes close to this analysis when he writes: "Beings therefore imitate divinity in being, acting out, what they are; *imitatio dei* consists in striving not to be God, but to be one's self, to emulate the being who is totally active, i.e., who totally is what he is" (1969, 60).

The important thing here is to see political ordering: the ordering of the polis that allows the philosopher to be the human who most fully and most often actualizes the identity of divine and human activity in his flashes of theoretical intuition. Aristotelian political physiology thus requires that the organism, whose masterly enslavement of the body is exemplified in the theoretician's rule of the appetites, be the judgment of God.

Kant

Given the complexities of the transcendental philosophy Kant initiates, which forbid us any theoretical or constitutive knowledge of God and of the organism, demonstrating what Deleuze and Guattari's saying the organism is "the judgment of God" holds for him will be considerably less straightforward than our previous treatment of Aristotle. Our analysis of Kant's theobio-politics will focus on his use of political terms—especially that of *Ge-*

walt, which means variously "force," "violence," and "authority"—in his writings on the organism, which we will extend to consider the relation of aesthetic judgment and moral reason to embodied inclinations.[11] In other words, we will focus on the organism both in a restricted, strictly biological sense and in a wider sense that includes Deleuze and Guattari's notion of the organism as politically attuned biological system. In our analysis, we will concentrate on the *Critique of Judgment* (Kant 1987) but will also include references to Kant's practical philosophy, presented in the *Critique of Practical Reason* (Kant 1956).[12]

In the architectonic of the Kantian system, as sketched in the preface and introduction of the *Critique of Judgment,* understanding legislates the constitutive cognition of nature, as we learn in the *Critique of Pure Reason,*[13] while reason legislates morality as the control of the power of desire, the concern of the *Critique of Practical Reason.*[14] To complete the system, judgment will mediate understanding and reason, just as its object, feeling, will mediate thought and desire (Kant 1987, Preface, 168, and Introduction, III, 178–79). The subject of the *Critique of Judgment* is no longer the merely theoretical knower of the *Critique of Pure Reason,* nor the rational moral agent of the *Critique of Practical Reason,* but a natural and embodied subject through whom surges a "feeling of life," *Lebensgefühl,* the raising and lowering of the intensity of which is felt as pleasure and pain (Kant 1987, ¶1, 204).

We must remember, however, that Kant distinguishes the purely mental feeling of life from physical "life forces" *(Lebenskräfte)* ("General Comment on the Exposition of Aesthetic Reflective Judgments," 274). Upon this distinction rests the entire critique of aesthetic judgment, which must distinguish empirical or physical interest in an object's possible effects on our health (physical life forces) from aesthetic disinterestedness focusing on the pure mental stimulation (mental feeling of life) occasioned by the presentation of an object.[15] Thus our analysis of bodies politic in Kant must take into account the way Kant's distinction of transcendental and empirical allows the distinction of the feeling of life and life forces to work, especially as it concerns the effects of reason in practical life and the effects of imagination in aesthetic judgment—and in, of all things, dreams.

The interplay between the felt intensity of life and life forces will be our guide to Kant's thought of bodies politic. We will pursue several themes: (1) Kant's use of *Gewalt* and other political terms in his bio-philosophy, (2) the intersection of biological thought with his aesthetics, and (3) the relation of these two to his practical philosophy.

We begin by noting that the feeling of life is affected in all registers corresponding to our higher powers: judgment, understanding, and reason. In addition to the pleasures and pains associated with aesthetic judgments of the beautiful and the sublime, we also experience cognitive and practical feelings. We feel a cognitive pleasure in discovering a harmony of laws of nature with our cognitive power, since we can unify heterogeneous empirical laws of nature under principles (Kant 1987, Introduction, V, 184; Introduction, VI, 187). Practical feeling, on the other hand, is twofold: we feel pain in the thwarting of the inclinations in the face of the moral law, but this very pain will produce respect for the moral law as a "positive feeling" (Kant 1956, Part I, Book I, Chapter III, 73–74).

When we come to the layout of the book itself, the *Critique of Judgment* has two main sections: a discussion of aesthetic judgment—the judgments of beauty and of the sublime—and a discussion of teleological judgment—the judgment of the "purposiveness" *(Zweckmässigkeit)* of organisms and of nature as a whole. A difficult concept, we will take natural purposiveness (what Kant will call "objective material purposiveness") to mean the way in which the whole is greater than the sum of its parts and, in fact, determines the meaning and function of the parts. Such a whole is one that for us must be the purpose of the design of the product so judged (Kant 1987, ¶65, 373). In other words, we must think of natural products as purposes of a designer, on the analogy of our own design practices. In thinking these teleological and aesthetic judgments, we are thus led to think of nature and art together, to mediate theory and practice, nature and freedom.

In moving to consider aesthetic judgment in more detail, we must remember that here we deal with reflective judgment, which in contrast to determinate judgment, does not subsume a sensory manifold under a pregiven concept, but instead arrives at its judgment, its way of making sense, in the very process of exploring the manifold given it (Introduction, VII, 190). In other words, reflective judgment is the escape from stereotyped cultural categories; it is provoked by the fresh encounter with the novel, an encounter that is felt before it is thought, or, even more radically, felt in excess of any recuperative thought. In Deleuze's terms, reflective judgment is provoked by affect. In the aesthetic judgment of beauty, an external object is judged as capable of provoking a harmonious interplay of imagination and understanding (¶9, 218; ¶23, 244); the sublime, on the other hand, is the judgment that an external object is capable of provoking a disharmony of imagination and reason (¶23, 245). In beauty, nature appeals to us as a pleasant stimulus, as provoking a disinterested nonsensuous pleasure; by contrast, the mathematical sublime provokes the feeling that nature is too big for us to comprehend, while the dynamical sublime provokes the feeling that nature overpowers us, that we are radically insufficient to match its physical power.

Aesthetic Judgment

The "Critique of Aesthetic Judgment" section has three main topics: beauty, sublimity, and morality. We will examine each in turn.

BEAUTY

Let us first consider the affective cognition of beauty, which is the free play of imagination and understanding. The body capable of judging beauty would seem to be the free body, one that avoids stilling the play of the sensory manifold by a conceptual ordering. But aesthetic judgment has not only to identify the free play of imagination and understanding in beauty (as well as the violation of imagination by reason in sublimity) but also to tell the difference between these pure spiritual motions (feeling of life) and the agreeable bodily vibrations of enjoyment or health-producing bodily motion (life forces) (Kant 1987, "General Comment," 274). For Kant, the distinction between spiritual motions and bodily vibrations can only hold because of a distinction between empirical and transcendental imagination. The distinction between aesthetic judgment and interest would be undone if mental movements provoke bodily movements and vice versa. To follow this lead we have to discuss the possibility of mistakes in the judgment of taste. Kant recognizes that it is always possible to fail to distinguish pure pleasure and sensuous enjoyment, that is, to fail to distinguish mental and bodily motion. This sometimes takes the form of our mistaking charms for form (¶14, 225). Now this ever-present possibility ruins our certainty in counting on another's assent to our judgment of taste (¶19, 237).

How are we supposed to make the distinction between pure mental pleasure and sensuous bodily enjoyment, between the feeling of life and life forces? The judger of taste "can be certain by merely being conscious that he is separating whatever belongs to the agreeable and the good from the liking that remains to him after that" (¶8, 216). Thus we have here a process of abstraction/subtraction, in which we are to become conscious of separation, of a difference in kind between bodily and mental movements. This becoming conscious of a differential pure pleasure is a sensation (*Empfindung*) of the "enlivening" or "quickening" (*Belebung*) of the two mental powers of imagination and understanding to an "indeterminate" (*unbestimmt*) but unified activity (¶9, 218). But the sensation of a differential pure pleasure of pure mental motion, in strict separation from bodily motion, is impossible without invoking the empirical/transcendental distinction, for the (empirical) imagination can provoke bodily movements, as we will see. Thus, on occasion one fails to observe these distinctions, mistakes bodily for mental motion, and makes an erroneous judgment of taste (¶8, 216).

For Kant, this mistaking of mingling for purity is only a mistaken application of an authority given us by a law and in no way annuls the authority itself (¶38, 290n). But the required separation involves "unavoidable difficulties" so that the subsumption "may easily be illusory" (¶38, Comment, 290–91). However, Kant insists, the "difficulty and doubt" about the separation of the bodily motion of the agreeable from the mental motion of pure pleasure in no way casts doubt on the principle of the legitimacy of the claim, just as one doesn't doubt logical judgments on the basis of incorrect application—although Kant admits that incorrect logical subsumption is not done "so often and so easily" (291). What is the source of the difficulty in making aesthetic judgments, in distinguishing mental and bodily motion? It is that imagination itself, which is part of the pure mental movement of aesthetic judgment, can also produce bodily motion in dreams. We come face to face with one of Kant's strangest concepts, that of the life-saving somatic action of the oneiric imagination:

> For when all the motive forces of the bodily kind *[körperlichen bewegenden Kräfte]* relax, dreams serve to thoroughly agitate the vital organs by means of imagination and its great activity (which in dreams usually reaches the level of an affect). . . . Therefore, if no such force moved us inwardly *[innerlich bewegende Kraft]* . . . sleep would even in a healthy person probably be a complete extinction of life. (¶67, 380)

There are several things to notice here. First, imagination can reach the level of an affect, that is, can induce mental motion (cf. "General Comment," 272, where an affect is the production of a mental motion). Second, this imaginal mental motion is an inward force, an inward force that can produce bodily motion. Since imagination is involved in the pure pleasure of mental motion, we can say that imagination is the forceful provocation of mental *and* physical motion. Of course Kant can try to recuperate this question of imaginal vibrations by distributing them across the empirical/transcendental divide. The question then becomes how one is to distinguish the workings of the transcendental imagination producing pure mental movements and empirical imagination provoking bodily motions.

We now reach the heart of the bodies politic underlying Kant's affective cognition of beauty, for, as we will see, to make those distinctions one needs a leisured body, a quiescent body, and leisure is distributed by position in a political structure enforced by *Gewalt*. To think of leisure one has to think of the production, distribution, and consumption of surplus time, which is dependent on the level of technological development of the social systems involved. With the notion of surplus time, we can think of the leisured aesthetic body as one enjoying a free relation to time, such that the imagination can playfully compose formations of the sense manifold by varying the temporal presentation of aspects of the object. These varying formations are submitted to the understanding for a check against its lawfulness. Beauty is thus the temporally playful experience of an object whose existence is not of interest, a purely temporal, mentally immanent object with no necessary reference to spatial existence.

On the other hand, the working, needy body must conceptually still the manifold into a recognizable—a cognizable—object whose spatial and temporal location can be verified so that its utility for meeting needs can be assessed. Thus the free body open to the aesthetic judgment of taste and the announcement of beauty, or to the experience of the sublime, is only possible through the organization of a commonwealth of taste or feeling that regulates the production of bodies politic by taking the logical possibility, open to all, of discerning pure spiritual free play from agreeable bodily vibration and assigns that to a probabilistic distribution among the leisured cultured and the hungry vulgar, a politico-economic distribution in which *Gewalt* plays a major role. In other words, *Gewalt* rules the civic and somatic bodies politic that allows the affective cognition of a leisured body capable of aesthetic judgment.

Let me expand upon this last point. On Kant's account it is a structural possibility of each person to engage in the free play of imagination and understanding, and thus achieve one condition of receptivity to beauty. The other condition is to disregard the agreeable and the good and so isolate spiritual or purely mental movement from bodily vibration. But the civic body politic, organized by coercion and enforced by *Gewalt*, takes these possibilities and distributes them to classes of people as probabilities. Through their roles in the social system, some are much more likely to be able to have leisured bodies and thus be able to appreciate the pedagogy of taste and so to achieve aesthetic receptivity. Others are too busy at work, or are hungry: "Only when their need has been satisfied can we tell who in a multitude of people has taste and who does not" (¶5, 210). The blitheness of this phrase might be forgiven Kant as the mere index of his belonging to a society of relative technological primitiveness, a sign that he couldn't even foresee the possibility of universal leisure. But Kant turns the social probabilities of being able to achieve taste into moral evaluation: interest in natural beauty is a sign of moral character (¶42, 298–99).

SUBLIMITY

Let us turn from beauty to consider the bodies politic underlying the affective cognition of the sublime. For Kant, the very physical insufficiency revealed in the sublime both provokes a violent torsion of our faculties and reminds us of our radical moral superiority to violent nature. Thus, sublimity becomes the feeling of pleasure through or even in painful violence to our animal nature: "The feeling of the sublime is a pleasure that arises only indirectly: it is produced by the feeling of a momentary inhibition of the vital forces *[Hemmung der Lebenskräfte]* followed immediately by an outpouring of them that is all the stronger" (Kant 1987, ¶23, 244). Furthermore, the liking for the (mathematical) sublime is linked to respect (¶27, 257) and comes about through "a subjective movement *[Bewegung]* of the imagination by which it does violence *[Gewalt]* to the inner sense" (¶27, 259). The harmony of the faculties resulting in a judgment of the beautiful produces pleasure directly; this is contrasted with an inner violence that provokes first pain and then an indirect pleasure in a judgment of the sublime.[16]

A certain spiritual tourism reveals the political affective cognition of the experience of the sublime. Rough men, unlike those with culture and developed moral ideas, would see only hardship were they to be forced to live in the mountains "we" find sublime:

> It is a fact that what is called sublime by us, having been prepared through culture, comes across as merely repellent to a person who is uncultured and lacking in the development of moral ideas. In all the evidence of nature's destructive force *[Gewalt]*, and in the large scale of its might, in contrast to which his own is nonexistent, he will see only the hardship, danger and misery that would confront anyone forced *[gebannt]* to live in such a place. (¶29, 265)

To undergo the experience of sublimity one must enjoy a socioeconomic position that enables one to visit a safe vantage point from which to see desolate places that would bring only misery to those unfortunates forced to try to live there. Our ability to not acknowledge the authority *(Gewalt)* of nature while still acknowledging its "might" *(Macht)* (¶28, 260)—and thereby acknowledging the *Gewalt* of reason over sensibility ("General Comment," 269, 271)—is thus an index of political affect, whereby sublimity is evoked in the fearfulness without fear that is open to those spiritual tourists who are merely passing through unruly nature.

Let us focus on the way the political affect of the spiritual tourism of the sublime is revealed in the formula "fearfulness without fear." The dynamic sublime is announced when nature's force is represented rather than directly faced, when a visit to a vantage point from which the wilderness is seen is the occasion for the thought of how dangerous this place might be if one were really to live here. Kant writes: "We can, however, consider an object *fearful* without being afraid *of* it, namely, if we judge it in such a way that we merely *think* of the case where we might possibly want to put up resistance against it, and that any resistance would in that case be utterly futile" (¶28, 260; emphasis in original). The actual exposure to nature's force results in fear; it is the mere thought of nature's force, open to those who can afford to visit a vantage point upon the wilderness, which enables the experience of the sublime.

Later, Kant's point is put in terms of the imaginative evocation of a fear that is not actual but is, instead, merely provoked by the safe sight of nature's force:

> Thus any spectator who beholds massive mountains climbing skyward, deep gorges with raging streams in them, wastelands lying in deep shadow and inviting melancholy meditation, and so is indeed seized by *amazement* bordering on terror, by horror and a sacred thrill; but since he knows he is safe, this is not actual fear: it is merely our attempt to incur it with our imagination. ("General Comment," 269; emphasis in original)

Again, the body politic affectively open to the experience of sublimity is the leisured and safe body of the spiritual tourist who visits the vantage points from which one safely sees nature's force, without real exposure to it, in order to provoke an imaginary fear, what Paul Guyer calls an "emotional vibration" (1996, 204). In this imaginary fear the supersensible vocation of reason is announced as that which *would be* untouchable by nature's force *were* one's body actually to be exposed to it. The political affect of the sublime is the experience of this counterfactual conditional by spiritual tourists.

MORALITY

We have spent considerable time dealing with the bodies politic, the affective cognition, and the political affect involved in aesthetic judgment. We have done so because of its close connection to morality, which as we will see is the culmination of Kant's bio-philosophy; this will confirm that for Kant, as well, the organism is the judgment of God. At the pivot of the book, the transition from aesthetic to teleological judgment, Kant writes that beauty is a symbol of morality. Symbolization is a way of presenting an analogy of concepts; for instance, a despotic state can be symbolized by a hand mill because, presumably, both contain the concept of mechanical determination of passive objects by a transcendent force, just as a constitutional monarchy can be symbolized by an "animate body" *(beseelten Körper)* because, presumably, both contain the concept of immanent self-organization (Kant 1987, ¶59, 352; see also Ginsborg 2004).

The symbolization of morality by beauty thus concerns an analogous relation of the faculties in both forms of judgment. One analogy is that of self-legislation. Regarding the way we judge a universal pleasure in the apprehension of the beautiful, Kant writes, "Concerning objects of such a pure liking *[eines so reinen Wohlgefallens]* it [judgment] legislates to itself, just as reason does regarding the power of desire" (¶59, 353). Furthermore, judgment of the beautiful and moral judgment both focus on the harmony of freedom and law: judgment of the beautiful focuses on "the freedom of imagination . . . as harmonizing with the lawfulness of the understanding," just as moral judgment focuses on "the freedom of the will as the will's harmony with itself according to universal laws of reason" (¶59, 354). In this way the lawful free play of faculties in judgments of beauty symbolizes the self-legislating freedom of practical reason. However, the direct pleasure of the aesthetic judgment of the beautiful must be contrasted with the pain of the moral law's stifling of inclination, while the rebound effect that produces the "positive moral feeling" of respect is, if anything, analogous to the pleasure through pain of the sublime. Thus we must supplement the notion of beauty's symbolic relation to morality with the notions of affective cognition we find in sublimity and morality, a parallel that explains Kant's focus in the "General Comment" on the close connection of sublimity and morality.

Teleological Judgment

Let us now consider teleological judgment. While Kant tells us there is no pleasure in teleological judgment as such (Kant 1987, "First Introduction," 228), we will see at the end of our discussion that pleasure and pain play large roles in the ultimate resolution of the Kantian system to which the discussion of bio-philosophy leads us. There is a long road ahead of us, as we must discuss teleological judgment as such: the teleological judgment of organisms and the whole of nature, the antinomy of teleological reason, and finally the solution of the antinomy in the relation of our discursive understanding to the negative idea of a nondiscursive understanding.

OVERVIEW

To make sense of organisms, given our cognitive makeup, we must use teleological judgment: we judge the whole as determining the parts ("downward causality"). We do not understand how such holistic determination can be brought about mechanically (i.e., using only the powers of matter), so we must use an analogy with our making of artifacts: the whole must be a design, and the designer must have a purpose in making that design. Now, in considering the peculiarity of our cognitive powers, we find we have a discursive understanding, but the very fact of this restriction to discursivity reveals the idea of a nondiscursive understanding (Kant 1987, ¶77). This nondiscursive understanding must be that which is capable of intuiting the relation of whole to part that we find in organisms. Thus, in the restricted, purely biological sense, the organism is the judgment of God.

The extended sense of this phrase comes from the following argument. When we consider the whole of nature as a system, we find that we can only posit man's culture—his ability to refine his skill and his discipline—as the ultimate end *(letzte Zweck)* within nature, and man's freedom—his status as moral agent—as the final end *(Endzweck)* of nature, standing outside nature (¶83, 431). We then see that we must further determine the nondiscursive understanding as the moral author of the world, whose purpose in designing nature is that the highest good (the deserved happiness of man qua moral agent) be possible. That the path to the extended sense in which the organism as judgment of God holds for Kant is now clear. The moral author is to rule as a "legislating sovereign *[gesetzgebendes Oberhaupt]* in a moral kingdom of purposes" (¶86, 444), just as pure practical reason is to rule in man as moral agent, who is prepared by a culture of discipline that will combat the "despotism of desires" (¶83, 432). Here we see Kant's theo-bio-politics most clearly.

THE RESTRICTED SENSE OF
"THE ORGANISM IS THE JUDGMENT OF GOD"

The details of the arguments presented in the critique of teleological judgment surpass our ability to provide a comprehensive treatment in this context. Nevertheless, we can provide some comments. First, we must discuss the relation of teleological judgments to judgments of natural causality in mechanical terms. Ginsborg 2004 is indispensable here. According to her reading, Kant means by "mechanism" a blind causality attributable to the attractive (gravitational phenomena) and repulsive (impenetrability) forces he thought belonged to matter as such. The problem is that biological phenomena seem to be inexplicable to us solely by means of mechanism, that is, the powers of unorganized matter. Although there are many twists and turns to Kant's argument, one of the keys from the very start is that teleological judgment will always be limited to a regulative use of reflective judgment. In other words, teleological judgments can guide our natural science as a presupposition—it can be a heuristic in generating principles to order phenomena so that they make sense to us—but we cannot assume that we have knowledge of things in themselves by means of teleology.

In keeping with this principle, Kant begins the critique of teleological judgment with the claim that such judgments are justified if we observe nature "by *analogy* with causality in terms of purposes, without presuming to explain it in terms of that causality" (Kant 1987, ¶61, 360; emphases in original). A "causality in terms of purposes" is a causality that works on the basis of an idea in the mind of a producer that is responsible for the production of that product (¶10, 220).

Teleology has three foci for Kant: the functioning organism, its development, and the whole of nature (Grene and Depew 2005, 94). Kant treats the organism in ¶64–66. At first, in ¶64, Kant "provisionally" defines individual things that are natural purposes as being *"both cause and effect of itself"* (370; italics in original). Kant distinguishes three senses of this overlapping of cause and effect. First, with regard to its species, a tree produces itself via generation of another tree of the same species, thus "ceaselessly . . . preserving itself as a species." Second, the tree produces itself in its growth through its assimilation of "matter," which thereby gains the quality of the tree. Third, mutual cause and effect entails the mutual dependence of parts upon each other.[17]

In ¶65 Kant renders his account more precise and brings the question of development to the fore; a thing is a natural purpose if "the connection of *efficient causes* could at the same time be judged to be a *causation through final causes*" (373; italics in original). Here, just as the parts exist as a result of the other parts (efficient causality), we can think that they exist for the sake of each other and the whole (final causality). This existence for the sake of the whole renders the part an organ that produces the other parts. (In our terms, organization entails synchronic emergence in which the whole constrains the parts and thereby enables systematic focus.) A natural purpose is thus "both an *organized* and a *self-organizing* being"; it is possessed of a "formative force" *(bildene Kraft)* that distinguishes it from a machine with merely "motive force" *(bewegende Kraft)*. The formative force of the organized being imparts form to form-lacking matter, thereby organizing it (¶65, 374; italics in original). The organized being is not merely an "analogue of art," so the self-organizing powers of nature evident in the organism, although (and because) inscrutable to us, should be called an "analogue of life," a being in which each part is both an end and a means of itself (¶65, 374). Strictly speaking, Kant continues, although natural self-organization "has nothing analogous to any causality known to us," we may, in restricting it to regulative use of reflective judgment, use a "remote analogy with our own causality" to guide our investigations of organisms (¶65, 375).

In ¶67, Kant shifts from the consideration of organisms to that of nature as a whole. Natural purpose or intrinsic organization or organism is not the same as a purpose of nature or something fit into an overarching scheme of nature. To construct such a scheme, we would need a final purpose of nature, and this would presuppose a supersensible end: "For the purpose of the existence of nature itself must be sought beyond nature" (378). But the concept of natural purpose does lead us to the idea of nature as a planned system, though as we should by now expect, this is only a regulative use of reflective judgment, a guide. Thus, teleological judgment does not detract from the use of mechanism in understanding nature, but we have still to solve the problem of how to relate teleological and mechanical judgments; we are faced with an antinomy.

The "antinomy of teleological judgment" presented in ¶70 states in its thesis that it must be possible for us to judge all natural phenomena in mechanistic terms, while its antithesis says that some products of nature cannot be judged mechanically; they require a notion of final causality. According to Ginsborg, recent scholarship runs against resolving this antinomy by relegating *both* principles, that of teleological causality and that of mechanical causality, to regulative and reflective status (as some have thought Kant to be doing in proposing a "preliminary" to the solution of the antinomy in ¶71), since the first critique had shown the necessity of making mechanical causality constitutive and determinative of all cognition of nature (Ginsborg 2004).

After Kant disposes of rival systems in ¶72–73, he takes up his argument again in ¶74. He reminds us that the concept of a natural purpose (that which is behind the principle of judging nature teleologically) cannot be used dogmatically for determinative judgment, but is merely regulative for reflective judgment (¶74, 396). The supersensible reference of the concept of natural purpose is essential, however, and this renders it off-limits to cognition; in the familiar Kantian move, it is thinkable but not knowable. In ¶75, we read that "Given the character of our cognitive powers . . . we are absolutely unable to form a concept of how such a [systematically organized] world is possible except by thinking of it as brought about by a supreme cause that *acts intentionally*" (399). Mechanism will never enable us to explain organisms and systematically organized nature; there will never be a "Newton" for a "blade of grass" (400).

In a key move, Kant tells us in ¶77 that the relegation of the idea of natural purpose to a regulative role in judgment (a relegation necessitated by the recognition of certain peculiarities of our cognitive power), rather than to a constitutive role in the understanding, presupposes "the idea of some possible understanding different from the human one" (¶77, 405). This peculiarity of our cognitive nature is the *discursive* status of our understanding, the fact that it does not determine the particular to be brought under the universal (rather, we receive the particular through our sensibility, formed by the a priori forms of intuition). Opposed to such a discursive understanding would be an intuitive understanding, one gifted with a complete spontaneity of intuition. (We must note that we have only a negative idea of such an intuitive understanding. We cannot understand how it operates; all we know is that it is possible to think of a nondiscursive understanding.) Rather than laboriously seeking, step by step, to unify all the particular laws of nature, as we are forced to do, an intuitive understanding would immediately intuit a necessary harmony of nature's biological diversity with universal physical laws. The harmony we find is contingent: universal physical laws *allow* for the particular laws governing biological diversity, but they do not, so far as we can tell, *require* those particulars; for an intuitive understanding, however, the fit of universal and particular would be necessary (¶77, 406; see also Ginsborg 2004).

A series of further reflections on our cognitive makeup leads Kant to claim that "the character of the human cognitive power forces us to seek the supreme basis for such combinations in an original understanding, as cause of the world" (¶77, 410). In working through the solution to the antinomy, Kant will explain how mechanism must be coordinated with teleology: we must have recourse to the supersensible as the possible, though not to us cognizable, ground of nature. This recourse to a "supreme understanding" allows us to "subordinate" mechanism to teleology (¶78, 414): we are to

investigate nature using mechanical terms as far as possible without los-
ing sight of the fact that the nature of our reason will "force" us to ultimately have recourse to teleological judgment—which for us presupposes
a design, a purpose, and a designer—in order to understand some "natural
products," that is, organisms (¶78, 415). We thus see how the organism,
in a restricted, purely biological sense, is the "judgment of God" for Kant:
our judgment must rely on a notion of purposiveness to understand organisms, but such recourse to purpose leads us to the notion of a nondiscursive
understanding as "nature's supersensible substrate" that allows a "recon-
ciliation" of mechanical and teleological causes (¶77, 414).

THE EXTENDED SENSE OF
"THE ORGANISM IS THE JUDGMENT OF GOD"

We are now in a position to see how the teleological judgment of nature's
purpose feeds into Kant's thought of the organism, turning it toward a
theo-bio-politics. While the cultural production of man's capacities for purposiveness is the ultimate purpose of nature here on earth (¶83, 431), the
final purpose of nature—that in virtue of which nature is planned—can
exist only outside nature, in man as moral subject (¶84, 435; ¶86, 443).
The purposive intelligence that would have the possibility of man's morality as its final purpose in arranging natural order must be a moral God.
Thus, nature and freedom are finally related in the thought of a moral ar-
chitect God, a "legislating sovereign in a moral kingdom of purposes," who
guarantees that nature must at least cooperate with our moral action (¶86,
444). The divine twist to Kant's thought of the human organism as body
politic comes into focus: "In this way *moral* teleology compensates for the
deficiency of *physical* teleology and for the first time supplies a basis for a *theology*" (¶86, 444; italics in original). The systematicity of nature, which we
may presuppose, results in the thought of God as a practical supplement.

The key to understanding this last aspect of Kant's thought of the body
politic is to consider culture. We must distinguish the culture of skill from
the culture of discipline while at the same time searching for the connection to *Gewalt* as force, violence, and authority. The culture of skill prepares our capacity to set ourselves purposes, while the culture of discipline is negative, consisting in the "liberation of the will from the despotism
of desires," which "rivets us to certain natural things" necessary for our
biological survival, that is, the furthering of our life forces (¶83, 432). In
effect, we are riveted to pleasure; freedom comes only through self-chosen
pain. Nature has given us our impulses so we would not "neglect or even

injure our animal characteristics" (¶83, 432). With the culture of discipline, however, we can develop our freedom to "tighten or to slacken, to
lengthen or to shorten" our impulses "as the purposes of reason require."
In an interesting twist, the way to the rule of reason is prepared by the pleasure of fine arts and sciences, which "make great headway against the tyranny of man's propensity to the senses and so prepare him for a sovereignty
in which reason alone is to dominate *[Herrschaft . . . in welcher die Vernunft
allein Gewalt haben soll]"* (¶83, 433).

Those purposes of reason are the painful establishment of the moral law
as the ground of action in a person, as we learn in the *Critique of Practical Reason.* The establishment of the moral law as ground of action, "by
thwarting all our inclinations, must produce a feeling which can be called
pain," while the moral law, as positive in itself, commands respect in "striking down, i.e., humiliating, self-conceit" (Kant 1956, Part I, Book I, Chapter III, 73). The pain of humility must be self-chosen, as Kant makes clear
in discussing humility, "a sublime mental attunement, namely voluntary
subjection of ourselves to the pain of self-reprimand" (Kant 1987, ¶28,
264). Here we see the political affect of morality parallel that of the sublime: the violent, painful striking down of our natural body will rebound to
reveal a supersensible vocation. As Paul Guyer puts it: "The painful frustration of our inclinations itself makes palpable to our senses the majesty of
the moral law, which produces a positive feeling of admiration for the principle of our own will and activity" (1996, 358–59).

In his moral philosophy, Kant objects to the propensity to make our subjective grounds of choice into an objective determining ground of the will,
self-love, a propensity that can even attempt to make our self-love into law,
the condition Kant calls self-conceit. Guyer expresses Kant's thought of the
body politic perfectly: "Human beings achieve their unique moral value by
elevating themselves above their inclinations, which is not to say by erad-
icating them but by ruling them through reason. . . . Kant's underlying
image is that what is unique to us is our capacity for self-activity, which can
be realized only through our self-governance, and that is where he places
our sole moral worth" (350; italics added). Thus respect for the moral law
reasserts the proper role of the rational moral law as sole legislator of the
kingdom of practical reason. Respect for the moral law is a disciplinarian
that through sublimely painful self-humiliation prevents the revolution
that would place self-love in charge.[18]

Whether or not the feeling of admiration for the purely rational will
and the feeling of respect for the moral law are pleasurable is a difficult

question. Guyer claims, "The feeling of respect is thus a complex but ultimately pleasurable state of feeling . . . grounded . . . in the recognition of the possibility of the realization of our own objectives" (360). These objectives in this case include "the objective of governing ourselves by reason rather than by inclination" (359). Just like the indirect pleasure of the sublime, this pleasure at the prospect of rational self-governance is produced on the basis of the immediate effect of pain produced by the moral law's effect on inclination. However, focusing on these immediate effects, Kant writes in the *Critique of Practical Reason*, "Respect is so far from being a feeling of pleasure that one only reluctantly gives way to it as regards a man" (that is, recognizing the morality of others is also painful to us) (1956, 77). Whether or not the feeling is that of pleasure, the focus on the rule of reason and the painful stifling of inclination is clear. Whether Kant's political affect of self-chosen pain, of sublime humility, and the moral crushing of the inclinations are ultimately hedonic is questionable, but that it is dolorous through and through is obvious.

We have seen that for Kant as well as for Aristotle the organism is the judgment of God. This is so in a restricted sense, whereby we can understand organisms only by positing God's nondiscursive understanding, and in Deleuze and Guattari's extended sense, whereby the politically attuned biological system—in this case, the rational moral agent ruling the body—is modeled on God's rule in nature: both are instances of the *Gewalt* of reason in its manifold senses of force, violence, and authority. In chapter 4 we will turn to Deleuze and Guattari's own thought of the organism as judgment of God, followed by a consideration of the body without organs.

Chapter 4　The Anorganic Body in Deleuze and Guattari

AFTER OUR TREATMENT of the theo-bio-politics of the organism in Aristotle and Kant, we now turn to Deleuze and Guattari. We have seen what it means to apply the strange-sounding dictum that the organism is the "judgment of God" to canonical works in the history of philosophy. For Deleuze and Guattari, "organism" is for the most part not a biological term;[1] it is instead a term that refers to political physiology, in which somatic bodies develop patterns of affective cognition that fit them into hierarchically ordered social bodies.

In this chapter I first trace their treatment of the organism in *Anti-Oedipus*. As wildly creative as that book is, Deleuze and Guattari up the ante in provocation when they say, in *A Thousand Plateaus*, "God is a Lobster" (1987, 40). In explicating this claim, I show how Deleuze and Guattari break with the divinely modeled political physiology we saw at work in Aristotle and Kant. Deleuze and Guattari are naturalists, but for them nature is not simply focused on perfection; it is bivalent, with a hierarchically ordered aspect named "stratification"—the expression of which is found in the saying "judgment of God"—and with an experimental, creative aspect found in the "line of flight."[2]

I then examine the counterpart to the organism, the anorganic or non-organismically ordered body, the "Body without Organs" (BwO), a body whose organs have escaped the constraints of the organism that previously integrated their functions and are now free to experiment with novel orderings. These experiments will be perhaps "reterritorialized" to produce another organism—one that functions properly in a hierarchical politics—or they may produce an immanently ordered body that functions in a new, self-organized, and democratic social system. But such experimentation is not guaranteed success; fascism is an ever-present danger to capitalist bodies politic on all three compositional scales: personal, group, and civic (Protevi 2000).

The Organism Is the Judgment of God (Who Is a Lobster)

Anti-Oedipus

Deleuze and Guattari derive the terminology for their thought of bodies politic—the organism and the Body without Organs—from the schizophrenic artist and writer Antonin Artaud, who writes: "The body is the body / it is all by itself / and has no need of organs / the body is never an organism / organisms are the enemy of the body" (Deleuze and Guattari 1984, 9). This passage requires a preliminary comment before we begin our reading of *Anti-Oedipus.*

My treatment of Deleuze and Guattari concentrates on the conceptual content of their work and underplays the performative effect of their writing. One of Deleuze's themes is to criticize the assumption that we like to think, that we are set up for thinking (Deleuze 1994, 131). Following Heidegger, Deleuze maintains that we are not yet thinking (144). For the most part, Deleuze holds, people go through life slotting things into categories (placing differences within a horizon of identity) and passing along clichés; "idle chatter," as Heidegger puts it. To push us out of our comfort zone, we must be forced to think, Deleuze maintains, in a fundamental encounter whose object cannot be recognized, that is, cannot fit into our preexisting categories (139).

One of the ways Deleuze and Guattari force us to think is their bizarre collection of sources. Why on earth are we reading the ranting of a schizophrenic like Artaud in a philosophy book? Better yet, why are we reading these not as examples of pathological thought but as providing the basic concepts of the work?[3] Another is their vulgarity, as in the infamous opening lines of *Anti-Oedipus:* "It is at work everywhere, functioning smoothly at times, at other times in fits and starts. It breathes, it heats, it eats. It shits and fucks *[Ça chie, ça baise].* What a mistake to have ever said *the* id" (Deleuze and Guattari 1972, 7/1984, 1). What kind of philosopher writes like that? A third performative effect is their humor, as when they mock Melanie Klein: "Say it's Oedipus, or I'll slap you upside the head *[sinon t'auras un gifle]*" (54/45; translation modified). There are many more passages like this; it is safe to say very few philosophy books contain as many jokes, puns, and double entendres as *Anti-Oedipus.* A fourth element in their performance is the gleeful coarseness of their polemics. Among many other examples, thinkers of the signifier are associated with the lap dogs of tyrants, members of the French Communist Party are said to have fascist libidinal investments, and Freud is described as a "masked Al Capone." All in all, the performative effect of reading *Anti-Oedipus* is unforgettable. I would not go so far as to say that *Anti-Oedipus* is written in a schizophrenic style, but it is not a normal philosophy book, and the effect of their writing cannot be adequately conveyed while discussing its conceptual content.

With that bracketing of performance in mind, let us turn to the key term of *Anti-Oedipus*, "desiring-production," which reveals Deleuze and Guattari's conceptual and terminological innovation in breaking open the field for the study of bodies politic. Crisscrossing Marx and Freud, they put desire in the ecosocial realm of production and production in the unconscious realm of desire. Rather than attempting to synthesize Marx and Freud in the usual way—by a reductionist strategy that either (1) operates in favor of Freud by positing that the libidinal investment of social figures and patterns requires sublimating an original investment in family figures and patterns (i.e., Oedipal triangulation) or (2) operates in favor of Marx by positing neuroses and psychoses as mere superstructural by-products of unjust social structures—Deleuze and Guattari call desiring-production a "universal primary process" underlying the seemingly separate natural, social, and individual realms. Desiring-production is thus not anthropocentric; it is the very heart of the world. All natural processes, even those well beyond the human, are processes of desiring-production: "Everything is a machine. Celestial machines, the stars or rainbows in the sky, alpine machines . . . nature as process of production" (1984, 2).

Besides its universal scope, we need to realize two things about desiring-production right away: (1) there is no subject that lies behind the production, that performs the production; and (2) the "desire" in desiring-production is not oriented to making up a lack, but is purely positive (1984, 25). Desiring-production is autonomous, self-constituting, and creative: it is the *natura naturans* of Spinoza or the will-to-power of Nietzsche. In our terms, desiring-production—or better, its repression in social production—is responsible for the construction of bodies politic: as we will see, social machines produce interlocking social and somatic systems by regulating material flows as they pass in and out of civic and somatic bodies politic, as well as patterning the affective cognition habits of subjects.

As we can see from this brief sketch of its key term, *Anti-Oedipus* is, along with its conceptual and terminological innovation, a work of grand ambitions: among them (1) an ecosocial theory of production, encompassing both sides of the nature/culture split, which functions as an ontology of change, transformation, or becoming; (2) a "universal history" of social formations—the "savage" or tribal, the "barbarian" or imperial, and the capitalist—which functions as a synthetic social science; and, to clear the ground for these functions, (3) a critique of the received versions of Marx and Freud—and their intersection in the attempts to synthesize them by analogizing their realms of application. In pursuing its ambitions, *Anti-Oedipus* has the virtues and the faults of the tour de force: unimagined connections between disparate elements are made possible, but at the cost of a somewhat strained conceptual scheme, to which we now turn.[4]

Anti-Oedipus identifies two primary registers of desiring-production: the natural, or metaphysical, and the social, or historical. They are related in the following way: desiring-production is that which social machines repress, but also that which is revealed in capitalism, at the end of history (a contingent history, one that avoids any sort of dialectical laws of history). Capitalism sets free desiring-production even as it attempts to rein it in with the institution of private property and the Oedipal patterning of desire; schizophrenics are propelled by the charge of desiring-production thus set free, but they fail at the limits capitalist society proposes, thus providing a clue to the workings of desiring-production. The psychiatric register, as an index of the natural-historical registers, is thus the key heuristic in *Anti-Oedipus*.

It is important at the start to realize that Deleuze and Guattari do not advocate schizophrenia as a lifestyle or as the model for a political program. The schizophrenic, as a clinical entity, is the result of the interruption or blocking of the process of desiring-production, its having been taken out of nature and society and restricted to the body of an individual where it spins in the void rather than making the connections that constitute reality. Desiring-production does not connect "with" reality, as in escaping a subjective prison to touch the objective; rather, it makes reality, it is the Real—in a twisting of the Lacanian sense of the term—in which we conceive it not as a reality that is produced as an illusory and retrojected remainder to a signifying system but simply as reality itself in its process of self-making. The schizophrenic is a sick person in need of help, but schizophrenia is an avenue into the unconscious, the unconscious not of an individual but the "transcendental unconscious," an unconscious that is social, historical, and natural all at once. Like lesion studies which move from damage to reconstruct normal function, Deleuze and Guattari study clinical schizophrenia as an indirect means to study normal subjectivity, that is, to study the way it cuts itself off, protects itself, from the often unbearable intensities of desiring-production. The self-protection of the ego is not necessarily cowardice; Deleuze and Guattari accept that in many cases prudence is indeed the better part of valor. While it is true that some formulations of *Anti-Oedipus* are utterly disdainful of the fixed subject— "Destroy, destroy" is one of the slogans for schizoanalysis (1984, 311)—a note of caution is clear in *A Thousand Plateaus*, where we read that "staying stratified . . . is not the worst that can happen" (1987, 161).

In studying the schizophrenic process, Deleuze and Guattari posit that in both the natural and the social registers desiring-production is composed of three syntheses: the connective, the disjunctive, and the conjunctive. These three syntheses perform three functions: production, recording, and enjoyment. We can associate production with the physiological, recording with the semiotic, and enjoyment with the psychological registers. While it is important to catch the Kantian resonance of "synthesis," it is equally important to note, in keeping with the poststructuralist angle we discussed previously, that there is no subject performing the syntheses; instead, subjects are themselves one of the products of the syntheses. The syntheses have no underlying subject; they just are the immanent process of desiring-production. Positing a subject behind the syntheses would be a transcendent use of the syntheses. Here we see another reference to Kant. Taking up Kant's distinction in transcendental philosophy between immanent and transcendent, Deleuze and Guattari propose to study the immanent use of the synthesis in a "materialist psychoanalysis," or "schizoanalysis"; by contrast, psychoanalysis is the transcendent use of the syntheses, producing five paralogisms or transcendental illusions, all of which involve assigning the characteristics of the extensive properties of actual products to the intensive production process (1984, 75).

As we have claimed, in Deleuze and Guattari's exploration of desiring-production, the psychiatric register is the key heuristic. Deleuze and Guattari posit a fourfold pattern in schizophrenics: paranoia, catatonia, divine contact, and multiple subjectivities. They feel persecuted, they break down, they feel in touch with the divine as they recover, and they identify with "the names of history." (As with their etiology of the schizophrenic patient, Deleuze and Guattari do not propose this pattern as meeting the standards of clinical psychiatry. They are not pretending to be physicians; they do not claim that all schizophrenics exhibit each one of these symptoms. Rather, they are philosophers attempting to use schizophrenic processes as clues to the workings of bodies politic.)

Before moving to discuss the schizophrenic process, two key concepts must first be elucidated: organs and desiring-machines. Organs are necessary for a living body; they produce a flow that is cut by another organ, just as they cut into the flows of other organs. Organs are flow-break couplings in which a matter-energy flow is interrupted, and part is siphoned off to flow in the economy of the body. In other words, organs are a body's way of negotiating with the outside and regulating the inside, appropriating and regulating matter-energy flow. Deleuze and Guattari call organs desiring-machines for two reasons. First, "machine" for them indicates any connection of organs, or a system of flow-breaks; mechanical or technological machines are only a type of machine. Second, schizophrenics often experience their organs as machines, in both the generic sense of flow-break connections and the specific sense of technological machines. Certainly there are notable cases in which schizophrenics actually connect their bodies with real technological mechanisms, but even when they do not actually do so, many feel their bodies are composed of machines that come from outside.

For schizoanalysis, the organs are "part-objects," which are formed by the connection of flows. The milk flow connected to the mouth, for instance, forms a desiring-machine or part-object. Part-objects are so named because they do not refer to whole persons. In the mouth-breast machine, the breast is experienced in itself, separate from the face of the mother, while the mouth is experienced in itself, separate from the excretory organs to which it is linked. Considered in their immanent function, the organs/part-objects/desiring-machines form a multiplicity: they are a field of difference in itself, the multiple with no relation to a superior coordinate system that allows localization and individuation. Put simply, the part-objects do not belong to persons; they are instead points of intensity, nodes in a network of material flows in and out of bodies, the connection of the ecosocial and the somatic. It is important for us to note that when they work, the desiring-machines form patterns of intensive flows: there is a certain probability that given one flow-break connection, another will follow. Thus a body politic is ordered; it fits into a scheme in which ecosocial flows enter and exit somatic bodies, attuning them to its pattern. But that pattern need not be rigid and in the service of a social machine as a transcendent unity; in other words, the body politic, while it must be ordered, need not be an organism.

While it is not my goal to bring all of Deleuze and Guattari's concepts into contact with current psychological and physiological research, there are some preliminary and interesting connections. First, in the ontological register, in keeping with the immanent use of syntheses, *Anti-Oedipus* is thoroughly materialist, perhaps even bordering on the reductionist. "We believe in the possibility of a biochemistry of schizophrenia," Deleuze and Guattari remark at one point (1984, 84). Second, a closer look can often resolve an apparent conflict. For instance, to consider the specific point at hand, Deleuze and Guattari claim that Melanie Klein's discovery of the part-objects was botched by their being referred to as pre-Oedipal, that is, as destined to be assigned to global persons in constituting the Oedipal triangle (44–45). In finishing off their critique of Klein, Deleuze and Guattari write: "Partial objects are only apparently derived from [*prélevés sur*] global persons; they are really produced by being drawn from [*prélevés sur*] a flow or nonpersonal *hylè*, with which they reestablish contact by connecting themselves to other partial objects. The unconscious is totally unaware of persons as such" (1972, 54 / 1984, 46). This seems to suggest that the infant is unable to distinguish between self and other, a notion that conflicts with recent research that confirms that infants possess a body schema that enables a self-other distinction.

To reconcile Deleuze and Guattari's notion of the infant as a multiplicity of part-objects with this research, it is important to distinguish here between body image and body schema. Gallagher 2005 is an indispensable resource here. Gallagher distinguishes the body schema as "a system of sensory-motor capacities that function without awareness or the necessity of perceptual monitoring" from the body image as "a system of perceptions, attitudes, and beliefs pertaining to one's own body" (2005, 24). The apparent tension between the new body schema research and Deleuze and Guattari's notion of a multiplicity of part-objects is resolved by distinguishing between bodies and persons. Persons in the psychoanalytic framework that is the target of Deleuze and Guattari's critique are global unities formed by their insertion in a family structure. Persons have learned to identify the momentary production of emotional states (more on this later) as belonging to an ego that takes its name and learns the proper pattern of its organ connections from its position in a family. All these higher-level cognitive functions refer to the body image, which is confirmed by Deleuze and Guattari's remark, "The body without organs . . . is the body without an image" (1984, 8). The later developments, which constitute the sophisticated political affect of the Oedipal triangle, should not be read back into the self-other distinction in the infantile body schema. The latter is certainly a necessary condition for the former, but there is no deterministic teleology here. From our developmental systems perspective, development of the body image is contingent upon input from social systems, and there are many ways a body's organ connections can be patterned that would not fit the definition of the Oedipalized body or organism. Surely no one wants to claim that Oedipal patterns are genetically determined, do they?[5]

To return to our narrative, we note that while the psychiatric is privileged as the key heuristic (that is, to use classical terms, first in the order of discovery), Deleuze and Guattari say that in fact the social is primary (first in the order of being). In other words, subjects qua persons are produced ontogenetically; they develop by being patterned by the society in which they are found. The study of bodies politic is the population study of such ontogenesis, the study of the differential implantation of patterns according to the political markers of gender, race, class, and other relevant factors. For Deleuze and Guattari, the ecosocial register of the connective synthesis is social production in which a system of flow-breaks is constructed: to use a Louisiana example, flows of fish are interrupted by nets and hooks and then connected to human mouths and stomachs. To produce those nets and hooks, flows of wood and fiber are connected with axes and needles (previously the product of flows directed by metallurgy), and so on. While social production does produce by means of the connective synthesis, it is a repression of desiring-production, since social production never simply follows the intensive flows of desiring-production but is always regulated in terms of persons, namely, nodes in the social network located at the intersection of lines of filiation (descent) and alliance (marriage).

Following the psychiatric register as their heuristic, Deleuze and Guattari first consider the paranoid moment of schizophrenia. In doing so, they isolate the first synthesis, the connective, and the first function, production. Again, the link of paranoia and the connective synthesis of production is heuristic only, not constitutive. Schizophrenics feel the connections that normally pass unnoticed in the physiological register. While for the normal subject these flows are unconsciously regulated, schizophrenics sometimes feel the material flows that are produced and cut by organs. The paranoid reaction consists in repulsing the desiring-machines, or sensed organ-flows, as an invasion; schizophrenics often feel themselves attract or "miraculate" the returning machines.[6]

To see how such to-and-fro of desiring-machines works, we turn to the second synthesis, disjunction, and the second function, recording. The second clue in the psychiatric register of schizophrenia, following paranoia and preceding divine contact, is catatonia. The body repulses the invading machines and shuts down. Physiologically, the flows through the organs drop in intensity, with the limit being intensity equals zero. Taking up Artaud's phrase, the moment of catatonia is the Body without Organs.[7] The body becomes an undifferentiated mass; it erases its previous patterns of flows-breaks among organs and is open to new patterning (compare the neurodynamics of "unlearning" in Freeman 2000a and 2000b.) As such a tabula rasa, the BwO is the site for the inscription of the social relations that regulate production; these relations determine which organs can connect with which others. The catatonic moment, the BwO, is thus a recording surface on which a social machine regulates the flows of its connections with (and in) somatic bodies. Social repression works by forming exclusive disjunctions so that organ connections are forced into fixed patterns: either this or that connection is possible, not both (as would be the case with inclusive disjunctions).

To see how such inscriptive regulation operates, we must follow the schizophrenic body as it recovers from catatonia, as the body renews itself in the moment of divine contact. The formerly catatonic body feels its organs spring to life; it seems as though the body is calling for the organs to renew themselves. In the rush back from the moment in which intensity is equal to zero, the body is suffused with a feeling of divine energy: this is the attractive, or miraculating, moment in which the body calls for the organs. Here the recording surface "falls back" on production and claims credit for it. In social production, Deleuze and Guattari call the attracting recording surface the socius. In keeping with the priority of the social, the individual, or somatic catatonic BwO, is "the ultimate residuum of a deterritorialized socius" (1984, 33). In other words, when socially regulated flows break loose, some somatic bodies overload and break down; when the schizophrenic comes alive again after the breakdown, he or she gets back in touch with desiring-production, attracting the organs to the body with an energy that is experienced as divine.

The relation between socius and organ patterning is the key to our reading of Deleuze and Guattari in terms of the notion of bodies politic. According to their "universal history," social life has three forms of socius, the social body that takes credit for production: the earth for the tribe, the body of the despot for the empire, and the capital for capitalism. According to Deleuze and Guattari's reading of the anthropological literature, tribal societies mark bodies in initiation ceremonies so that the products of an organ are traced to a clan, which is mythically traced to the earth or, more precisely, one of its enchanted regions, which function as the organs on the full body of the earth. The signs in tribal inscription are not signifiers: they do not map onto a voice but enact a "savage triangle forming . . . a theater of cruelty that implies the triple independence of the articulated voice, the graphic hand and the appreciative eye" (1984, 189). In this way, primitive meaning codes regulate the territorialization of material flows, that is, the linking of those flows with the earth.

Empires overcode these tribal codes, tracing production back to the despot, the divine father of his people. When tribal signs are overcoded, the signifier is formed as a "deterritorialized sign" allowing for communication between the conquered and the conquerors. Signifiers are a "flattening" or "bi-univocalization": two chains are lined up, one to one, the written and the spoken (205–6; cf. Derrida's notion of phonocentrism). The body of the despot as imperial socius means that workers are the hands of the emperor, spies are his eyes, and so on. The material flows of despotic empires are thus deterritorialized: they are no longer bound to the earth, but are freed from earthly circuits and reterritorialized on the body of the despot, which saturates the social field.

Capitalism, however, is the radical deterritorialization of the material flows: they are no longer bound to the body of the absolute monarch (or even onto that of the guild or city) but freed as capital and labor. This deterritorialization proceeds alongside a radical decoding that is absent from the despotic overcoding: here is the notorious loss of meaning in capitalism, as "all that is solid melts into air." While previous social machines had zealously coded signs that made sense of flows by associating them with the earth or with the body of the despot, capitalist production is credited to the "body" of capital, so that this form of recording works by the substitution of an axiomatic for a code: in this context an axiomatic means a set of simple principles for quantitative calculation of differences between flows rather than elaborate rules for qualitative judgments that map the flows and their organs onto the socius. Capitalism's command is utterly simple: connect deterritorialized flows of labor and capital and extract a surplus from that connection. Thus capitalism sets loose an enormous productive charge—Connect those flows! Faster, faster!—the surpluses of which the institutions of private property try to register as belonging to individuals. Those individuals are primarily social (as figures of capitalist or laborer), but they are represented and experienced as private (as family members). Whereas organs of bodies were socially marked in previous regimes (as belonging to the clan and earth, or as belonging to the emperor, as in the *jus primae noctis*), body organs are privatized under capitalism and attached to persons as members of the family. In Deleuze and Guattari's terms, capitalism's decoded and deterritorialized flows are reterritorialized on "persons," that is, on family members as figures in the Oedipal triangle.

To understand such Oedipalized personalization as subject formation, we must turn to the third synthesis, conjunction, and the third function, enjoyment. Following the psychiatric register as their heuristic, Deleuze and Guattari work backward from the phenomenon of multiple subjectivities to the process of normal subject formation. At each connection of organs, a little bit extra—a surplus value—is produced and consumed in enjoyment. Schizophrenics feel no compulsion to relate the multiple episodes of enjoyment to a single ego; Deleuze and Guattari call this phenomenon the nomadic subject. Physiologically, subjective enjoyment arises from the flow of energy through different singular states of the body. In schizophrenics, the privatization of experience demanded by capitalism fails; there is an immediate libidinal investment of the social field, and the subject as singular experience receives "one of the names of history." Personalization is the habit of registering all these experiences under the same name, the same "I." Under capitalism, recording brings out the moment of private property; when this is combined with personalization as ego formation, we find the cry "The surplus value of this flow belongs to me!" and the "me" is constituted by its position in the Oedipal triangle, which determines which organs it can connect with.

This notion of multiple levels of subjectivity, with the fixed subject as a production of identity out of difference, is not as strange as it might first sound. Consider the connection with Damasio's somatic marker theory of emotion in which a subject of intense emotional experience arises from a singular state of the body. In Damasio 1999 we find three selves. First, there is a "proto-self," defined as "the state of activity" within "an ensemble of brain devices which . . . continually represent, *nonconsciously*, the state of the living body, along its many dimensions" (Damasio 1999, 22; italics in original). Second, there is the "core self," which we can identify with Deleuze and Guattari's "nomadic subject," which Damasio defines as "a transient entity, ceaselessly re-created for each and every object with which the brain interacts" (17). In other words, with each organ connection—or more precisely, at each body state as its multiple organs connect with their flows—a core self or nomadic subject arises. And third, there is the production of individual, personalized, socialized, and familial fixed subjectivity, the "autobiographical self," which "depends on systematized memories of situation in which core consciousness [correlated with the core self] was involved in the knowing of the most invariant characteristics of an organism's life—who you were born to, where, when, your likes and dislikes . . . your name, and so on" (17). Here we see a correlation with the Oedipal subject of Deleuze and Guattari.

This is not the occasion for a full-fledged comparison of Deleuze and Damasio's notions of the self and the subject, but we should note that both insist on the primacy of affect in both the core self and the nomadic subject. Damasio writes concerning the core self: "You rise above the sea level of knowing, transiently but incessantly, as a *felt* core self, renewed again and again. . . . The first basis for the conscious *you* is a feeling which arises in the re-representation of the *nonconscious proto-self in the process of being modified* within an account which establishes the cause of the modification" (1999, 172; italics in original). Compare with Deleuze and Guattari's discussion of the nomadic subject: the hallucinations (I see, I hear) and delirium (I think) of schizophrenics "presuppose an *I feel* at an even deeper level" (1984, 18). Life and lived experience are not representative of family images; an "actual, lived emotion" comes out of living your body as "nothing but bands of intensity, potentials, thresholds, and gradients" (19). Despite all the differences regarding the status of representation and the value of fixity we might discuss, both Deleuze and Damasio agree that the subject, at the level of the core self or nomadic subject, is continually born and reborn as the body passes through singular configurations of its multiple dimensions or, as modeled in complexity theory, as the trajectory of the body passes through points in its phase space.

Another connection of Deleuze and Guattari and Damasio can help us explain how it is that Oedipal patterning works. An organism, or Oedipalized body, permits itself some connections while forbidding itself others. While Deleuze and Guattari do not provide any details on the psychological mechanisms involved in this patterning, we could further speculate that the positive and negative somatic markers associated with possible futures provides the unconscious emotional valuations that mark off some organ connections as prohibited. Damasio 1994 develops the "somatic marker hypothesis," whereby scenarios of future situations are marked by flashes of as-if body images: images that are produced by an imagined scenario of what it would be like to live through the imagined situation.[8] The feeling of what this or that future would be like to live through—as these memories of the future are formed in association with past training as the application of pain or the allowing of pleasure—thus serves to shape the phase space of the body into zones of the permitted and the prohibited, the pleasant and the nauseating. Unconscious emotional premonitions thus assign an emotional weight to the imagined scenarios, and these connections are policed by exclusive disjunctions. In other words, in entertaining the possibility of organ connections marked as deviant, a negative emotional weight is unleashed which turns the body away from that possible connection and back to other patterns with more positive emotional weights. Such patterning could be modeled in complexity theory terms as the set of singularities determining the layout of attractors in the phase space of affective cognition capacities. Deleuze and Guattari put it like this: "The points of disjunction [the singularities marking borders of basins of attraction] on the body without organs [the phase space of the body] form circles [the basins of attraction] that converge on the desiring-machines [the attractors as patterns of organ connection]; then the subject—produced as a residuum alongside the machine . . . passes through all the degrees of the circle, and passes from one circle to another" (1984, 27). The subject follows the patterns of organ connection, which are set up by inscription by a social machine.

To sum up, the "neurobiologico-desiring machines" (Deleuze and Guattari 1984, 63) form an "organism" when their patterns produce a body that serves its social machine. The organism as Oedipalized body is a selection of a subset of the possible connections of the body, orienting it to docile reproductive labor. What is reproduced? Either products at work (connect your organs with those of the technical machines of the capitalist) or species reproduction via heterosexual penile-vaginal intercourse (connect your organs the way they should be connected to make babies). In other words, to use the terms of the "philosophy of difference," Oedipalization means the fitting of difference into a preexisting categorical scheme or horizon of identity whereby recognition of identities, especially those of gendered personal identity, is possible.

We have barely scratched the surface of the rich text of *Anti-Oedipus*, but we have shown at least the outlines of its notion of the organism. Now let us turn to *A Thousand Plateaus*, where the organism is named the judgment of God, and thereby put ourselves in position to finish our brief exploration of the way bodies politic have appeared in the history of philosophy.

A Thousand Plateaus

Let me say a few words about the difference between *A Thousand Plateaus* and *Anti-Oedipus*. First, we can note that while *Anti-Oedipus* is concerned with the ecosocial, the emphasis is on the social. By contrast, *A Thousand*

Plateaus has a much more consistently wide range of registers: cosmic, geologic, evolutionary, developmental, ethological, and so on. Second, while *Anti-Oedipus* has a classical conceptual architecture—chapters that develop a single argument—*A Thousand Plateaus* is written as a "rhizome," as allowing connections between any of its points. Just as it is an exaggeration to say that *Anti-Oedipus* is written in a schizophrenic style, there are some definite patterns to *A Thousand Plateaus* that detract from its purely rhizomatic status. Nonetheless, there is a sort of mapping of form and content as *A Thousand Plateaus* tries to produce a rhizome; it tries to "make" the multiple, as Deleuze and Guattari put it (1987, 6). Finally, the results of the paralogisms of *Anti-Oedipus* become strata in *A Thousand Plateaus:* the organism (the unification and totalization of the connective synthesis of production, or the physiological register); the signifying totality or *signifiance,* which we can render as "signifier-ness" (the flattening or biunivocalizing of the disjunctive synthesis of recording, the semiotic register); and the subject (the reification of the conjunctive synthesis of consummation, the psychological register).

To understand how Deleuze and Guattari think of bodies politic as organisms in *A Thousand Plateaus*— as the political patterning of a somatic system—we must first understand that for them the biological sense of organism, the natural sense of the organism, is already political; *A Thousand Plateaus* operates with a notion of political physics. I mean that in *A Thousand Plateaus* natural processes are bivalent for Deleuze and Guattari, that nature incarnates an abstract machine of stratification and destratification. While stratification reduces complexity in producing a body composed of homogeneous layers, destratification increases complexity by allowing consistencies or assemblages, instances of transversal emergence. In other words, a consistency or assemblage is a functional whole that preserves the heterogeneity of its component parts and enables further rhizomatic connections (positive affects as increase in *puissance*), as opposed to a stratum, which relies on the homogeneity of components. The "abstract" part of the strange term "abstract machine" simply means that the processes of stratification and destratification occur in many material registers, from the geological through the neural/subjective. A machine binds parts into a functional whole; an abstract machine is the diagram for processes that form functional wholes in different registers. Nature forms strata or systems composed of homogeneous parts layered into a functional whole, but it also breaks down such strata, freeing parts to form connections with heterogeneous others, thereby forming consistencies or assemblages whose operation preserves the heterogeneity of its components. Nature operates in, on, and between the strata, and also beyond them, on the plane of consistency, that is, destratification as the condition for the formation of assemblages.

Professor Challenger, the narrative subject of the "Geology of Morals" chapter of *A Thousand Plateaus*, tells us that the abstract process of stratification works by means of a "double articulation" of content and expression, each of which has both substance and form. (The two "pincers" of content and expression thus explain the figure of the "lobster"; the reification of the abstract process of stratification results in a "God" who seemingly performs the operation.) The abstract machine of stratification has four processes in two articulations. Deleuze and Guattari use the example of sedimentary rock, but the stratifying abstract machine operates in many different registers, social as well as natural. The first process is sedimentation, which determines (a) substance of content, that is, the selection of homogeneous materials from a subordinate flow; and (b) a form of content, that is, the deposition of these materials into layers. The second process is folding, in which there is (c) a form of expression, that is, the creation of new linkages; and (d) a substance of expression, the creation of new entities with emergent properties (1987, 43).[9] Constructing an organism out of a body (patterning its organ connections to render the body useful to a hierarchical social machine) is one of the three principal strata separating humans from the plane of consistency, the condition for the production of new transversally emergent bodies politic. The other strata that keep us from such experimental creativity are significance and subjectivity, that is, the lures of endless interpretation ("What did that mean?" instead of "Into what flows did that intervene?") and passionate egocentricity ("It's me, I tell you, it's me. I'm the one to blame / get the credit!" instead of participating in an encounter that surpasses our ability to identify our contribution to it).

As a stratum, the organism can be explained using the terminology of form-substance and content-expression, though we must remember that on the organic stratum, content and expression must be specified at many different scales: genes and proteins, cells, tissues, organs, systems, organism, reproductive community, species, biosphere. Skipping over several scales (cells, tissues, organs) for simplicity's sake, let us focus on the level of organic systems (e.g., the nervous, endocrine, and digestive systems), where the substance of content is composed of organs and the form of content is coding or regulation of flows within the body and between the body and the outside. The form of expression at this level is homeostatic regulation (over-coding of the regulation of flows provided by organs), while the substance of expression, the highest level emergent unifying effect, is the organism, conceived as a process binding the functions of a body into a whole through coordination of multiple systems of homeostatic regulation.

As we have seen in our discussion of *Anti-Oedipus*, organs are points of intensity of matter-energy, a place of activity differentially related to the flows in the environment and in the body's other organs. An organism, then, is a particular organization of organs, one that is centralized and hierarchical, appropriating the matter-energy of the organs and funnel-ing a surplus portion of them to the benefit of the organism as a transcen-dent entity relative to its organs, a superior body that has appropriated the organs as labor. Through its organization of the organs, each one biting into and regulating a flow, an organism is a thickening or coagulation of flows of biomass and genetic material. The organism is thus a stratum with regard to those flows, "a phenomenon of accumulation, coagulation, and sedimentation that, in order to extract useful labor from the BwO, imposes upon it forms, functions, bonds, dominant and hierarchized organizations, organized transcendences" (1987, 159). The organism profits from the labor of the organs.

To pick up our theoretical background laid out in chapter 1, the organ-ism is an emergent effect of organizing organs in a particular way, a "One" added to the multiplicity of organs in a "supplementary dimension" (21, 265). The organism is the unifying emergent effect of interlocking homeo-static mechanisms that quickly compensate for any nonaverage fluctua-tions below certain thresholds to return a body to its normal condition (as measured by species-wide norms; hence Deleuze and Guattari's sense of "molar"). The organism as unifying emergent effect is a stratum on the BwO, a construction, a certain selection from the virtual multiplicity of what a body can be, and hence a constraint imposed on the BwO: "The BwO howls: 'They've made me an organism! They've wrongfully folded me! They've stolen my body!' " (159). While all intensive bodies are "ordered"—contain some probability structure to the passage of flows among their organs (only the empty BwO, at intensity equal to zero, has removed all patterning among its organs)—the organism is "organized"; its habitual connections are centralized and hierarchical. In the terminology of *Anti-Oedipus*, the organs of an organism are patterned by exclusive disjunc-tions, which we render here as a series of virtual singularities actualized in such a way as to preclude the actualization of other, alternative, patterns; in other words, an organism, in complexity theory terms, is locked into a basin of attraction or, better still, a stereotyped set of such basins. As a fixed habitual pattern locked onto normal functioning as determined by species-wide average values, thinking of biological reality in terms of the organism deadens the creativity of life; it denies the concrete reality of developmental plasticity, so that it is "that which life sets against itself in order to limit itself" (503). Like all stratification, however, the organism has a certain value: "Staying stratified—organized, signified, subjected—is not the worst that can happen" (161), although this utility is primarily as a resting point for further experimentation.

For Deleuze and Guattari, organisms occur in at least two registers, biological and political, at once. Their treatment of the organism is thus thoroughly naturalizing, for the same abstract machine of stratification, the same Lobster-God, operates in any register from geological to social as the way to appropriate matter-energy flows and build a layer that slows down the flow and funnels a surplus to an organized body. The abstract machine of stratification is biological and political at once; we can say that the geology of morals set forth by the Lobster-God is a bio-political organization. The political sense of organism means the Oedipalized body of *Anti-Oedipus*, one whose desire (pattern of organ connection) has been captured and overwritten by a social machine. The organism as Oedipalized body is a selection of a subset of the possible connections of the body, orienting it to docile reproductive labor.

Culture, or the multitude of concrete socializing practices, produces the body politic as "organism." Cultural production of bodies politic is a recompensatory reterritorialization or stratification to make up for a previous deterritorialization on the organic stratum, the freeing of humans from instinct. Cultural practices—in Deleuze and Guattari's terminology, machinic assemblages operating on the human strata of organism, significance, and subjectification—select from a vastly larger pool of potential connections, opened up due to the deterritorialization of some of our organs (61). The production of the organism (its actualization from the virtual field of practices, or in model terms, the production of habitual attractor layouts) also has a diachronic dimension. *Anti-Oedipus* argues that Oedipalization is not universal but is only the capitalist form of that reterritorialization. As stratification—selection and consolidation—the social machine selects from the set of potential organ connections and consolidates them, via a series of exclusive disjunctions, into fixed and seemingly irrevocable patterns of allowable organ connections. As such a fixed pattern that provides a centralized and hierarchical organization of material flows useful to a social machine, the organism is the judgment of God.

When we now turn to the phrase that qualifies God for them, Deleuze and Guattari appear as philosophical jokers or provocateurs when they say God is a lobster (1987, 40). As refreshing as Deleuze and Guattari's introjection of humor into philosophy is, they are also serious about the Lobster-God. In keeping with Deleuze's Lucretian, Nietzschean, Spinozist heritage, Deleuze and Guattari are committed to the immanence of natural processes. For Spinoza, God and nature were equivalent *(Deus sive Natura)*. Deleuze and Guattari's commitment to Spinoza is not to his notion of God, but to his insistence on the immanence of natural processes. Given his historical context, which defined God as transcendent, Spinoza's insistence on immanence was seen as atheism. If for us God is defined as transcendent, then Deleuze and Guattari and Spinoza are indeed atheists. Deleuze and Guattari do not, however, say that the abstract machine is God, rather that God is a lobster. The lobster is doubly articulated, the result of the process of stratification symbolized by the Lobster-God. But the abstract machine of nature is bivalent: not just stratification producing organisms but also destratification producing the plane of consistency. So the Lobster-God is neither transcendent nor all of nature; it is only one aspect of nature as abstract machine of stratification and destratification. The partiality of the Lobster-God must be acknowledged.

For Deleuze and Guattari, when the term "God" is not being used to signify stratification, it is the name of a transcendental illusion sometimes occurring in various cultures. In the "universal history" section of *Anti-Oedipus,* the overcoding of tribal territorial codes pushes the social recording surface onto the body of a despot filiated with a sky god (1984, 194). All credit for production goes to the despot and/or to the transcendent God. But this is a transcendental illusion produced by an immanent process of invasion, conquest, and semiotic overcoding (the historical origin of the signifier, according to Deleuze and Guattari [1984, 207–8]). Adopting a Kantian practice, Deleuze and Guattari view critique as the refusal to use concepts derived from products to discuss their own production process. Thus the ground cannot resemble that which it grounds: the virtual cannot resemble the actual. The stratification process as part of the abstract machine of nature does not resemble strata; God as part of the abstract machine, as the Lobster-God of stratification, is responsible for, but does not resemble, that which is produced, namely, God as the transcendent unitary entity on which the organism is modeled. Thus for Deleuze and Guattari's thought of bodies politic, "God is a lobster" is a critical statement that exposes the illusion of the organism as the judgment of God.

The Body without Organs

We turn now from the organism to focus on the Body without Organs, or BwO, one of the most difficult of Deleuze and Guattari's concepts to grasp. We must first appreciate that the term "Body without Organs" is a misnomer and is responsible for much confusion. It would have been better to call it by the more accurate but less-elegant term "the anorganic body," as Deleuze and Guattari freely admit: "The BwO is not at all the opposite of the organs. The organs are not its enemies. The enemy is the organism" (1987, 158). A BwO retains its organs, but they are released from the habitual patterns they assume in its organism form; insofar as the organism is a stratum (a centralized, hierarchical, and strongly patterned body), a BwO is a destratified (decentralized, dehabituated) body. Adding to the potential confusion is a significant change in the term "full BwO" from *Anti-Oedipus* to *A Thousand Plateaus*. In *Anti-Oedipus*, the BwO is "full" when it is catatonic, a mere surface across which desiring-machines are splayed and upon which a nomadic subject moves (1984, 8). As such a surface, the full BwO allows for the recording of desiring-production; in the social register it is the socius (10). In *A Thousand Plateaus*, however, the full BwO is positively valued; it is the "empty" BwO that must be avoided (1987, 150). The full BwO allows for connection with other destratified bodies, while the empty BwO is a black hole for subjectivity, where nothing happens (citing Burroughs, the junky is a prime example here [150]).

Although the organism is a stratum imposed on the BwO, it is equally true that a BwO is an object of construction, a practice; it is "what remains after you take everything away" (151), after you take away all the patterns imposed on the BwO. A BwO has ceased to be content for an expression; that is, it has ceased working as part of a functional structure and has entered a plane of consistency, a condition in which it is now open to a field of new connections, creative and novel becomings that will give it new patterns and triggers of behavior. In other words, the BwO is the organism moved from equilibrium or a fixed set of habits to an intensive realm where it has changeable, "metastable" habits.

The relation of intensity to the BwO is complex and the key to understanding the different aspects of the term BwO, which we will designate as follows, using our own terminology. We should distinguish four types of BwO, considering both the singular and the universal. First, we have a single BwO as (1) an "intensive" BwO, a body whose entry into a nonequilibrium state enables experimentation with patterns that distinguish it from an organism's fixed patterns; and as (2) a "virtual" BwO, the limit of destratification of any one body (and hence its virtual register or phase space). Then we have the "universal" BwO as (3) intensive, that is, as the plane of consistency, the condition for the construction of all assemblages (equals the Earth) (72); and as (4) virtual, as the plane of immanence or absolute deterritorialization, the freeing of matter from form and function (equals the Cosmos).

An "intensive" BwO is "populated by intensities" (153). This means that in a "molarized" population of organisms (what Foucault would call a "normalized" population) one can determine a standard measure or extensive property—an "order word"—that will trigger production (producing such uniform reaction is the goal of disciplinary training). On the other hand, with an intensive BwO, only experimentation with the cartography of a body, its immanent relations of flows (longitude), will determine the triggers of production (affects or latitude) (260–61). With a "virtual" BwO, we see that insofar as any intensity of flow among the organs of a body will actualize a certain series of singularities indicating a pattern or increased probability of connection among organs, a BwO is a body at zero intensity of its flows (153). In this way a BwO is the state space of a body, its virtual realm. The "universal" BwO, then, is the plane of consistency of all bodies and, hence, the arena in which all connections are possible and where ethical selection must occur (153–54).

A (singular) virtual BwO is not reached by regression, for a BwO is not the infantile body of our past but the virtual realm of potentials for different body organization precluded by the organism form.[10] Thus it is reached by a systematic practice of disturbing the organism's patterns, which are arranged in "exclusive disjunctions" (specifying which organs can ever meet and outlawing other possible connections). A virtual BwO is the result of having counteractualized the exclusive disjunctions of the organism to reach the virtual field where multiplicities are series of singularities ordered in "inclusive disjunctions," that is, series in which any possible connection is equally probable. Since all actual bodies must make choices, the key ethical move is to construct an intensive body in which patterning is flexible—that is, where a virtual BwO can more easily be reached—so that any one exclusive disjunction can be undone and an alternate patterning accessed.

Constructing an intensive BwO is done by disturbing the organism, that is, by disrupting the homeostatic feedback loops that maintain organismic patterns by a shift in intensity levels or by a change of habitual practices; in complexity theory terms, such a shift is modeled as a move out of a basin of attraction that thereby leaves behind the layout of singularities that unifies bodily patterns at an emergent level. In this way a body of purely distributed, rather than centralized and hierarchized, organs can be reached, sitting upon its underlying matter-energy flow. In other words, an intensive BwO is purely immanently arranged production, defined as matter-energy flowing without regard to a central point that drains off the extra work, which is the surplus value of the organs for an emergent organic subject in a "supplementary dimension" (265) to those of the organs (159). As an object of practice reached by starting from the organism, an intensive BwO needs to be cautiously constructed by experimentation with body practices. It never hurts to come back to this phrase: "Staying stratified—organized, signified, subjected—is not the worst that can happen" (161). Nor is the intensive BwO an individualist achievement: "For the BwO is . . . necessarily a Collectivity [*un Collectif*] (assembling [*agençant*] elements, things, plants, animals, tools, people, powers [*puissances*], and fragments of all of these; for it is not 'my' body without organs, instead the 'me' [*moi*] is on it, or what remains of me, unalterable and changing in form, crossing thresholds)" (1980, 200/1987, 161).

At this point, we can now see that the (actual) organism is the limit of a process, just as a (virtual) BwO is the limit of a process. The organism and the BwO are limits of the opposed processes of stratification and de-stratification. There is no such thing as an organism or a BwO. Both are representations of limits of processes. "An organism" is only a representation of pure molar fixity, just as "a BwO" is only a representation of pure molecular flow. The organism versus the BwO is only a de jure distinction, but Deleuze and Guattari insist that such ideal purity never obtains in the world. All we have are de facto mixes, bodies consisting of varying ratios of stratifying and destratifying. After all, a stratum is itself only a ratio of capture versus escape. Neither the organism nor the BwO exists.

Why are there only representations of bodies that have reached the limit of the process of stratification (an organism) and destratification (the body without organs)? Because of the relation of actual and virtual: we expand the actual by incorporating more of the virtual, but the two can never fully overlap; the virtual must remain as adjacent, as the road not taken, and the nagging reminder of what might have been. Thus working toward your BwO is not regression; rather, it is tapping into previously deselected potentials, a refreshing dip into the pool of the virtual in order to reorganize in a non-organismic fashion, to gain a new non-organism body, an intensive BwO. That not all such bodies are ethically worth selecting is not the point here, as we will see in the concluding paragraphs. The organism is pure actuality, pure selection that has dispensed with disturbance from the virtual deselected option, while a virtual BwO is the never-never land of never having to make choices. Neither exists. We thus see the nonequivalence of the actual and the virtual.

To note the nonexistence of organism and virtual BwO is not to say that bodies cannot move toward either limit. Approaching the virtual BwO by intensifying the flows in a body entails incorporating avenues of access to the virtual into the order of the body with inclusive disjunctions that do not shut off a potential, even when another is temporarily selected. A body must be ordered to some extent: it must have a coordination of organs that negotiate with the external flows. But with inclusive disjunctions those organs can have roles that shift about, experimentally, over time. Approaching the organism, on the other hand, is ordering a body with exclusive disjunctions so that, once the organism's pattern of organs is set up, its virtual options are forbidden. The difference between inclusive and exclusive disjunctions in ordering is easy to see in the political sense of organism as Oedipalized desire; in this context, inclusive disjunction is nothing more than the ability to make connections that are not reproductive. The incorporation of the virtual via inclusive disjunction is then the criterion of ethical selection for the production of bodies politic.

Although it is not our major focus, a brief discussion of the universal BwO in relation to the questions of transversal emergence and organic form is in order. In dialogue with Ansell Pearson 1999, Hansen 2000 points to the need to distinguish timescales; he claims Deleuze and Guattari conflate the macro-evolutionary timescale of symbiogenesis with the timescale of ontogeny or individual development. At stake is the relation of the universal virtual BwO of life as self-ordering and creative to the portion of the virtual field relevant to an organism (a virtual BwO, the BwO of the organism, as what this particular body "can do"). Hansen claims Deleuze and Guattari neglect the constraints of the viability of organic form in favor of what he calls their "cosmic expressionism." That is, Hansen believes Deleuze and

Guattari postulate a completely open "molecular" field for any possible combination of organic forms, without regard to the conservation of viable organic form in species-wide norms. Thus even organic form is a haecceity, or arbitrary selection from an open and heterogeneous virtual field. The key complaint is that Deleuze and Guattari consider individuation as (synchronic) haecceity while neglecting diachronic emergence from a morphogenetic field, which needs the constraint of natural kinds channeling development. Hansen pinpoints Deleuze and Guattari's identification of "life" with the universal virtual BwO, as plane of immanence and absolute deterritorialization, neglecting the constraints on the universal intensive BwO as plane of consistency, that is, a condition of bodies politic formed by relative deterritorialization always accompanied by reterritorialization, or in other words, developmental plasticity constrained by the necessity of viability.[11]

Hansen is onto something here. As a fixed habitual pattern locked onto normal functioning as determined by species-wide average values, the organism deadens the creativity of life, the possibilities of diachronic emergence; it is "that which life sets against itself in order to limit itself" (Deleuze and Guattari 1987, 503). The organism is a construction, a certain selection from the virtual multiplicity of what life can be and, hence, a constraint imposed on the universal virtual BwO as the virtual realm of life, the set of all possible organic forms. Like all stratification, however, the organism has a certain value, as we have had occasion to stress repeatedly: "Staying stratified—organized, signified, subjected—is not the worst that can happen" (161). We should recognize that for Deleuze and Guattari this utility is primarily as a resting point for further experimentation, the search for conditions that will trigger diachronic emergence. Hansen is correct: Deleuze and Guattari's insistence on caution in experimentation only recognizes individual organism survival as a negative condition for further experiment without giving any positive role to the organism-level self-organizing properties of the morphogenetic field.

The only thing to say on behalf of Deleuze and Guattari is that Hansen's analysis is organic, all too organic. While the statement about staying stratified not being the worst thing is negative, we also have to remember that all the strata intermingle (1987, 69); that the body is a body politic; that in the context of bio-social-technical transversal emergence, "organism" is a political term, referring to body patterns being centralized so that "useful labor is extracted from the BwO" (159). We see that "organism" is a term for a particular type of body politic when we realize that for Deleuze and

Guattari, the opposite of the organism is not death but depravity: "You will be an organism . . . otherwise you're just depraved" (159). That is, being an organism means that your organs are Oedipally patterned for hetero marriage and work. Getting outside the organism does not mean getting outside homeostasis guaranteed by a certain organic form so much as getting outside Oedipus into what Oedipal society calls "depravity." Furthermore, the thought of bodies politic means we have to think the body *(le corps)* as socially embedded, as an example of transversal emergence: we are all a corps of engineers. When a body links with others in a bio-social-technical assemblage, it is the complex, transversally emergent body that increases *its* virtual realm; that is, it is the intensive BwO of the bio-social-technical body that is at stake, not that of each individual organism or somatic body. So the experimentation that Deleuze and Guattari call for is not so much with somatic body limits (although that is part of it) but with bio-social-technical body relations in diachronic transversally emergent assemblages, what Deleuze and Guattari will call a "consistency" or a "war machine."

Part III **Love, Rage, and Fear**

Chapter 5   **Terri Schiavo:**
The Somatic Body Politic

WE BEGIN OUR CASE STUDIES with the Terri Schiavo case, which provides us with a point of intensity of the personal-level and short-term temporal scale of bodies politic. The "personal and short-term" nature of the Schiavo case is only a convenient and abstract label; we will see in the concrete case the imbrications of all compositional and temporal scales of bodies politic. In particular, we will see how the Schiavo case is a paradigm example of a restricted sense of "political physiology," that is, the way in which government institutions are employed to control nonsubjective physiological processes. Nonetheless, it is fitting to place the Schiavo case under the personal rubric, for two reasons. First, Terri Schiavo's parents were trapped in a pseudoempathy triggered by phenomena of faciality; their love conflicted with the love that Terri herself had for them and for her husband and that led her to express her desire not to receive tubal feeding. Second, in discussing the legal issues surrounding the enforcement of her desires, we will develop a notion of the legal person based on the Deleuzian concept of singularity rather than on the traditional legal category of rationality.

While in our other cases we will focus on the relation of basic emotions to subjectivity, with the limit cases being the evacuation of subjectivity by the triggering of affect programs (rage and panic in the Columbine and Katrina cases, respectively), in the Schiavo case real organic damage permanently destroyed the neural bases of her subjectivity, resulting in a diagnosis of persistent vegetative state, or PVS. We thus have an opportunity to study political physiology as what contemporary theorists call "biopower," the direct political control of homeostatic processes of organic life. Here the organism is less the judgment of God than the object of political control in an immediate and brute imbrication of the social and the somatic.

The Schiavo case is the latest high-profile right-to-die case in the United

States. Its denouement came in a Florida hospice in March 2005, providing a strange mix of the juridically mundane, the legislatively bizarre, and the mediatically spectacular. The case is a particularly complex problem in the Deleuzian sense; it is a concrete instance that links various Ideas or multiplicities in a singular way, creating a problematic field that expresses a perspective on the virtual realm. Its solution, which took more than fifteen years, actualized lines from legal, medical, biological, political . . . multiplicities. The ellipsis indicates the impossibility of completely delimiting the forces at work in any case (the virtual as endless differentiation), just as it indicates the necessity of cutting through them in making any one solution work (actualization as differenciation). Thus, that actualization—a creative resolution of the problem—brought some aspects of the virtual into distinctness, while others faded into momentary obscurity (Deleuze 1994, 214; Williams 2005, 132–34). The elements functioning most intensely in the Schiavo case cut across the fields of right, medical discipline, and biopower, hence at the intersection of sexuality and racism, as Foucault explains (1978, 2003; Agamben 1997). For the American courts, the Schiavo case was a typical right-to-die case; it concerned neither assisted suicide nor euthanasia, only the by-now solidly established ability to exercise by proxy the right to refuse treatment. Precious few would have noticed it except for the small matter of the constitutional crisis that the passage by the U.S. Congress of "Terri's Law" almost provoked and the national, if not global, media frenzy that ensued.

With the passage of time, the case offers the opportunity to establish some differences between Agamben and Foucault concerning biopower, biopolitics, sovereignty, law, and medical discipline, as well as to advance some ideas on jurisprudence—in particular, the use of the Deleuzian concept of singularity to rethink the notion of privacy. The turn to a liberal notion of the right to privacy as the right to die is never simple, for we remain trapped at the intersection of discipline and biopower if we ground that right in the sovereign rights of personal autonomy and bodily integrity. The challenge to a Deleuzian jurisprudence is to creatively transform that right to show its basis in depersonalization. In other words, only in an extraordinary, ethical situation, living along the fault line between organic or "bare" life and personhood, does one feel the intensities pulsing through a person and revealing the impersonal individuations and pre-individual singularities that the person actualizes and that allow for a judgment as to the medical treatment appropriate for him or her, whether that judgment is rendered by him- or herself or by proxy. Here it is not a matter of a "judgment of God"—the application by a disembodied mind of a transcendent standard to the facts of a case—but judgment as felt intensity at a singular point, allowing lines of a problematic field linking virtual multiplicities to be actualized as the solution of a problem. In other words, here we see judgment as felt intensity of that which surpasses a person, depersonalizing him or her, rather than as the exercise of a sovereign will.

Deleuzian Jurisprudence

Several scholars have called attention to Deleuze's remarks on jurisprudence (Patton 2000; Smith 2003; Lefebvre 2005 and 2008). They all refer to the following comments, which Deleuze made in an interview: "Codes and pronouncements are not what creates rights *[ce qui est créateur de droit]* but jurisprudence does. Jurisprudence is the philosophy of right *[du droit]*, and proceeds by singularity, by prolonging of singularities *[procède par singularité, prolongement de singularités]*" (Deleuze 1990b, 209–10 / 1995, 153; translation modified). He also says something along these lines that is of particular interest to the Schiavo case: "People are already thinking about establishing a system of right for modern biology *[le droit de la biologie moderne]*; but everything in modern biology and the new situations it creates, the new course of events it makes possible, is a matter for jurisprudence. We don't need an ethical committee of supposedly well-qualified wise men, but user-groups *[groupes d'usagers]*. This is where we move from right into politics *[du droit à la politique]*" (1990b, 229–30 / 1995, 169–70; translation modified).

Deleuzian jurisprudence (as practice of law, and reflection on that practice, rather than a theoretical inquiry into legal concepts and principles) is the "philosophy of right" in the sense that it countereffectuates the actual legal system *(les lois)* by moving to the virtual multiplicity of rights *(le droit)* and proceeding back down in novel creations. Each precedent is a singularity that is "prolonged" to cover a series of ordinary decisions that fall under its control. There are profound differences, of course, between the French system—with its codes, rooted in Roman law—and the American system—rooted in British common law but constrained by a constitution articulating abstract principles of justice as well as requiring federalism and separation of powers.[1] But as we will see, certain aspects of American jurisprudence relevant to this case accord well with Deleuze's notion of creative differenciation—something bitterly hated by those who decry judicial activism, a hatred that has led some to go even so far as to attack the very principle of judicial review.

The ruling precedent in the Schiavo case[2] is *Cruzan v. Director, Missouri Department of Health*, 497 US 261 (1990), in which the U.S. Supreme Court justices "assume that the United States Constitution would grant a competent person a constitutionally protected right to refuse lifesaving hydration and nutrition" (497 US at 279). Given certain standards of evidence, this right can be exercised by proxy. The court notes that lower courts have grounded this right in the common-law right to informed consent, or in both that right and in a constitutional right to privacy developed in the modern substantive due-process tradition.[3]

Justice David Souter's concurrence in *Washington v. Glucksberg* 521 US 702 (1997) is a good primer in the substantive due-process tradition, which accords well with a Deleuzian notion of jurisprudence. According to Souter's reading of the post-*Poe* dissent tradition, "the business of such review is not the identification of extratextual absolutes but scrutiny of a legislative resolution (perhaps unconscious) of clashing principles, each quite possibly worthy in and of itself, but each to be weighed within the history of our values as a people" (521 US at 764). Except for the "perhaps" modifying "unconscious" (Deleuze would prefer "always," I think), we see here the necessity of moving from the actual (the resolution) to the virtual (the clash of principles) as that virtual realm of principles changes in relation to the series of actualization (the history of our values as a people).

Souter cites a particularly Deleuzian passage from Harlan's *Poe* dissent on which I will comment in brackets.

> Due process has not been reduced to any formula, its content cannot be determined by reference to any code. [Our social life is not governed by codes but regulated in territories, which are realizations of an axiomatic.] The best that can be said is that through the course of this Court's decisions it has represented the balance that our Nation, built upon the postulates of respect for the liberty of the individual, has struck between that liberty and the demands of organized society. [The regulation of those territories comes about through the actualization as differenciating resolution—balance—of conflicting virtual principles. The term "balance" might not sound Deleuzian, but I think it can be distinguished from "reflective equilibrium," which aims to justify by establishing coherence among intuitions and principles. In jurisprudence, we aim to establish a precedent as a creative resolution that will be open to revision in a living tradition.] If the supplying of content to this Constitutional concept has of necessity been a rational process, it has certainly not been one where judges have felt free to roam where unguided speculation might take

them. [Deleuze is not against reason, only against reason construed solely as deduction from first principles, which Souter and Harlan abjure as well. While "unguided speculation" might sound like absolute deterritorialization, we must remember that there is nothing wrong with relative deterritorialization accompanied by a reterritorialization that keeps open the occasion for further deterritorialization, which we will find in the last sentence of this passage in the evocation of a "living" tradition.] The balance of which I speak is that balance struck by this country, having regard to what history teaches are the traditions from which it developed as well as the traditions from which it broke. That tradition is a living thing. [Differenciating actualizations, as resolutions of problems, change the virtual with which they are in mutual presupposition, so that each evolve and change in creative ways.] (367 US at 542)

Souter's next formulation stresses the need for concrete appraisal rather than abstract reasoning: "It is a comparison of the relative strengths of opposing claims that informs the judicial task, not a deduction from some first premise" (521 US at 764). So we see that in the view of one of the members of the Supreme Court, American jurisprudence in the substantive due-process tradition insists on concreteness and singularity as creative resolutions of the conflicting principles at the heart of the Idea of liberal society, or ordered liberty. Souter goes on: "The process of substantive review by reasoned judgment . . . is one of close criticism going to the details of the opposing interests and to their relationships with the historically recognized principles that lend them weight or value" (521 US at 769). This puts this tradition firmly in line with common-law method, which, again, insists on concreteness and singularity in making creative resolutions to complex problems involving virtual principles: "Common law method tends to pay respect . . . to detail, seeking to understand old principles afresh by new examples and new counterexamples" (521 US at 770).

I am not claiming, of course, that the actual practice of American jurisprudence in the substantive due-process tradition has always worked in the way Souter claims it should in the ideal case. Souter himself points out the problems in the Dred Scott decision and the Lochner-era economic decisions. And Souter's methodology of looking to resolutions of conflicting principles is itself at odds with Justice Antonin Scalia's methodology that first asks if what is at stake is a fundamental right, one basic to the history of the United States, before applying a heightened scrutiny test of compelling state interest rather than merely a rational state interest. Despite these caveats, we do see how a Deleuzian jurisprudence might work. Let us now move to the right to privacy in a biopolitical era with advanced medical technology.

Biopower and Biopolitics

Substantive due-process liberty interests, no matter how singular the case and detailed the argumentation, are not absolute and must be weighed against countervailing state interests. The court ruled in *Cruzan* that Missouri was allowed to impose a clear and convincing evidence standard in determining a patient's wishes in order to protect a countervailing state interest in "the protection and preservation of human life" (497 US at 280). The court expanded on this by saying that "a State may properly decline to make a judgment about the 'quality' of life that a particular individual may enjoy, and simply assert an unqualified interest in the preservation of human life to be weighed against the constitutionally protected interests of the individual" (497 US at 282).

Here we must distinguish between Agamben and Foucault; that is, we must distinguish between biopower and biopolitics, between material production and (quasi) legal predication (Fitzpatrick 2005). For Foucault, *biopower* is modern and productive, "fostering life or letting die"; this affirmative productivity distinguishes it from sovereign power, with which it today coexists, whose negativity is expressed in the formula "kill or let live" (Foucault 1978, 138). Biopower is material production, producing capacities in individual bodies as it regulates populations; we can say it positively patterns bodies politic, channeling flows at the somatic and civic/national levels. Sovereign power, on the other hand, can only slice into material flows via a *prélèvement* that subtracts from an already-established flow without being able to augment or direct the production process of the flow (136; see also Fitzpatrick 2005).

While Agamben acknowledges the Foucauldian thesis of the modernity of *biopower*, he will claim that sovereignty and *biopolitics* are equally ancient and essentially intertwined in the originary gesture of all politics; sovereignty is the quasi-legal power ("law's threshold or limit concept" [Agamben 2005, 4, 23]) to decide the state of exception whereby bare life or *zoē* is exposed "underneath" political life or *bios* (Agamben 1997 passim; 2005, 4, 87–88). Grounded in the "biopolitical tradition of *auctoritas*," which "immediately inheres in the living person of the *pater* or the *princeps*," the sovereign power of deciding the exception shows that "law and life must be tightly implicated in a reciprocal grounding" (Agamben 2005,

84–85). Agamben finds in the concentration camp the modern biopolitical paradigm, in which the state of exception has become the rule (Agamben 1997), and we have all become (potentially) bearers of exposed bare life in that we are all subject to what I will call a depoliticizing predication: to use the current American jargon, being named an "enemy combatant" (Agamben 2005, 3). The converse of that depoliticizing predication is a politicizing predication—often implicit or assumed—existing only by the grace of not being depoliticized: in other words, the retention of the rights of a citizen. Let's call this complex concept (de-)politicizing predication. Finally, let us note that Agamben also sees the concentration camp as a material *biopower* experiment, producing the bare life of the *Muselmann* (Agamben 1999a, 85, 156). We will interrogate the relation between biopower and biopolitics in Agamben's writing on the concentration camp.

We can also note a difference of method. Agamben reveals the political logic of the originary imbrication of sovereignty and biopolitics via a reading that is something like a Heideggerian gesture of locating an originary decision. Such a decision founds an epoch that is now exhausted and flattened out into totalitarian management, a complete revelation that hides the very condition of its appearance ("invisible in its very exposure, all the more hidden for showing itself as such" [Agamben 1999a, 156; see also Sinnerbrink 2005]), albeit with a Derridean emphasis on imbrication and "zones of indistinction." Foucault, on the other hand, provides a materialist genealogy of modern state biopower, detailing techniques of medical discipline and population management operating at the intersection of sexuality and racism.

I will argue that Agamben's concept of (de-)politicizing predication, despite its considerable utility in thinking biopolitics, cannot handle biopower, either in the case of the *Muselmann* nor in the Schiavo case and other similar cases of end-of-life issues, because of its lack of purchase on real material change as opposed to the "incorporeal transformation," or the change in juridical status effected by (de-)politicizing predication. What we need is Foucault's materialist genealogy of biopower's investment in real bodies. An analysis of biopolitics is not enough; we need an analysis of biopower. Agamben accepts Foucault's materialist genealogy into his system, but Agamben's own contribution—the concept of (de-)politicizing predication—does not help us understand what happened to Terri Schiavo's body, nor does it help us think how we should transform our jurisprudence to change the dualist ontology behind the phrase "Terri Schiavo's body." I will discuss the biopower aspect of the Schiavo case using the concepts developed by Deleuze and Guattari in *A Thousand Plateaus*, so that "bare life" is the human being destratified below the stratum of subjectivity to that of the organism. A key difference here from Agamben's analyses is that Terri Schiavo suffered a real, ontological destratification, while Agamben is concerned with the "incorporeal transformation" or change in juridical status that reveals bare life.[4]

Taking Issue with Agamben

I see two key problems in thinking through the Schiavo case with Agamben's concepts. First, Agamben's perspective does not provide a handle on a corporeal rather than an incorporeal materialism. In addition, Agamben underemphasizes trapped bare life in favor of a near-exclusive focus on exposed bare life.

CORPOREAL MATERIALISM

To understand the Schiavo case, we need a notion of ontological destratification (Deleuze and Guattari 1987, 160), that is, a notion of corporeal materialism, for the destruction of Terri Schiavo's cortex was a real change that preceded her diagnosis, which then removed her from the philosophical category of conscious subject and its legal counterpart, the competent person. With (de-)politicizing predication, however, Agamben gives us only a notion of what Deleuze and Guattari would call an "incorporeal transformation" (80) or change in juridical status that exposes or protects bare life. To understand the incorporeal nature of the (de-)politicizing predication, we might also here refer to what Foucault calls in his inaugural address to the Collège de France an "incorporeal materialism," in which "the event is not of the order of bodies [*l'événement n'est pas de l'ordre des corps*]" (Foucault 1972, 231; translation modified from "the event is not corporeal").

What we need in the Schiavo case, though, is precisely a corporeal materialism in order to understand changes to a body in and through an event. A (de-)politicizing predication attaches itself to a body that remains materially unchanged by the act of predication, even though the exposure of bare life thus affected might open that body up to profound changes by means of the action of other bodies. In other words, a change in incorporeal biopolitical *status* can open a body up to a different set of corporeal biopower *practices*. Here are three examples of a quasi-legal (de-)politicizing predication opening a body up to different material biopower practices.

(A) A person is first named "non-Aryan," then "Jew," then "deportee," and then "camp prisoner." These are all different grades of depoliticizing predication, producing different statuses. Shock, overwork, exhaustion, and malnutrition might drive this person to the point where he is named *Muselmann*, but we must note two things here: (i) the term "Muselmann" is informal concentration camp jargon, unique to Auschwitz, not an official biopolitical designation (Mills 2005); (ii) such informal naming follows the physical changes that follow upon the original official depoliticizing predications. In other words, the term "Muselmann" functions like a *diagnosis*, an evaluation of a state; it is not a transforming predication but caps what has already happened to a body, rather than opening that body up to what is to come.

The shunning of the *Muselmänner*, I would argue in reading Agamben 1999a, was caused by the behavior of the bodies, not by their having been named as such. While being named "camp prisoner" transformed the status of the person and allowed the exposure of bare life and degradation to the condition of *Muselmann* (the last stage of degradation, the "living dead" of the camps), the act of being so named did not open the body up to different treatment; it was an acknowledgment of their having been differently treated; it was an acknowledgment that nothing else could be done, that no further degradation of depoliticizing status or material condition was possible. Agamben interrogates the figure of the *Muselmann* of the camps as another zone of indistinction, "the non-human who obstinately appears as human: he is the human that cannot be told apart from the inhuman" (1999a, 56–59, 82). Rather than Agamben's insistence on the representational/conceptual notion of indistinction, a corporeal materialism uses the notion of physiological threshold to indicate the point at which an ontological rather than juridical change occurs (see also Vogt 2005 and Mills 2005).

(B) A person is named by the government of the United States an enemy combatant. He or she might then be put into "stress positions" that can produce pain as long as, in the words of then Counsel to the President Albert Gonzales in his August 1, 2002, memo, "Standards of Conduct for Interrogation under 18 USC §§ 2340–2340A," the "specific intent" of the interrogator is not to cause pain "equivalent in intensity to the pain accompanying serious physical injury, such as organ failure, impairment of bodily function or even death" (Greenberg and Dratel 2005, 172). Other treatments might include forced watching of gay porn, exposure to strobe lights, and/or excruciatingly loud American music (Brown 2006; ACLU 2006), since, again according to Gonzales, the "mental harm" of these practices does not come from "threats of imminent death; threats of infliction of the kind of pain that would amount to physical torture; infliction of such pain as a means of psychological torture; use of drugs or other procedures designed to deeply disrupt the senses, or fundamentally alter an individual's personality; or threatening to do any of these things to a third party" (Greenberg and Dratel 2005, 172). Someone with the sensibilities of a Donald Rumsfeld might discount the severity of these practices—just as he compared his work at a standing desk (236–37) to the standing punishment or Field Punishment No. 1 for the WWI-era British Army (BBC 2006)—but there is no gainsaying the psychophysical destruction that prolonged exposure to such treatments wreaks on persons in the detention facilities of the New World Order, as with, to cite just one instance of what happened to a U.S. citizen, the case of José Padilla (Richey 2007).

(C) Agamben seems to be under the impression that a diagnosis of brain death means that a body "must be abandoned to the extreme vicissitude of transplantation" (2004, 15). But to my knowledge, such a declaration of brain death only allows for the exercise of the person's previously expressed wishes regarding organ harvesting and transplantation. Such a diagnosis is thus *not* a depoliticizing predication. Furthermore, the official medical diagnosis of PVS that Terri Schiavo received, like the informal social categorization of *Muselmann,* follows upon real change; they are both diagnoses, and diagnoses do not themselves provoke change in the body. The particular diagnosis of PVS is far from a depoliticizing predication, for the import of the *Cruzan* decision is that PVS, far from removing rights, does *not* remove the right to privacy involving refusal of life-sustaining medical treatment, including feeding tubes. The diagnosis of PVS leaves the person's legal status unchanged and allows them the same exercise of rights as other citizens, albeit by proxy. It does not necessitate the removal of feeding tubes by state action any more than the diagnosis of brain death requires organ harvesting but only allows it, following appeal initiated by a person. Agamben writes movingly of the physical changes suffered by the concentration camp prisoners, but he can only use everyday concepts to do so; there's nothing in his specifically philosophical concepts that covers these changes, as there is in, for instance, Deleuze's dynamic materialist ontology of complex systems. But it is precisely a corporeal materialism that is needed to think of the material changes that occur in and through the action of a physiological event such as that suffered by Terri Schiavo.

TRAPPED BARE LIFE

My second point in criticism of Agamben is that it is not just judgments as to brain death authorizing organ harvesting or inferior quality of life authorizing euthanasia that concerns us in biopower (again, any such judgment in this case was Terri Schiavo's own, and so, if anything, it was a matter of passive assisted suicide rather than euthanasia), but also the construction of an inescapable state interest in fostering the life of the favored group, those graced with an implicit politicizing predication. While it is true that the politicizing predication is part of Agamben's conceptual system, virtually all of his analyses in *Homo Sacer* and *Remnants of Auschwitz* concern the way in which bare life is exposed, excluded from law, threatened, while *bios*, politically informed life, is protected. But in the Schiavo case, we are concerned not with exclusion of *zoē* but with its inclusion, with a bare life that the law holds close. We find here a sphere of protected bare life, a biosphere, into which the out-group cannot penetrate—its bare life is exposed via a depoliticizing predication—and from which the in-group can never escape. Again, the relative neglect of the notion of trapped bare life is not so much a conceptual problem for Agamben as it is a matter of emphasis.

The limits that exclude the out-group—limits that create exposed bare life—are currently formed by the state of exception regarding the "enemy combatants" (so that the Guantánamo camp is the state of exception become rule, the spatialization of the state of exception); the limits of the in-group—trapped bare life—are formed by the October 21, 2003, Florida state law allowing the governor to order the reinsertion of the feeding tube in the Schiavo case. More precisely, the bodies of those in the out-group are excluded from the protection of law so that the bare life inherent therein is exposed, while the bodies of those in the in-group are ordered by law to be subjected to the most intense medical interventions. In highlighting the subjection of the in-group to medical intervention aimed at keeping trapped bare life going (to be distinguished from Agamben's analysis of the exposure of bare life of the "experimental persons" of the Nazi concentration camps for the sake of knowledge that would purify and strengthen the body politic of the German *Volk*), we see how we need Foucault's genealogy of materialist biopower, to which we now turn.

Foucault's Genealogy of Material Practices

I will focus on three areas in which Foucault enables us to think through the Schiavo case in ways that are not the focus of Agamben's work: (1) medical intervention and the administrative supplement in hospital/hospice palliative care; (2) sexuality and racism elements in the Schiavo case; and (3) hints as to a transformation of right to privacy jurisprudence away from the sovereignty paradigm.

MEDICAL INTERVENTION

In *"Society Must Be Defended"* Foucault mentions the 1976 Franco case as an example of medical intervention creating an encompassing biosphere of trapped bare life (Foucault 2003, 248–49; see also Agamben 1999a, 83). With Franco—and in the United States, the contemporaneous *Quinlan* case (70 NJ 10 [1976])—we see the establishment of a disciplinary (and hence individualizing) medical power able to defer somatic death, and with which our sovereignty-based jurisprudence struggles. Who is to decide the end of treatment? But just as prison administration provides what we could call a carceral supplement to legal power in the criminal system (Foucault 1977, 16, 246–47), so does hospital administration, in the form of palliative care, enable the system to operate: everyone has to die, sometime; care has to stop, sometime. Since the ruling distinction is active versus passive procedures, rather than the intent to cause death, hospital and hospice care can aim only to relieve pain rather than intend to hasten death (Rawls et al. 1997). Of course, there is sufficient gray area here in establishing dosage guidelines so that palliative care can have the unintended consequence of hastening death (hastening, that is, as compared with a completely tendentious "natural" standard) as long as the intention was solely pain relief. This day-by-day hospital work escapes legal and media attention except in the rare cases—like Schiavo's—where a "mediastorm" occurs.

SEXUALITY AND RACISM

The intersection of medical discipline of individual bodies and biopower regulation of the population, Foucault reminds us, occurs in sexuality and in racism (Foucault 1978, 149–50; 2003, 257–63). The Schiavo case confirms the sexuality angle: her bulimia can be analyzed—following Bartky 1988 and Bordo 1993—as a mode of governmentality, as self-discipline of female corporeality, the "tyranny of slenderness" (Chernin 1994). We need to note that the 1992 malpractice suit brought by Michael Schiavo was against the fertility doctors Terri Schiavo was consulting to help her get pregnant. They should have diagnosed her bulimia as being the cause of her having stopped menstruating, the jury ruled. This lapse in medical discipline regulating fertility led to Terri Schiavo's breakdown and to her body being caught in a medical assemblage, with the feeding tube being only the most famous component—but nevertheless a significant one, as it necessitates entry into the body. The right to refuse medical treatment is grounded in the common-law right of informed consent, in turn grounded in sovereign control of bodily integrity. And with bodily integrity, we obviously touch upon central and profound gender issues related to the construction of bodies politic. Who has entry to her body? Who has control over that entry?

Regarding the intersection of gender and race, we must also note that the people at the heart of the three most famous American right-to-die cases—Karen Quinlan, Nancy Cruzan, and Terri Schiavo—were all middle-class white women, each childless at the time of her accident. We might go so far as to say that the culture of life—as the antiabortion forces label themselves in their current PR campaign—enveloped them, refusing to let them go. Potential givers of white life at a time when the white race faces being outbred by other races, they were in need of phallic domination: give her the tube of life whether she wants it or not. An ugly thing deserves an ugly name: we might even have to call the forced insertion of a feeding tube "tube-rape" (Beyerstein 2005). The racism in some biopower decisions can be overt: Sun Hudson, the first patient to be taken off life support under a Texas law (signed by George W. Bush while governor) that allows hospitals to remove life support from indigent patients over family objections, was black (Mayo 2005). But in the American case, it is more often the social racism that Foucault talks about (Foucault 2003, 261), directed against the economically unproductive, the marker of that unproductivity being their lack of insurance. They can't compete, they are weighing us down, their death purifies our body politic as we compete in the global market. Many of these economically unproductive are black, but many of them are white as well.

JURISPRUDENCE

The Schiavo case was resolved by means of the right to privacy as the right to die, but we want to be wary here, for we remain trapped at the intersection of discipline and biopower if we ground that right in sovereign rights of personal autonomy, which is the theoretical base of current American jurisprudence on end-of-life issues. Strictly speaking, the law concerning assisted suicide that formed the basis of *Washington v. Glucksberg* (521 US 702 [1997])[5] or hospital removal of life support in futile care, as in the Sun Hudson case, are tangential to Schiavo because they concern terminal cases. Of course, you could argue that Terri Schiavo was always terminal, and the medical intervention in her case is only death prolonging rather than life sustaining. In all seriousness, we will have to rethink the horror movie cliché of the undead. But to understand that claim, we have to turn to the medical and biological issues.

Personality, Personhood, Organic System

Terri Schiavo suffered a heart stoppage in February 1990 brought on by a drastically low potassium level. The heart stoppage cut off oxygen to the brain. The cortex suffers permanent damage after six to seven minutes, but the brain stem can survive for up to twenty minutes without oxygen. The paramedics summoned by an emergency 911 call by Michael Schiavo arrived in that interval between cortex destruction and cessation of function of the brain stem.[6]

The anoxia resulted in PVS, a bizarre and frightening condition. As we will see, much of the pain, anger, and sadness in this case came from one particular quirk of the human constitution that provides a compelling case study in affective cognition.

That quirk is that reflexive facial movements can both provoke a protoempathic identification and be interpreted as indicating subjectivity. With the latter, we see the Deleuzoguattarian concept of faciality at work (Deleuze and Guattari 1987, 167–91). Faciality is the reterritorialization of the signifier on the face, behind the white walls and black holes of which subjectivity is projected. Many of you by now have seen the videos of Terri Schiavo's face. Many people, but her parents most of all, looked at Terri Schiavo's face and both felt a powerful emotional bond (protoempathic identification) and read subjectivity behind it (in what philosophers of mind call a theory of mind).[7] This sort of identification and projection is well placed in forming an emotional bond and in beginning a subjectivity loop between infant and caregiver. Hendriks-Jansen 1996 provides a fascinating discussion, with extensive citations of the relevant literature, of caretaker-infant interaction as a feedback loop that scaffolds emergent subjectivity out of a "core self" (252–77). As the infant's subjectivity is not yet fully present, I would prefer to call this a "primary corporeal inter-ipseity" rather than the more common "primary intersubjectivity" (Stern 1985; Gallagher 2005). In addition to scaffolding subjectivity, the affective importance of such early parent-child bonding cannot be overestimated; part of its power is that it is a repetition of emotional bondings that stretch back throughout human and primate history and that provide the basis for more developed forms of empathy (de Waal 2006; Joyce 2007).

We can see in the Schiavo case how protoempathic identification, projection of subjectivity, and perception of the face are intimately linked.

But the provoking of protoempathic identification and the projection of subjectivity in this case were a cruel trick, an evolutionary adaptive capacity perversely out of place in PVS. Face-provoked emotional bondings with infants helped the species survive and form the basis for more-expansive moral sentiments, but the infant will develop, whereas Terri Schiavo never would once she fell into the state named PVS. The infant is a potential person; the organic system that still bore the name Terri Schiavo would never again be a person. A lot of sad affect was generated from saying "They are starving a person to death," but this comes from applying the proper name of a person, "Terri Schiavo," to an organic system. It is neglecting the drastic destratification suffered in this case, an irreversible move from the subjective or alloplastic to the organic.

The key in understanding this destratification is to consider the behavior pattern of the system and to distinguish personality, personhood, and organic system. On one level, considering the organic system in the hospice bed, there is no personality as singular pattern of subjective interaction. Singular social interaction patterns (unique mannerisms and sense of humor and so on) are a marker of personality, that which distinguishes persons from each other. As the organic system in the hospital bed offers only generic physiological behavior (heartbeats, lung movements, reflex muscular withdrawals of limbs from positions in which cell damage occurs—not movement in reaction to pain, if pain is properly held to be subjective synthesis of nerve signals traveling in pathways other than reflex withdrawals), in that sense, there is no personality in the hospice bed, but that's only an a fortiori conclusion from the claim there is no person there.

If you want to distinguish personhood from the state of being an organic system, what you want are generic responses in the social, rational, and hedonic domains, for a person is a generic member of society, a generic rational being, a generic pleasure seeker. We don't want considerations of personality to influence personhood any more than we want considerations of racial, religious, or sexual categories. We define personhood generically in order to protect the diversity of personalities. Here we must distinguish between legal personhood and legal competence. A legal person is an entity recognized by the state as belonging to the category of person, and a legally competent person is a subset of that category. A child is a legal person but not a legally competent person; the same is true for people who for one reason or another cannot meet the criteria for legal competence. A legally competent person will display consistent repetition of generic responses in social, rational, and hedonic interaction (the person can answer to his or her name just like everyone else, can reason like everyone else [cf. the "reasonable man" legal standard], can pursue and/or defer pleasure like everyone else).

The question is whether to treat PVS cases—which clearly do not now meet the criteria of legal competence as a person, though they once did—or whether we should propose another category for them. In PVS, we see only singular production of endogenously generated activity or singular reaction to subsocial stimuli (sounds or noise rather than social signals). The pattern of blinks and smiles and other reactions displayed by an organic system in PVS is utterly singular, unique to that system and its degree of damage, length of time from injury, and so on. Granted, given enough time, these blinks and smiles will coincide now and again with the production of social signals, leading to the faciality machine we described earlier: the projection of an illusion of subjectivity, a false protoempathic identification, a horrible discrepancy between a widespread human capacity deeply rooted in our evolutionary past and deeply connected to love and empathy and the irreversible condition known as PVS.

This projection of subjectivity, this false protoempathic identification, was not limited to the family of Terri Schiavo: a reading of the medical report of one of the doctors supporting a diagnosis of a minimally conscious state (MCS), rather than PVS, reveals such false identification and misplaced projection; we will undertake such a reading shortly.

The problem with the distinction between legal competence and legal personhood, and the retention of personhood by PVS cases, is that the damage suffered in PVS destroys all that we want to protect by the concept of person: what Kant called rational humanity, and what the utilitarians call the potential for pleasure.[8] (We can argue that extending the category of person to children or those adults with temporary disruptions of legal competence is done to protect their potential for competence.) I certainly do not want to argue that the PVS material system surviving the end of legal competence is unworthy of any legal and moral protection, but simply that such protection need not be extended to "persons." Here we have to think of the category of the "undead" if we want to avoid the dualistic notion of an immaterial person whose interests survive the disabling or the death of the body (or the person as a bundle of immaterial interests that were formerly incarnated in a now disabled or dead body). As a materialist, then, I would say personhood is an emergent property of a body recognized by the community as taking part in generic social, rational, and hedonic interactions, and that surviving interests consist of a social agreement to honor the wishes expressed by legally competent persons. I would further claim that the material system in PVS is neither a person nor a corpse, but undead; what we are struggling to do is rethink the categories bequeathed us by thousands of years of medical impotence in the face of death, categories now useless in PVS and coma cases.

While a material system in PVS is alive, and not a corpse, we might look to our treatment of corpses for hints as to how to regulate the bodies of those who once were persons but who are now undead. If we temporarily bracket the notion of surviving interests, we legally regulate the treatment of corpses either for Kantian reasons, to protect the humanity of those who handle corpses, or for utilitarian reasons, to protect the chance for happiness of those who might suffer from those who have been coarsened by maltreatment of corpses. Furthermore, we legally regulate the treatment of animals, for those reasons as well as to prevent useless suffering. But the latter is irrelevant to PVS because the synthetic functions necessary for registering pain are quite complex and beyond the capacity of PVS systems. To repeat, the experience of pain is a cognitive function to be distinguished from the reflex withdrawal of body parts from sites of cell damage.

Thus we have only a homonymic relation between Terri Schiavo the (legally competent) person, who ceased to exist when the system bearing her name slipped past a threshold of oxygen deprivation that destroyed her cortex but spared her brain stem, and Terri Schiavo the material system, the assemblage of body and tube, in the Florida hospice. You could translate it in the following manner, but it is the sort of dualistic language the material systems perspective seeks to avoid: what was in the hospice bed was only the body that used to support the (legally competent) person of Terri Schiavo. Thus, all the emotion generated by the trope of "starving a person to death" is a category mistake: what is being done is ceasing to support autonomic processes that at one time supported a (legally competent) person but now only support themselves. More precisely, and less dualistically, we have a material system that once took part in generic social, rational, and hedonic interactions but now only displays the behaviors of bare organic function. What used to be a person is now only an organism. This means that far from being a case of euthanasia, the Schiavo case wasn't even a case of assisted suicide, if suicide is a person targeting the organism in order to withdraw from social interactions, to cease being a person.

PVS cases have *already* been withdrawn from singular and generic social interaction. Here the person targets the organism, which is something like the remains of the person, just as the corpse is the remains of the organism (McMahan 2002).

Excursus: The Cheshire Affidavit

William P. Cheshire Jr., M.D., was asked to investigate charges of possible abuse of Terri Schiavo (Cheshire 2005). Although no such abuse was found, Cheshire goes on to say that he believed he had found reason to doubt the PVS diagnosis and to prefer a diagnosis of MCS (minimally conscious state). He begins by noting a study that showed a 40 percent misdiagnosis rate for PVS versus MCS (Andrews et al. 1996). He neglects to mention that only three of the seventeen misdiagnoses (out of forty total subjects) remained misdiagnosed after four years, and that the study called for, as a remedy to such misdiagnoses, diagnosis by a multidisciplinary team of specialists experienced in PVS diagnosis, as well as assessment over a long period of time—precisely the sort of diagnostic assessment that Terri Schiavo received. Cheshire then cites Gianino et al. 2002 to show that MCS is a diagnostic entity of recent origin. Of note is that one of the authors of that article is Ronald Cranford, who in his testimony in the 2002 trial on Terri Schiavo's medical condition had rejected the MCS diagnosis in favor of reaffirming the PVS diagnosis that had stood for twelve years. Of further note is that in reviewing Terri Schiavo's medical records, Cheshire does not mention the EEG tests that had played a role in establishing and reaffirming the PVS diagnosis.

Cheshire visited Terri Schiavo five days after her feeding tube had been removed. His visit lasted ninety minutes and consisted only of visual observation, not a formal medical exam. In describing his visit, he does everything he can to interpret behavior as indicating consciousness. For instance, "Although she does not seem to track or follow visual objects consistently or for long periods of time, she does fixate her gaze on colorful objects or human faces for some 15 seconds at a time and occasionally follows with her eyes at least briefly as these objects move from side to side." But this occasional and intermittent behavior is precisely consistent with PVS and should not count as evidence of consciousness. It is the intermittency and short duration that should be emphasized, not the occasional tracking. Cheshire goes so far as to interpret unprompted pain behavior as evidence of consciousness rather than, more plausibly, its absence. In describing a videotape he observed, he notes that after a physician has told her parents that Terri will be moved: "She vocalizes a crying sound, 'Ugh, ha, ha, ha,' presses her eyebrows together, and sadly grimaces. It is important to note that, at that moment, no one is touching Terri or causing actual pain." One would ordinarily be expected to conclude that unprompted pain behavior counts against a consciousness interpretation and in favor of an interpretation of endogenous, random production. Instead, Cheshire advances the interpretation that "she appears to comprehend the meaning of Dr. Hammesfahr's comment and signals her *anticipation* of pain" (italics in original). This is surely remarkable, and it indicates that for Cheshire anything can be interpreted as evidence of consciousness: intermittency is overlooked in favor of occasionality, and absence of stimulus is interpreted as anticipation of stimulus.

Cheshire then cites what he calls pain issues in Terri Schiavo's treatment and argues that pain is indicative of an MCS rather than a PVS. He further argues that a diagnosis of MCS would make "an enormous difference in making ethical decisions on Terri's behalf," without mentioning that such third-party judgments are irrelevant in privacy right cases. Furthermore, he neglects to argue against the view that such pain—even if it were present—would produce a best interest argument, if one were to be made, which was never attempted in the Schiavo case, against reinsertion of the feeding tube. (The unsupported interpretation of Terri Schiavo's ability to feel pleasure inserted at the end of the document is simply that, unsupported, and even if it could be supported, it would necessitate a utilitarian pleasure/pain calculus to determine best interests, if one wanted to avoid an even more difficult argument about the value of suffering.)

The conclusion of Cheshire's report is equally remarkable. "To enter the room of Terri Schiavo is nothing like entering the room of a patient who is comatose or brain-dead or in some neurological sense no longer there. [But no one ever claimed she was comatose or brain-dead. The diagnosis was PVS.] Although Terri did not demonstrate during our 90 minute visit compelling evidence of verbalization, conscious awareness, or volitional behavior [but these are the criteria for an MCS, even if they need only be intermittent], yet the visitor has the distinct sense of the presence of a living human being who seems at some level to be aware of some things around her."

After this paragraph, the pseudoclinical language of "the visitor" is dropped (although if he were to have been consistent with this stance in the previous paragraph, "Terri" should have been "the patient"), and Cheshire completely personifies his narrative, giving both his false protoempathic identification and his projection of subjectivity free rein: "As I looked at

Terri, and she gazed directly back at me, I asked myself whether, if I were her attending physician, I could in good conscience withdraw her feeding and hydration. No, I could not. I could not withdraw life support if I were asked. I could not withold life-sustaining nutrition and hydration from this beautiful lady whose face brightens in the presence of others." Here we see the complete overlooking of court findings that the removal of the tube was done in accordance with Terri Schiavo's wishes. The story shifts from Terri Schiavo's wishes to what Cheshire could or could not do in good conscience to this "beautiful lady." If she were in an MCS, Cheshire concludes, his judgment is that "it would be wrong to bring about her death by withdrawing food and water." But, assuming Cheshire had any standing to advance a best interests/quality of life argument, this presupposes that an MCS provides a better quality of life than a PVS, which is not at all evident—or even plausible, frankly, given the pain issues he describes and to which we will return.

Life, Destratification, Sacrifice

If you define all organic processes that take place in us as human life, then you get a potential conflict between the wishes of a person and the self-valuing of an organism, and the resolution of that conflict through the refusal of hydration and nutrition in PVS is suicide, even when directed from before a collapse into legal incompetence and thus must be considered assisted suicide.[9] From a Varelean autonomous systems perspective, a conatus-like self-valuing, a production of sense, appears in all life, even unicellular organisms, via the restoration of homeostasis in response to environmental change.[10] But such self-valuing is not sufficient for personhood, though it may be worthy of respect in some cases. Surely the use of antibacterial agents to aid ailing persons has to outweigh the consideration we might want to extend to bacterial self-valuing.[11]

The conatus of organic life can come into conflict with the surviving interests of a person due to the differential decay rates of organ function. In PVS cases, this comes from the assemblage character of the brain and the greater sensitivity to oxygen deprivation of the cortex relative to the brain stem. The organism as assemblage means death becomes scattered throughout the organism, as Foucault observes in reading Bichat, distinguishing between morbidity as death of the organism and mortification as death of organs.[12] Although our previous investigation of Deleuze and Guattari's notion of the organism centered on its status as a body politic, we can say in a more-restricted biological register that for Deleuze and

Guattari, as well as for the theory of autopoiesis, the organism is an emergent structure, a homeostasis-conserving systematic relation of organic subsystems (Maturana and Varela 1980). Autopoietic theory distinguishes between the (virtual) organization and the (actual) structure of organisms. Organization is the set of all possible relationships of the autopoietic processes of an organism; it is hence equivalent to a virtual field or the Body without Organs of that organism (Maturana and Varela 1980, 88, mentions autopoietic "space" [scare quotes in original]). Structure is that selection from the organizational set that is actually at work at any one moment (xx, 77, 137–38). Perturbation from the environment in "structural coupling" leads to structural changes that either reestablish homeostasis or result in the destruction of the system qua living (81). Homeostatic restoration thus results in conservation of autopoietic organization.

The key difference between the position of Maturana and Varela and that of Deleuze and Guattari is that between the recursive epistemology of Maturana and Varela and the stacked ontology of Deleuze and Guattari: because organs themselves are emergent structures of cells, when organs die, component cells have differential death rates. (We are restricting our attention to Maturana and Varela's early collaboration. Later, Varela [1991] will restrict autopoiesis, strictly speaking, to the level of the cell and speak of the organism as an interlocking network of processes including neurological and immunological ones, alongside those of cellular autopoiesis.) To return to our concerns in interpreting the Schiavo case, if there is something human about an organism, why not about organs or cells? What makes a liver something human? Only that it can be transplanted into another human organism and come to function therein. An organ is human only insofar as it is potentially a component of a human assemblage, only insofar as it can be subordinated to the sovereign unity of a somatic body politic.[13]

A brain stem–controlled organic system in PVS is thus human only potentially, in the case it could be a subordinate part of a whole and hence support a person and perhaps a personality. Below the personal stratum it is no longer human, but precisely organic. The human qua personality, as belonging to the alloplastic stratum, can take part in singular social interactions even though it is recognized as a person via its generic social, rational, and hedonic interactions. Think of it in complexity theory terms: the singularity we treasure as personality comes from the production of novel patterns, thresholds, and triggers that form consistencies or positive affect–producing assemblages in which each component is empowered to create new consistencies (here we see "power" as *puissance*). But an organic system can return only to homeostasis. It is locked onto species-wide norms.

The glory of a personality, and the reason it trumps the organic system from which it emerges, is that it is free from automatic self-valuing and can value others, sometimes even to the extent of sacrificing its own organic system. Sacrificing. Making holy. In confronting biopower we have to preserve room for the sacrifice some might wish to make. Another confrontation with Agamben is necessary here. For Agamben, bare life is exposed by an incorporeal transformation, a change in juridical status, so that the bearer of bare life can be "killed, but not sacrificed." That is, bare life is beyond both human and divine law, and the killing can come from outside with impunity. But in PVS we see a real ontological destratification rather than an incorporeal transformation or change in status, and the killing is not even suicide but, to coin an awkward word for a strange situation, "organismcide," the future targeting of the organism by the personality. It's sacrifice, but not self-sacrifice, if by "self" we mean the coincidence of organism and personality.

Should anyone say there is no evidence Terri Schiavo wanted to make such a sacrifice, I say there is no evidence she did not, and all the paternalistic speechifying about Terri's best interests robs her memory of the dignity of an other-directed motivation in not wanting to continue tubal feeding after the death of her person. It is possible Terri Schiavo did not want tubal feeding simply to prevent the horror of the MCS, insofar as that approaches a full-blown locked-in condition, but to allow some peace of mind to come to her loved ones. In other words, in wanting to die if ever trapped in a PVS, it is possible that her concern was not with herself but with her loved ones—husband, parents, and siblings.

To appreciate this distinction, we first have to realize that an MCS and a locked-in state are two entirely separate medical conditions. In an MCS, severe cortical damage has occurred, but some minimal cognitive function remains. A catatonic locked-in syndrome occurs with no cortical damage—hence full cognitive function—but with a closing off of motor control (Laureys, Owen, and Schiff 2004). I speculate that most people fear a locked-in condition when they don't want tubal feeding, though the only reason to believe an MCS is any better than being locked in would be the lowered cognitive function.

An other-directed motivation for refusing tubal feeding would be not to avoid the horror of the locked-in state (though that is horror indeed) but to allow some peace of mind, closure, and the ability to grieve to come to our loved ones. We should not "err on the side of life" as the slogan would have it, but err on the side of saving room in this world for sacrifice, namely, freedom from the blind and automatic self-valuing of organic systems when that self-valuing, supported by technology far beyond the imagination of the culture in which traditional moral intuitions are formed, would cause an irresolvable pain not to the organic system or any vestigial or minimal consciousness clinging to it, but to the others the person loves. Note I did not say "pain" *simpliciter* but "irresolvable pain," the pain of not being able to grieve. I would even go so far along those lines as to say the default setting should be an opt-in position: only those people who specifically request extraordinary measures in futile situations as defined by current medical science and safeguarded by ethics boards should get them. Thus, only if you want to tie your family's hands and exhaust the family wealth in waiting for a miracle or in offering your body to quack therapies would you be able to subject them to that.

Intensity, Singularity, Privacy

The turn to rights is never simple in the context of medical discipline and biopower, for their relations with sovereignty are not innocent, as Foucault reminds us in his great 1976 lecture course *"Society Must Be Defended"* (Foucault 2003). Sovereignty means control over a unit, whether geographical or corporeal.[14] The new right we search for in our Deleuzian jurisprudence cannot be founded on privacy as control, on the subject as unified person, but on singularity, as exposure to intensities that perform a depersonalization. The person is viewed not as a sovereign unit, within which he or she can decide on a state of exception that would expose his or her own bare life, but as negotiating the line between personality and organic system, and depersonalization as opening to the virtual via the intensity of affect. But just as this antidisciplinary right cannot be that of sovereignty, any right we would turn to against biopower cannot be that of a judicial system infiltrated by normalization procedures (Foucault 1978, 144). In *History of Sexuality: Volume 1*, Foucault tells us that the initial recourse to the new-found intersection of discipline and biopower was the right to life: "Against this power that was still new in the nineteenth century, the forces that re-sisted relied for support on the very thing it invested, that is, on life and man as a living being. . . . What was demanded and what served as an objective was life. . . . The 'right' to life, to one's body, to health, to happiness . . . this 'right' . . . was the political response to all these new procedures of power" (144–45).

Foucault describes this "bottleneck" formed by the intersection of the right to life, medical biopower, and personal sovereignty in *"Society Must Be Defended":*

> And it is precisely in the expansion of medicine that we are seeing . . . a perpetual exchange or confrontation between the mechanics of discipline and the principle of right. . . . The only existing and apparently solid recourse we have against the usurpations of disciplinary mechanisms and against the rise of a power that is bound up with scientific knowledge is precisely a recourse or a return to a right that is organized around sovereignty. . . . [A]t this point we are in a sort of bottleneck . . . having recourse to sovereignty against discipline will not enable us to limit the effects of disciplinary power. . . . We should be looking for a new right that is both antidisciplinary and emancipated from the principle of sovereignty. (2003, 39–40)

The second stricture, against normalized right, is relevant here, for Terri Schiavo's wishes not to receive tubal feeding in a severely compromised situation were subject to two tests, one explicit—were they her wishes?—and the other implicit—were those wishes in accordance with American norms? Judge Greer notes in his February 11, 2000, ruling as to Terri Schiavo's wishes that "the testimony of Ms. Beverly Tyler, Executive Director of Georgia Health Discoveries, clearly establishes that the expressions made by Terri Schiavo to these witnesses are those types of expressions made in those types of situations as would be expected by people in this country in that age group at that time." Thus it is the very normalized nature, the generic nature, of Terri Schiavo's statements that made them plausible. The subject of law, the person, is the generic member of society, the one conforming to the norm of what "would be expected." But that cannot be what we are looking for in Deleuzian jurisprudence.

For Deleuze and Guattari in *A Thousand Plateaus*, it is the haecceity, or assemblage, not the person, which deserves a proper name (1987, 260–65). A person as subject is modeled on a substance with properties. It is fixed in the actual; it sits comfortably in those normalized habits that render it a generic member of society. But it is only in extraordinary situations, singularizing situations, that we move from being a person as a generic member of society to being a becoming, a haecceity or consistency, a person undergoing depersonalization by opening to the intensive processes at whose intersection the person appears as the line between personality and organic system. That is, it is only in singular situations, at turning points in our lives, that we touch upon the processes that produce us as bodies politic. This singularity is marked by political affect, as a primary "I feel," or better yet, "There is a feeling in me."

It is this intensity generated by concrete processes forming bodies politic that lies behind the justification of privacy as singularity. The user-groups, the parties to a case, are those who feel most intensely and accurately; that is, they bring forth or express a certain singular relation of Ideas forming the problematic field of any one case. It is this singularity that both defeats morality as the laying down of abstract rules and requires that we articulate a principle of singularity for jurisprudence. It is not abstract reasoning about the sanctity of life but the intensity and accuracy of affect generated by exposure to the extraordinary that is our guide. If you want to feel something of that intensity and accuracy, you can try a substitution thought experiment involving your own loved ones: how would you want them to feel if you were in a PVS? (Please note that I'm not asking what you would do for a loved one in a PVS, but what you would want them to do if you were in a PVS.) In other words, how much do you want them to suffer from your condition? Such a thought experiment would be neither Heideggerian nor Levinasian, though it might be closer to the latter. It is not Heideggerian, for it does not concern the impact of the thought of your death on your actions; nor is it Levinasian, for it does not concern the effect the death of the other will have on your subjectivity. The thought experiment will not give you back to yourself in Heideggerian authenticity, but it will (we would expect) depersonalize you via the depersonalization undergone by your loved ones as you imagine how they would be exposed to a singular and intense situation. It will, I would expect, knock you out of your habits of thought: the intensity and accuracy of the affect would shock you to think as you think about how your loved ones would feel.

What is the name of this mutual depersonalization, this intensive becoming, for Deleuze and Guattari? Love. "Every love is an exercise in depersonalization on a body without organs yet to be formed, and it is at the highest point of this depersonalization that someone can be named, receives his or her family name or first name, acquires the most intense discernability in the instantaneous apprehension of the multiplicities belonging to him or her, and to which he or she belongs" (1987, 35). One of the ways to the new right we search for must be through such love, the sacrificial love that Terri Schiavo had for her loved ones—for her husband and for her parents and for her siblings—a love that, obscenely, we glimpsed in the media spectacle to which they were subjected.

Chapter 6   **The Columbine High School Massacre: The Transverse Body Politic**

WE CONTINUE OUR SERIES of case studies with the Columbine High School massacre of 1999. Considering it as a point of intensity of the group level and mid-term temporal scale, we will show the confluence of military techniques enabling close-range killing with freelance experiments in political physiology enabling the killers to overcome any protoempathic identification they might have felt—at least during the time of their killing spree. The ability of law enforcement and the military to kill in a planned, systematic manner is the key to sovereignty conceived as the monopoly on the legitimate use of violence in a territory; the seepage of the ability to implement systematic killing outside government institutions constitutes a category beyond mere crime of passion, necessitating the categories of mass murder (when the motivations are private) and/or terrorism (for political motivation [Cole 2003]). Though the Columbine killers are clearly in the first category, we will try to get at their experiment in political physiology by investigating military techniques, since the details of their own training are lost in the morass of fantasy writings they left behind.

Some excellent reporting has been done on the Columbine massacre (Cullen 1999, 2004; Watson 2002). I assume the basic facts will be recognizable in outline: two white teenage boys, Dylan Klebold and Eric Harris, open fire in an affluent suburban Colorado high school on April 20, 1999, killing thirteen others and, finally, themselves. The assault followed extensive planning and assembling an arsenal of firearms and bombs. The original plan was to detonate bombs in the school cafeteria and to wait outside in the parking lot to shoot fleeing survivors. However, the bombs failed to detonate, and so Klebold and Harris entered the school, choosing the library as their initial point of attack. They killed the students over a period of sixteen minutes, and after a thirty-minute quiet period they killed themselves. Cullen's work has dispelled many myths about the killers including the idea that they were complete outcasts (in fact, they had a good-sized circle of friends with whom they partied; they even went to the prom); that they had been victims of extreme and continuous bullying (not true; they were fringe types, but not daily victims, as were some other school shooters); that there was a connection to the Trench Coat Mafia (a separate group); that they targeted jocks, African-Americans, and Christians (Klebold and Harris were indiscriminate haters who even included racists among their most hated objects); and the "unlikely martyrdom" of Cassie Bernall, who was allegedly asked whether she believed in God and when she said yes, she was killed (in fact, it was another girl who was asked this question—*after* she had been shot—and though wounded by the initial attack, she survived) (Watson 2002).

Columbine's impact on American culture has been widespread. To pick one of many examples, on April 20, 2004, 404 of the 1,074 students enrolled at the Dutchtown High School in Ascension Parish in southeastern Louisiana skipped school. The reason many gave for their truancy was that it was the fifth anniversary of the Columbine massacre. This was not in solidarity with the victims, but because two of their classmates, who were free on bond, had been arrested in January for "terrorizing"—a felony according to Louisiana criminal law, punishable by up to fifteen years in prison. According to the police, the two had made "elaborate plans" to re-create the Columbine massacre. As it turned out, the day was uneventful: "I felt fine," reported one student. "The only difference was the number of students who were out of school and that teachers had to lock classroom doors."[1]

What does this anecdote say about contemporary high school students? How is it that students could report that they "felt fine" during a lockdown? Is this just adolescent bravado, showing off for the reporters interviewing them? Or is there something of political affect at work here? Browse a few issues of *Inside School Safety: Effective Management Strategies for School Administrators* and you will see fascinating experiments in surveillance being conducted on high school students—networked video cameras; face-scanning technology linked to databases of missing kids and sex offenders; metal detectors, both permanent and handheld; K-9 patrols; drug testing of urine samples; psychological profiling; and other techniques—turning the high school into one of the most securitized spaces in contemporary American society. Besides the ubiquitous war on drugs, many school districts cite Columbine and other school shootings as rationales for the increased security measures they implement. We do not know whether and to what extent these security measures are themselves anxiety producing; we would need some empirical testing. But where are we going to find a non-anxiety-ridden population in the post-9/11 United States to use as a control group?

As fascinating as this little slice of Americana is, I want to move back from the Dutchtown incident to examine the Columbine massacre itself in terms of the construction of bodies politic. In doing so, I am going to switch the usual philosophical approach from a focus on death as an event to be suffered to the act of killing. Just as the act of killing rather than the passion of death has been neglected in Western philosophy, we see a similar neglect of the killer; other than the analysis of the body of the guardian in the *Republic*, there has been precious little philosophical analysis of the killer, the one who deals death to others. By contrast, the psychology or even physiology of killing has been a deep and abiding theme in Western literature, from the *Iliad* onward, from the war epic through crime fiction. Now, with our approach, the field for the philosophical study of political physiology in the act of killing opens up.

Beyond the Moral / Intentional Analysis of Columbine

Most Columbine coverage has been mired in moral/intentional analyses of motivation and blame. If Klebold and Harris weren't simply dismissed as bad seeds, a host of cultural culprits were put forward as causes, generating a list of the usual suspects, everything from classics like Godless atheism, as Ronald Reagan might have put it, to current favorites, violent music and video games. Actually, the last two are not so far-fetched. The problem is that too many commentators contented themselves with vague hand waving about social influences on the minds of the shooters without any understanding of political affect. If music and video games did play a role in Columbine, it was in shaping the bodies politic of Klebold and Harris—and that means their affective cognition—not simply as causal factors that triggered their behavior. We must avoid the search for unidirectional causality, whether the causes proposed are genetic predispositions or bad social environment, or a blended interaction of the two. It is not so much the number of causal factors put forth that we object to but the linear causality attributed to them.

Missing from the discussion has been a treatment of the dynamic and complex constitution of their bodies politic, an analysis of their political physiology, which would enable answers to the question "how" rather than the question "why." What is needed is not an examination of the mechanics of the killing, the ease of access to firearms, the availability of bomb plans on the Internet, and so forth, but answers to questions: How did the bodies politic of Klebold and Harris negotiate the intensity of the act of killing? How did they produce such bodies politic for themselves? In what corporeal practices did they engage to prepare themselves for the act of killing?

Perhaps the most troubling thing about the killings is how Klebold and Harris could accomplish them as subjects: how they could plan them rationally and how they could carry them out in a state at least close to that of "cold blood." Klebold and Harris were neither in a blind or berserker rage nor in the trance-like fugue states claimed to be operative in the case of other school shooters. They interacted with their classmates, questioning them, taunting them, even in the act of killing. They retained their subjectivity rather than fleeing it in a fugue state, which is a species of dissociation, along with daydreaming on one end of the spectrum and multiple personality disorder on the other. They retained their subjectivity rather than retreating from it into a blind or berserker rage, the activation of an evolutionarily shaped rage agent. In considering the Columbine massacre, I am not sure what is more troubling: that Klebold and Harris could kill the way they did, as subjects, or that other humans have been launched into murderous rages or, even more bizarrely, murderous trances. To provide a contrast for the subjective presence in the predatory actions of Klebold and Harris, we need to wrest the asubjective phenomena of the murderous rage and the murderous trance from their banality. How do these rages and trances work? Where do they come from? What can we do about them? How do they relate to what we would usually consider normal subjectivity? We will concentrate here on rage and leave the mysterious phenomenon of fugue states for another study.

Rage

Current neuroscientists—and those psychologists and philosophers who accept the concept of basic emotion—unanimously agree that rage is a basic emotion and that it is not to be confused with aggression, though it sometimes is at the root of aggressive behavior.[2] A leading neuroscientist investigating rage is Jaak Panksepp, whose *Affective Neuroscience* (1998) is a standard textbook in the field. In discussing rage, he cites Kenneth Moyer's well-known taxonomy of seven forms of aggression: fear-based, maternal, irritable, sexual, territorial, intermale competitive, and predatory; Panksepp stresses that these behavioral complexes do not equal brain subsystems (193). In that regard, he argues that aggression is wider than anger

(187), distinguishing at least two forms of "aggressive circuits" in mammalian brains: predation and rage (188).[3] Predation is based in what Panksepp calls the "seeking" system, which is activated by physiological imbalances, those that can be experienced as hunger, thirst, or sexual need. In predatory hunting, based in seeking, the subject is still operative; there is an experience to hunting, what "it is like" to hunt. Insofar as they retained their subjectivity in interacting with their victims, the Columbine killers, it seems, though they were in some ordinary sense rageful and hateful, were indeed hunting when roaming the library looking for victims. We must be careful about too strictly distinguishing predation and rage in the act of killing, concrete episodes are most often blends of anger and predation. As one expert puts it: "Real-life encounters tend to yield eclectic admixtures, composites of goal and rage, purpose and hate, reason and feeling, rationality and irrationality. Instrumental and hostile violence are not only *kinds* of violence, but also violence qualities or *components*" (Toch 1992, 1–2; italics in original).

By contrast, it is important to note that in a blind rage the subject drops out.[4] We take the Viking berserker rage as a prototype, a particularly clear or pure expression of the underlying neurological rage circuits. It is not that the Vikings as subjects presented simply a stage for the playing out of these neurological circuits. To provoke the berserker rage, the Vikings, through a variety of training practices embedded in their customs, distributed traits for triggering the berserker process throughout their population; one researcher cites possible mushroom ingestion as a contributing factor (Fabing 1956). There is no denying that the social meaning of rages differs across cultures—how they are interpreted by others and by self after waking up—as do triggers and thresholds. But I think it is important to rescue a minimal notion of human nature from extreme social constructivism and hold that the rage pattern is the same across cultures—or as much as can be the same given variation in genetic inheritances, environmental input, and developmental plasticity. Even with all that variation, there is remarkable similarity in what a full rage looks like, though how much it takes to get there, and what the intermediate anger episodes look like (emotion scripts), can differ widely. Even Averill, a leading social constructivist, relates running amok in Southeast Asian societies to Viking berserker rages. Averill writes, "Aggressive frenzies are, of course, found in many different cultures (e.g., the *'berserk'* reaction attributed to old Norse warriors), but amok is probably the most studied of these syndromes" (Averill 1982, 59; italics in original). It is the very *commonality* of "aggressive frenzies" that we are after in our notion of pattern. (See also Simons 1996 on the startle reflex.)

I propose that in extreme cases of rage a modular agent replaces the subject. As we saw in chapter 1, a common term for rage and other basic emotions is "affect program." Affect programs are emotional responses that are "complex, coordinated, and automated . . . unfold[ing] in this coordinated fashion without the need for conscious direction" (Griffiths 1997, 77). They are more than reflexes, but they are triggered well before any cortical processing can take place (though later cortical appraisals can dampen or accelerate the affect program). Griffiths makes the case that affect programs should be seen in light of Fodor's notion of modularity, which calls for a module to be "mandatory . . . opaque [we are aware of outputs but not the processes producing them] . . . and informationally encapsulated [the information in a module cannot access that in other modules]" (93; my comments in brackets). Perhaps second only to the question of adaptationism for the amount of controversy it has evoked, the use of the concept of modularity in evolutionary psychology is bitterly contested. I feel relatively safe proposing a rage module or rage agent since its adaptive value is widely attested to by its presence in other mammals, and since Panksepp is able to cite studies of direct electrical stimulation of the brain (ESB) and neurochemical manipulation as identifying homologous rage circuits in humans and other mammalian species (Panksepp 1998, 190).[5] Panksepp proposes as adaptive reasons for rage agents their utility in predator-prey relations, further sharpening the difference between rage and predator aggression. While a hunting attack is by definition an instance of predatory aggression, rage reactions are a prey phenomenon, a vigorous reaction when pinned down by a predator. Initially a reflex, Panksepp claims, rage reactions developed into a full-fledged neural phenomenon with its own circuits (190). The evolutionary inheritance of rage patterns is confirmed by the well-attested fact that infants can become enraged by having their arms pinned to their sides (189).

The Act of Killing

Dave Grossman's fine work on military history and corporeal technologies, *On Killing* (1996), shows that overwhelming evidence in military history points to a deep-seated inhibition against one-on-one, face-to-face, cold-blooded killing on the part of some 98 percent of soldiers. The biggest problem of military training is how to overcome this deep inhibition. It is not that societies have to stop a natural impulse to murder—far from it. Armies instead need elaborate training to compel the vast majority of soldiers to kill, and even past basic training, elaborate social technologies such as the firing squad are needed to facilitate cold-blooded killing. The blindfold enables the shooters rather than soothes the victim; the blank cartridge allows plausible deniability to each of the shooters (Grossman 1996; Ehrenreich 1997). Indeed, so deep is this inhibition that traditional military drill, when conducted as target shooting at bull's-eyes, produced only a 15–20 percent *firing* rate among American infantry troops in World War II, excluding machine gunners (Grossman 1996, 3–4, citing Marshall 1978). A firing rate does not indicate willingness to kill, as Grossman explains. The usual fight-or-flight dichotomy is falsely drawn from *inter*-species conflicts; *intra*-species conflicts are also marked by display and submission, which along with flight are much more likely to occur before fight (especially fight to the death).[6] Hence, much of the firing rate was display rather than fight.

How can we ground this inhibition? Antonio Damasio, in *Descartes' Error* (1994) has developed a theory of the link of reason and emotion in which the key is the "somatic marker hypothesis," whereby scenarios of future situations are marked by flashes of body images, images that make us feel what it would be like to live through the imagined situation.[7] The feeling of what this or that future would be like to live through serves to shape the phase space of planning into zones of the plausible and the implausible, the pleasant and the nauseating, the thinkable and the unthinkable. Unconscious emotional premonitions thus cut down on the possibilities for which one needs to use classical reasoning by assigning an emotional weight or valence to the imagined scenarios.

I propose several factors to account for the wide distribution of the inhibition on killing among humans, each of which depends on what is at least a protoempathic identification.[8] We need not decide here on the mechanism of that emotional contagion or shared affective state, for which, as we saw in chapter 1, there are two major explanations in the current literature: simulation theories (relying on mirror neurons) and phenomenological theories. Either approach seems superior in accounting for this inhibition on killing to Theory Theory (agreeing here with the emphasis on affect found in Maibom 2007). Rooting the sort of intense identification we find in cases of anticipation or recollection of close-range killing—consider the trembling limbs, the intense nausea, the bouts of vomiting that we find here—in a cognitive inference via the observation or anticipation of outward behavior (in this case writhing in agony and clutching at spilled guts) so that we *attribute* the emotional state of agony to the *mind* of another person seems rather thin soup: thin soup that is akin to the folk cognitivism of media reports that describe waterboarding as the production of the belief in the mind of the victim that he or she is drowning. We should rather describe waterboarding as triggering an evolutionarily preserved panic module that acts by means of a traumatizing biochemical cascade. We here see the link of internalist or cognitivist approaches and a certain neurocentrism: it is only by bracketing the endocrine system in favor of an exclusive focus on the central nervous system (and there, focusing on electrical activity somehow abstracted from its biochemical milieu of neurotransmitters and hormones) that one could think of beliefs here. Whether it is a simulation or an embodied intersubjectivity, there is a fundamental linkage of affect, body image, and bodily integrity in the experience of protoempathic identification. Anecdotal evidence is clear that seeing someone else's blood and guts spill out of them is powerfully felt by many soldiers (Kirkland 1995; Kilner 2000).[9]

The inhibition on killing, then, that I would propose in combining Grossman and Damasio comes from sensing what the intensity of the fight to the kill would be like. In other words, the inhibition occurs because a true attack, an attack beyond a certain threshold—the threshold mutually recognized as that indicating display—might provoke a deep panicked self-defense (rather than submission).[10] That is to say, we do not want to take the risk that a full-fledged attack will trigger a panicked fight for life on the part of opponents who are willing to submit when faced with an attack that can be read as display calling for submission. Or, more precisely, the body politic does not want this, since we are dealing with embedded corporeal inhibitions that constrain subjective action. Past a certain threshold of biochemical parameters correlated with the sense-making activities of affective cognition, antagonistic muscles fire and punches are pulled, fingers release their strangleholds, well beyond and against subjective will. Try it, you'll see.

Thus it is not who is willing to kill that counts but who is *able* to kill; that is, which body politic has been developed to the point that it can overcome or bypass the inhibition on close-range personal killing, an inhibition in which protoempathic identification plays a major role. In contrast to the Schiavo case, this time it is not just the face that is important but the gut: the viscero-motor centers mapped by pain-recognizing mirror neurons would seem here to be very important (Singer et al. 2004). Seeing or even simply imagining the guts of the other must then trigger a scenario in which "What if that's *me* with *my* guts hanging out?" is entertained. But just as that somatic marker must carry with it powerful attendant inhibitions, it most likely also generates complex psychophysiological rewards, since at the same time that the as-if scenario generates its somatic maker, a real somatic marker is being generated with its "everything is still okay" message.

With this complex interplay of somatic markers in the as-if and real modes, it should be evident why the "body" and "subject" terminology is awkward and why a concept of corporeal agent is needed. Any first-person account of rage is self-defeating at a certain point, for it must include an account of how the highest order of consciousness, personal subjectivity, fades away in extreme rage. At the peak of a towering rage, humans no longer speak, they only howl and spit and growl. If we assume, as seems reasonable, that subjectivity and language are intimately linked, then we are no longer able to relate these acts to a personal memory; that is, they no longer seem to have come from "me."[11]

At this point, the switch to a second-person perspective or to an inferential process is needed in order to account for the replacement by rage of autobiographical, fully subjective, consciousness. It seems either that other people must tell you what "you" (your body) did while you were "blind" (unconscious) with rage, or that you must piece together retrospectively what must have happened from the changes in the world from when you last remember being there. These inferences result from the adoption of a third-person perspective about yourself, in which you attribute causal efficacy to "yourself" (your body) while in the rage. Theweleit 1987–89 cites reports of people waking up from a rage and wondering who it was that did all that damage. The accounts go something like this: "This person wasn't dead before, I'm the only one here, I've got blood all over me, I remember getting really mad at him—I must have been the one who killed him!" As Nietzsche's *Genealogy of Morals* tells us, a long history of the development of personal responsibility is enfolded in this identification of the actor of the events with the "me" of the narrator.

Thus, in rage there is no hyperintense or transgressive experience; there's no subject to the experience, only to the aftermath. The body politic —the socially developed body, the crossing of certain thresholds of which triggers the evolutionary rage pattern—is the agent, with an absent subject. The evolutionary module theory developed here gives another sort of third-person account, this time a neurophysiological explanation of the takeover of the control of the body by a rage agent. Thus in the embodied inhibition against extreme violence we see a nonsubjective desire to avoid the intensity of a rage state due to the flashing somatic marker developed in a quick as-if scenario. A further boost to the inhibition against extreme violence comes from a similar somatic marker / as-if scenario operation: the felt need to avoid the intensity of revulsion after killing. It is as if living with having been a killer would be too much. The nausea that would be the somatic marker of that image would then be prospectively a nonsubjective inhibitor and retrospectively the base for the subjective guilt the soldiers feel for having done that to someone else. "How would you like it if I did that to you?"—the guilt machine of the Golden Rule.

Professional Techniques of Killing

How, then, do armies get soldiers to kill? The political physiology of military killing entails articulating the patterns, thresholds, and triggers of the military unit with the patterns of intensity, the thresholds of inhibition, and the triggers of command embedded in the soldier's body. Let's go through the hierarchy of thresholds embedded in most people's bodies, noting that thresholds can be both too high or too low, a difference that destroys the putative unity of the concept of aggression. Self-defensive violent behavior can be provoked by the misperception of a threat on the part of a person with lowered thresholds resulting from trauma, while predatory or utilitarian violence can result from the development of high thresholds, opening up a person's as-if somatic markers to realms of action outside the norm, resulting in antisocial or psychopathic behavior (Niehoff 1999; Blair, Mitchell, and Blair 2005). We must also note the dynamic/autonomous systems perspective necessary in all studies of bodies politic: the intensity required to push a system to a threshold depends on the recent and developmental history of the system; we all recognize that the last straw is not an objective or fixed trigger but varies according to how you are feeling at the moment, and on what you have been through in your life.

With these caveats in mind, let us arrange the thresholds from easiest to most difficult, following Grossman 1996: violent thought, revenge fantasies, resentment, and so forth; the push in the back, arm, or chest; the body punch; the slap in the face; the punch in the face; the slash with nails or knife (prosthetic nails) in the back, arm, chest, and face; the overhand stab with a knife in the back, arm, chest, or face; the disemboweling underhand stab in the gut or genitals; the kill with bare hands or teeth on neck, face, and eyes. The most difficult killing, then, is hand-to-hand between isolated opponents who can identify with each other.

What enables military killing? The most well-known factors are distance, technology, teamwork, command, and dehumanization. In Deleuzian terms, these variables form an Idea or multiplicity, that is, as we saw in the introduction, a set of differential elements, differential relations, and singularities. All these factors are sociosomatic corporeal techniques, which when combined in a solution or machinic assemblage—when articulated with somatic bodies politic, each with its own singular developmental system constituted from genetic endowment and ecosocial environment—lower the intensity of the act of killing so that, in most cases, it falls below the threshold that would inhibit close-range killing with the hand by untrained agents. Distance (or more precisely, the differential relation of rates of change of advance and retreat) and technology (or more precisely, the assemblages composed between humans and machines such as guns, knives, etc.) combine so that for many trained corporeal agents or bodies politic, it is not a very intense act just to push a button when far away from the killing. Teamwork and command (horizontal and vertical social relations that are differentially composed and strewn with singularities) will combine to disperse the intensity among a larger social body so that it is not *me* killing *you*, but my group (phalanx, legion, battalion) fighting yours.[12] Finally, with dehumanization, the intensity of the act of killing an animal is below the threshold of inhibition for killing a human—the whole point behind Grossman's distinguishing of fight-or-flight (*inter*-species) from display and submission (*intra*-species). Repetition in training serves to lower the intensity even more. Artillery and aviation troops have such great enablers from distance, technology, teamwork, and command that they achieve close to 100 percent fight-to-kill rates without even much need to resort to dehumanization of the enemy.[13]

Without the enablers of distance, technology, teamwork, command, and dehumanization, most soldiers must leave the state of cold blood in order to kill one-on-one at close range: they have to dump their subjectivity. They burst through the threshold of inhibition by supercharging their bodily intensity. Thus the tried-and-true method for killing in close combat is the berserker rage, the frenzy of killing anything that enters the death zone immediately in front of the berserker. In the berserker rage, the subject is overwhelmed by a chemical flood that triggers an evolutionarily primitive module that functions as an agent that runs the body's hardware in its place. The Greeks called it "possession by Ares" (Harris 2001). It is important to understand that such rage is itself traumatic: it sets your endorphin release thresholds so high that only more combat will get you off (Bloom 1999; Van der Kolk and Greenberg 1987).

Two common triggers of the berserker rage are the death of a comrade and panic over engulfment (Theweleit 1987–89; Shay 1995). I speculate that the flashing somatic marker of future pain (separation from and mourning for the comrade), coupled with the memory of pleasure tagged to the comrade, triggers such rage. The wrenching shift between the pleasant memories and the painful future triggers rage, a notion that dovetails with Panksepp 1998, where frustration, as the curtailment of the free use of seeking and play systems, triggers rage. A third trigger, at which we have already hinted, is direct and immediate threat to life, the panicked self-defense reaction that display and submission seek to avoid. There are, of course, many other triggers that we cannot discuss here, among them abandonment, as when domestic violence escalates from beating to killing, which often happens only after separation. The military problem of the berserker rage is how to disengage it in combat, or at best, keep it controlled so that it is released only on command.

As we have seen, the vast majority of soldiers cannot kill in cold blood and need to kill in a de-subjectified state, for example, in reflexes, rages, and panics. But who does the killing when reflexes, rages, and panics are activated? Zahavi 2005 and Gallagher 2005 distinguish agency and ownership of bodily actions. Ownership is the sense that my body is doing the action, while agency is the sense that I am in control of the action, that the action is willed. Both are aspects of subjectivity, though they may well be a matter of prereflective self-awareness rather than full-fledged objectifying self-consciousness (Zahavi 2005).

Alongside subjectivity we need also to notice emergent assemblages that skip subjectivity and directly conjoin larger groups and the somatic. To follow this line of thought, we should recall our previous discussion of basic emotions as modular affect programs (Griffiths 1997) that run the body's hardware in the absence of conscious control. As with reflexes, ownership and agency are only retrospectively felt, at least in severe cases of rage in which the person wakes up to see the results of the destruction committed while he or she was in the grips of the rage. In this way we see two elements we need to take into account besides the notion of subjective agency: (1) that there is another sense of agent as nonsubjective controller of bodily action, either reflex or basic emotion, and (2) that in some cases the military unit and nonsubjective reflexes and basic emotions are intertwined in such a way as to bypass the soldiers' subjectivity qua controlled intentional action. In these cases the practical agent of the act of killing is not the individual person or subject but the emergent assemblage of military unit and nonsubjective reflex or equally nonsubjective affect program.

Excursus: On the Warrior Body

Homer is the greatest of all students of the warrior body. Consider the trash talking in the *Iliad*. The physiology of fighting is that to overcome an inherited and universal *intra*-species inhibition on close-range killing warriors need rage. Rage will release endorphins, which reduce anxiety and act as analgesics, or painkillers. The repetition of such rages is traumatic, however: they produce chronic high endorphin levels, which set a high threshold for new endorphin release. Putting yourself into danger, and the trash talking that accompanies it, thus has to escalate: you need more and more stress, more and more danger, in order to get the same rush. Normal life triggers will not be enough to push the body past the threshold of endorphin release. Thus, outside of battle—think of Achilles' sulking when he deprives himself of battle throughout most of the *Iliad*—the warrior feels "dead": there's no joie de vivre. In fact, he (I am using the masculine pronoun here, but let's not forget the Amazons) is objectively deprived of endorphins. There's a lot to think about here in terms of affect and experience, physiology and consciousness, affect and cognition: was Achilles thinking straight when, in his depression, he allowed Patroclus to fight in his stead?

High-intensity training is needed for noble single combat: consider the relative capital investment for an agricultural society to produce an aristocratic warrior. To produce such warrior bodies you need to traumatize them by lots of intensive hunting and fighting as boys: think of Odysseus's scar from his adolescent rite of passage, the boar hunt (*Odyssey* 19.549–52). Phalanx training was intermediate between aristocratic single combat and naval rowing; it is less intense than single combat because of teamwork, that is, emergence. In the phalanx, you stand by your comrades rather than surge ahead. Recall Aristotle's definition of courage as the mean between rashness and cowardice: in concrete terms, rashness for the phalanx is standard behavior for the warrior, while phalanx courage—staying with your comrades—would be mediocrity if not cowardice for the warrior.[14] And this standing together is the key to the eros of the phalanx as ecstatic union with an emergent body politic. McNeill 1995 and Freeman 2000b allow us to account for this human bonding in terms of resonance and entrainment of asubjective physiological processes triggering endorphin release. Remember the discussion in the *Symposium* about Homer's not being explicit about sex between Achilles and Patroclus. Later Greeks, soaked in the eros of the phalanx, assumed sex between them; their only question was who was lover and who was beloved.

Homer is the great ancestor of all students of political affect in his treatment of Achilles, Hector, and Odysseus. Achilles' rage triggers include insult to honor. But honor is not a sentiment for Homer's Greeks. *Timé* is stuff: tangible and visible signs of esteem, usually in the form of women and gold, but also the best cuts of meat and wine. Recall the dialogue between Sarpedon and Glaucus: "Why do we fight? For the meat, the wine, and the land" (*Iliad* 12.320–42). In materialist terms, the meat is for muscle building, the wine is for coming down off the high of battle, and the land is to produce these inputs.

Homer's portrayal of Hector's dilemma concerning glory is incomparably nuanced. When asked by Andromache in book 6 (and later by Priam and Hecuba in book 22 [40–114]) to fight from the walls, he replies, "I would feel a terribly great shame before the Trojan men and the Trojan women, with their flowing robes" (6.440–42). We might even say Homer has what Damasio would call a somatic marker, a flashing scenario of what it would be like for his body to experience the removal from his being bathed in the positive feedback of admiring glances that keep his pleasure flowing. Without the reinforcement of those glances, he would have no triggers for his positive emotions and would become depressed. He flashes onto this future, this way in which he would die of shame. (Just as we have a folk ontology of complex systems, I think we also have a folk political physiology: we've always known you can die of shame or of a broken heart, that is, that the social and the somatic are intimately linked; it is just the Cartesian dualist ontology, the folk ontology of mechanistic medicine, that overlooks this or is troubled by it.)

Thus Hector's choice to fight is really the choice of the form of death. He does not have Achilles' choice: a short glorious life or a long dull one. Hector's choice is a short glorious life or a short depressed and inglorious life. His warrior body would need a long reprogramming to be a soldier and fight from the walls. Soldier fighting is *poietic*: done for the sake of something greater outside the action, that is, the safety and glory of the polis. Soldier fighting done in the phalanx is of a lower intensity: group eros versus the high of warrior fighting done in a rage. Warrior fighting is praxis: it is done for its own sake, or more precisely, it is done in order to deal with the traumatized warrior body, to get the next endorphin fix. Its necessity is immanently produced rather than transcendently imposed.

In his voyages Odysseus undergoes just the sort of long deprogramming Hector could not. In crying on the beach of Calypso's island for seven years, he is mourning his death as a warrior; he is reprogramming his joy/endorphin triggers, which are set at a very high level due to the intensity of battle. This is what all mourning is, finding new endorphin triggers. This is why "breaking up is hard to do": love is an intense state in which high levels of endorphins are released only in the presence of the beloved. This sets your endorphin release threshold very high. Thus everyday life is boring (its triggers cannot push you past that threshold of endorphin release), and you neglect your friends. "You never call since you met him/her!" But when the love trigger is disengaged, then you have no triggers at all that can reach the high threshold for endorphin release. That is why your friends recommend a hobby, meeting new people: you have to form new triggers. And Ares and Aphrodite are a couple because war and love can both be intense, erotic-ecstatic, physiologically traumatizing, and addictive experiences. Madonna showed her pop-culture genius in 1991 when she called General Norman Schwartzkopf "the sexiest man in America," thereby positing herself as Aphrodite.

Contemporary Military Techniques

As fascinating as they are, rages are not very effective in modern military action. A second strategy for facilitating killing by soldiers, a major innovation in military training perfected by the U.S. Army in the Vietnam era, is not to overwhelm the inhibition threshold with the chemical flood of rage but to bypass it by operant conditioning that triggers an unconscious, automatic "read and react" mode in which soldiers fire individually on whatever human-shaped targets appear in their range of vision (Grossman 1996, 177–79). Not a berserker rage, but a conditioned reflex. Here, the subject is bypassed by direct access of the military machine to reflexes embedded in the spinal cord of the soldier—as clear an instance of political physiology as one could imagine.

With this new corporeal technology the U.S. Army greatly increased firing rates in Vietnam; Grossman's thesis is that this increase was purchased at the price of a huge spike in post-traumatic stress disorder (PTSD), as increasing the percentage of soldiers able to kill also increased the percentage of soldiers who had to face the consequences of having killed. Bypassing the subject by plugging the spinal cord directly into the military machine still means soldiers have to deal with the aftereffect when the subject reappears. In one way the small percentage of willing killers prior to this conditioning were self-selected: the ability to kill also guaranteed an ability to handle the sight of the victim.[15] This makes sense based on our hypothesis that the nauseating body marker of the imagined scenario of the victim's mangled body isolates the singularity "to kill" in a no-go zone of the virtual for most soldiers. We have to be clear that guilt is only one aspect of PTSD; many of the problems have to do with the sustained high cortisol levels and the high endorphin-release thresholds of the traumatized body. In other words, PTSD is at least as much physiological as it is psychological disturbance, though neither one nor the other exclusively (Van der Kolk 1996).

Contemporary military training cuts subjectivity out of the loop so that most soldiers' bodies are able to *temporarily* withstand the stress of the act of killing. The first aspect is affective: soldiers are acculturated to dehumanize the enemy by a series of racial slurs. This acculturation is especially powerful when accomplished through rhythmic chanting while running, for such entrainment weakens personal identity to produce a group subject (McNeill 1995; Burke 2004). At the same time as the group subject is constituted, the act of killing is rhetorically sterilized by euphemisms. "Most soldiers do not 'kill,' instead the enemy was knocked over, wasted, greased, taken out, and mopped up. The enemy is hosed, zapped, probed, and fired on. The enemy's humanity is denied, and he becomes a strange beast called a Kraut, Jap, Reb, Yank, dink, slant, or slope" (Grossman 1996, 93). Desensitization is merely an enabling factor for the role of classical and operant conditioning in modern training. Such training enables most soldiers to kill reflexively. In doing so, they bypass the widespread inhibition on killing we have noted earlier.

The major problem of modern military training that reconfigures reflex action lies in going beyond what the restored subjectivity of many soldiers can withstand. The "shoot on sight" or "free fire zone" protocol begins in Vietnam with the application of human silhouettes rather than concentric targets in basic training; this new training produced a significant rise in kill-to-fire ratios (Grossman 1996, 181). In effect, such pattern-recognition training increases the distribution of a "hunter agent" in the population of soldiers, so that the sight of human-shaped targets triggers a shoot reflex. However, the increased distribution of hunting agents is incompatible with the widespread protoempathic identification we discussed previously. Unless this protoempathic identification is sufficiently desensitized, many soldiers are psychologically traumatized because in the aftereffects of battle they see the enemy's corpse—produced by their implanted hunting agents—as human, as someone "that could have been

"Light them up"

me" (Lifton 1973; Grossman 1996). In combination with the physiological effects of long-term stress (in particular, elevated cortisol levels), such psychological trauma is linked with PTSD (Shay 1995; Van der Kolk and Greenberg 1987).

Vietnam-era reflex training is good only for free fire zones. With urban warfare, more-sophisticated cognition is necessary: the shoot/no shoot instant decision. With the advent of digital and video simulator training for urban warfare, we see true cyborg killing. Military training has very often involved simulated combat conditions—training dummies—to develop motor skills. While it succeeds in this, the transfer to real combat often falters because of affective limitations. Traditional simulation training puts soldiers in an everyday world of three-dimensional objects; however, the difference between the dummy and a real person is clear, so "killing" the dummy does not desensitize protoempathic identification. Digital and video simulation (live action figures with a computer-generated image, or CGI, backdrop) develops individual motor skills, but we can speculate that they also increase the desensitization effect of training. Because images are so lifelike, they activate the protoempathic identification present in most. Repetition of the training attempts to produce the desired desensitization. In other words, simulation-trained contemporary soldiers have already *virtually* experienced killing before *actually* having to kill (Macedonia 2002; McCarter 2005). But they have not experienced the transition from the simulated environment to real life: we speculate that even though simulations can desensitize to some extent, they cannot override or completely extinguish the protoempathic identification capacity in a good number of soldiers.[16]

In addition to the affective aspect of heightened desensitization, simulation training constitutes a new cognitive group subject. The instant decision of shoot/no shoot is solicited by the presence or absence of key traits in the gestalt of the situation. Such instant decisions are more than reflexes, but they operate at the very edge of the conscious awareness of the soldiers and involve complex subpersonal processes of threat perception (Correll et al. 2006). In addition to this attenuation of individual agency, cutting-edge communication technology now allows soldiers to network together in real time. With this networking we see an extended/distributed cognition culminating in "topsight" for a commander who often does not command, in the sense of micromanage, but who observes and intervenes at critical points (Arquilla and Rondfeldt 2000, 22). In other words, contemporary team-building applications through real-time networking are a cybernetic application of video games that goes above the level of the subject (Fletcher 1999). In affective entrainment, instant decision making, and cognitive topsight, the soldiers produced by rhythmic chanting and intensive simulation training are nodes within a cybernetic organism, the fighting group, which maintains its functional integrity and tactical effectiveness by real-time communication technology. It is the emergent group with the distributed decisions of the soldiers that is the practical agent here, operating at the thresholds of the individual subjectivities of the soldiers.

The Columbine Killing Machine

After this survey of military training techniques for producing bodies politic capable of killing behavior, we can return to the Columbine High School killers. When considering the Columbine killers in detail, given our prior analyses, we have six factors to account for: (1) cold-bloodedness, (2) bodily intensity, (3) thresholds of violence, (4) planning the unthinkable, (5) breakdown, and (6) suicide.

With regard to cold-bloodedness, bodily intensity, and thresholds of violence, we should note that Klebold and Harris were subjects in the act of killing: they verbally interacted with their classmates. Is this an indication of cold-bloodedness (they lowered the intensity of the body state in the act of killing) or raised thresholds (they were able to maintain subjectivity even at body intensities that for others would have triggered the nonsubjective rage agent)? I am drawn to the latter hypothesis. Cullen 2004 cites the conclusion of a psychiatrist and the FBI agent in charge of the Columbine case that Harris was a psychopath (hence low-intensity, cold-blooded, stimulus hungry) and Klebold a "rage-filled depressive." That Harris was too cold and Klebold too hot means they complemented each other, with Klebold's rages providing Harris with stimulation and Harris's planning capability keeping Klebold in line. Harris by himself might have been cold-blooded, but I speculate that the complex system he formed with Klebold was a raised-threshold system. This combination created its own psychophysiological dynamic as it worked within a machinic assemblage or transversally emergent body politic, the Columbine killing machine consisting of Klebold-Harris-bombs-guns-school. The practical agent of the act of killing here was that machine, which includes the reflexes and quasi-reflexes we speculate that their training induced in them. Subjects they were, but trained subjects working in tandem with technological extensions.[17]

With regard to planning the unthinkable, this chapter may be as disturbing for you to read as it was for me to write. Yet it apparently was not at all difficult for Klebold and Harris to concoct their elaborate plans. Somehow they were able to operate below the threshold of horror and explore rationally the planning space of mass murder. This is unthinkable to most of us: we would be nauseated if these were real plans. If not unthinkable, then at least undoable. This whole chapter is anticathartic: violent fantasies, purely internal or externalized as video games, are thanatographic techniques; they are desensitizing and enabling, not cathartic. (To repeat, I define "thanatography" as representations of violence provoking physiological changes, analogous to the provocation of physiological change with pornography.) The analysis of thanatography needs to be differential and population based: there are no simple linear functions here; rather, there are patterns, thresholds, and triggers distributed in a population.

The questions of breakdown and suicide are linked. Klebold and Harris could keep up the killing for only sixteen minutes. After the massacre in the library, they lived for another thirty minutes, with lots of available targets. Why the inability to continue? Why did they end the quiet period with their own deaths? Remorse is too moral/intentional to be the only category of use here. If they were remorseful, a materialist would have to say that was the conscious reflection of a corporeal depression coming off the high of the killing. The physiological intensity of the kill must have burned them out: raising thresholds allows only a short endurance of hyperintensity. But this depression would only aid, not cause, the suicides, for we cannot forget that the suicides were planned all along. Why? Did they have a premonition—a feeling of the somatic marker of this scenario—that facing everyday life after such a high would be too depressing? In other words, that the killing would be so intense that their whole lives afterward would be just too dull to face? Perhaps they were caricatures of warriors, who want to "live fast, die young, and leave a beautiful corpse"? Is there an analytic link between living fast (the rush of killing) and dying young (the inability to face the relative depression of ordinary life)?

We cannot know what happened to provoke the planned suicide the Columbine killers carried out on themselves. We should not completely discount the remorse angle, though I do not think we should be satisfied with it totally. We can remark upon the tenacity of retrospective guilt produced through the "My God, what have I done?" effect. Even when the practical agent of the act of killing is the assemblage of an emergent killing machine (Klebold-plus-Harris-plus-bombs-plus-guns) and distributed nonsubjective reflexes, rage agents, or awareness-threshold decisions, we can see a centripetal power to subject constitution, drawing to itself responsibility for acts it never committed in isolation. At least in many military contexts, it seems many soldiers paradoxically just cannot help taking responsibility. If there is a centripetal power to the subject that we need to consider, perhaps Klebold and Harris found it biting into them during their quiet period.

As we can never know the details of the case, let us conclude with some (I hope responsible) philosophical speculation, based on the analyses of Deleuze and Guattari in *Anti-Oedipus*. We can say that Klebold and Harris constructed a paranoid desiring machine; it runs for a while and then breaks down in a flameout, a solar nihilism (Protevi 2000). They were subjects, but subjects experimenting in political physiology, seeing what somatic intensity they could withstand in coupling technological machines with biochemical rush, fueled by and enabling the use of guns, bullets, and bombs to release flows of flesh and blood from their normal organs.

We can quickly identify some rather obvious enabling factors for their killing machine: (1) teamwork, (2) machinics (bombs and guns versus knives and hands), (3) video game and chat room desensitization. I am willing to speculate, however, that the key factors are the thrill of judgment and the rush of taunting. Even if Klebold and Harris had not been taunted for years, they were, simply by being high school students, constantly judged and found lacking. In the terminology of *Anti-Oedipus*, they invested in the superior/inferior hierarchy from a paranoid perspective, putting themselves on top. Harris's hatred was generated by contempt: he hated people for their "stupidity" above all (Cullen 2004). It is important to remember that Klebold and Harris were not "prejudiced" and that Columbine was not a hate crime, a crime in which the victim is chosen and attacked for his or her membership in a despised group. In Deleuzoguattarian terms, traditional stereotyping and bigotry are molar, aimed at members of groups, but the up-close killing at Columbine was molecular. Let me explain.

We begin with the alleged martyrdom of the Christian girl. In fact, *all* the victims in the library were taunted before being shot at, including a fat boy and one with glasses. Furthermore, the answers of the victims were completely unrelated to their deaths (they weren't killed because their answers betrayed membership in a despised group), and they were not searched out for their characteristics. They were only available objects, seeds that enabled a crystallization of the free-floating hate of Klebold and Harris.

From this perspective, the taunting was not gratuitous cruelty but physiological necessity, as in the warrior's boasting in the *Iliad*. Despite all their training at raising thresholds and operating subjectively at high intensity, Klebold and Harris needed one last jolt to enable the act of killing. They found that jolt in judgment: having been judged and found wanting their whole lives, Klebold and Harris became judges on the spot. The judgment machine ("to be done with the judgment of God" is a profound Deleuzian wish) operates in many of our social machines. In "control society," it is a matter of constant checking and modulation, of dispersed self-enforced surveillance and improvement (Deleuze 1995, 177–82). Advertising is obviously one of the major stimulants of judging that one's own organs are faulty and in need of commodified improvement: "Ask your doctor if Zoloft [Lipitor, Vioxx, Levitra . . .] is right for you." Thus judgment is a catalyst of production, a provoker of flows, a vector of desire. We know high school is a particularly intense locus of judgment. (An excruciatingly vivid somatic marker is attached to that sentence for many readers, I would say!) And since everyone falls away from the norm (that is, everyone has a "becoming-minority") all Klebold and Harris had to do was simply look at their victims to identify their weaknesses; they were able to find a failure everywhere—you're black, you're Christian, you're fat, you've got glasses. Particularly enraging was the attempt to turn an inferior organ into a social advantage: "Do you think those glasses make you look cool?" was one of their taunts. Perhaps one of the ultimate targets of Klebold and Harris—certainly an unconscious one—was thus the judgment machine itself.

It should be clear that the taunting was not a cool categorization but a felt rush of superiority faced with inferiority. The secret of the Columbine killers, the answer to "how?" is the vast disinhibiting effect of finally operating the judgment machine for their own benefit, of being the trigger points of all that desire. The somatic marker of the scenario of the victim's death must have been that of the sheer joy of finally being the judge after having been judged so often, a rush that raised the threshold of inhibition and allowed them to enact the unthinkable. That their killing machine finally broke down, that the bodies of Klebold and Harris could not sustain the intensity, indicates they weren't really cold-blooded, but hyperintense: they did not lower the intensity of the act of killing; rather, they raised the threshold at which a nonsubjective rage agent would have kicked in. The breakdown of their machine highlights the difficulty of maintaining a subjective presence while enacting the bodily intensity necessary for the act of killing, while the fact that it ran for sixteen minutes warns us of the dangers of subjects willing to undergo such extreme experiments in political physiology.

Chapter 7   **Hurricane Katrina:**
             The Governmental Body Politic

AFTER OUR INVESTIGATIONS of intense cases of the personal and group levels and the short- and mid-term temporal scales of bodies politic, we turn now to the civic and the long-term with our study of Hurricane Katrina. In keeping with our focus on affective cognition in a social context, we will find a racialized fear on the part of government forces clashing with a protoempathic identification expressed as the communal solidarity of the people of New Orleans. The concentrated presence of many African-Americans first provoked racialized rumors and then, in response, a militarized response on the part of the government, reflecting a neoliberal and neoconservative assumption of an atomized population in need of top-down control (Wendy Brown 2006). Perversely enough, the militarized response first had to stop the community response that led the people of New Orleans to rescue themselves and their neighbors; Katrina in New Orleans thus shows that a neoliberal and neoconservative government has to create the very atomized and passive citizenry that supposedly legitimates its top-down control.

As we conclude our study of cases of political physiology, we should recall that our study is naturalistic. This means not only that we are anti-humanist, in that we do not accept special nonbiological categories for discussing political affective cognition, but also that we need to take seriously the ecological and not just social embeddedness of bodies politic. Our study of Hurricane Katrina illustrates this ecosocial embeddedness, for it was both an elemental and a social event. To understand its many aspects, you have to understand the land, the river, the sun, the wind (air), and the sea; you have to understand earth, wind, fire, and water; you have to understand geomorphology, meteorology, biology, economics, politics, and history. You have to understand how they have come together to form, with the peoples of America, Europe, and Africa, the historical patterns of life in Louisiana and New Orleans, the bodies politic of the region. You have to understand what those bodies could do, what they could withstand, and how they intersected the event of the storm. In this chapter, simply for the sake of time and space constraints, I will concentrate on New Orleans; the stories of the Mississippi Gulf Coast or of the Saint Bernard, Saint Tammany, and Plaquemines parishes in Louisiana are complex and dramatic as well. I mean "dramatic" in the Deleuzian sense, indicating the intensive morphogenetic processes or spatiotemporal dynamisms that actualize virtual Ideas or multiplicities, as well as in its normal sense of fascinating narrative (Deleuze 2004).

The Elements

The Land and the River

We could start by talking about plate tectonics or, for that matter, stellar nucleogenesis, for at the limit, everything is connected, and to tell the story of Katrina would be to tell the story of all of the earth, all of the cosmos (Wood 2004). So let us begin, as always, in medias res, and talk about the land of Louisiana. To do that, we have to talk about the river. The Mississippi drains a vast swath of the North American land mass. Almost all of the water that falls between the Appalachians and the Rockies, from the Allegheny River in upstate New York to the Missouri River in Montana (that which does not evaporate or stay in the soil or in a lake) drains down the Mississippi, the "father of waters."[1]

Like all rivers that flow into the sea, the Mississippi snakes about at its head, creating a delta as it floods its banks and lays down sediment picked up upstream. How much sediment depends on how fast the water flows, and how fast the water flows depends on how much is behind it, pushing it, and on how big a channel it flows through. The bigger the mass of water and the narrower the channel, the faster the flow and the more earth it carries, and the greater the chance the river will overflow the banks and drop that sediment as it slows down and trickles over the face of the earth. As the water flows, it eddies and swirls, depending on the configuration of the banks and bed, and sometimes a singular configuration triggers a different pattern of flow. The relation of turbulence and smooth flow varies, not by calculable laws, as would velocity in a perfectly smooth channel, but according to singular points in the configuration of bank and bed. This process has gone on for some time, as these singularities of the configuration determined which actual pattern of the river's flow would emerge from the differential relations (velocity and turbulence) of the elements (water and earth). At another level, they also determined the historical pattern of that emergence of actual flow, the rhythm of the river's flow and flood.

After European settlements progressed, flood control via levee construction began. The Europeans built military outposts and then cities on the edge of the river, to the north on the bluffs above the river (Baton Rouge, Natchez, Memphis), and to the south in the swamps along the edge of the river, between the river and the inland sea they called Lake Ponchartrain (New Orleans). When the river floods repeatedly, as it does as part of its natural cycle, it leaves a ridge of sediment, highest on the banks and sloping gently away down toward the swamps, the heaviest sediments dropping out first, building up the natural levee, which tends to subside as it dries out. It is on that natural levee that Bienville founded New Orleans in 1718. The floods still came, of course, since the ridge was a *natural* levee. On top of that levee the Europeans used their slaves to build more levees, all up and down the river.[2] What happens when you build levees upstream? You change the actualization structure of the water flow, the values that incarnate the multiplicity, the set of linked rates of change and its singular points. There are many ways a flow can occur, given its differentials and singularities, the way its elements intersect the configurations of its channel. In this case, you squeeze the same amount of water into a narrower channel (for now you contain the same relation of mass and velocity that would have flooded the previously lower banks), so the water downstream rises still higher. And so you build higher levees. As this positive feedback loop continues, you break the river's old rhythms, you change its relation to the earth around it, you deterritorialize it, to use Deleuze and Guattari's terminology.

But you cannot stay ahead of the river all the time. Researchers have found that river systems tend toward a state of self-organized criticality, producing a power-law distribution regarding riverbank failures and flooding. In other words, one of the guiding principles of human ecology (analogous to treating forest fires) should be that with levee construction you can stop many little floods, but when the river finally does flood, that flood will be a big one (Fonstad and Marcus 2003). The most famous and destructive of those big floods happened in 1927, and to save New Orleans, the powers that be, out of panic, dynamited the levee southeast of the city, flooding Saint Bernard Parish and destroying the livelihoods of many poor people.

(In fact, levee failures upstream the very next day meant that the city was never really in danger. We will discuss failures of judgment in panic situations later.) In response to 1927, the relation of the federal government to the states changed, for another factor was then in place: the mass media. Radio, newspapers, telegraph, photos transmitted the verbal and visual images of the flood's effects—which were even more severe in Mississippi's Delta region than in Louisiana—to the rest of the nation. Among the most striking images were those of thousands of African-Americans stranded on levees for days with no food or water and later herded into relief camps. The consequent distress of the viewers and listeners in other parts of the country created a demand to control the river even more. So the U.S. Army Corps of Engineers, along with state and local boards, built more and better and bigger levees, enough, they said, in the case of New Orleans, to withstand a Category 3 hurricane, determining that level of protection to be adequate after conducting a cost-benefit analysis (USACE 2005).[3]

The effects of the Corps' projects on the river and the land were profound. First, there is the problem of subsidence as the sediment that would ordinarily build up the land is stopped by upstream dams that trap it and by levees all along the river that prevent flooding. Exacerbated by New Orleans's canal and pump system, untreated subsidence means the city is sinking ever faster, as pumping the city dry means drier, more-compacted soil, which creates a positive feedback loop that makes the city even more vulnerable. Furthermore, many ship channels and canals were cut into the wetlands. In particular, a deep channel (the notorious Mississippi River Gulf Outlet) was created close to New Orleans so that oceangoing ships would have a short, direct path from the Gulf of Mexico to New Orleans, where they could intersect another flow carried by the river's water flow: the flow of goods from the middle of the country (Fischetti 2001; Bourne 2000; Tidwell 2004). Coupled with the denial of flooding, this shipping channel (plus hundreds of smaller canals and channels created by the oil industry) changed the ratio of salt water to freshwater in the bayous, killing many species of plants and animals. The cypress trees were logged, another insult to the wetlands, for sediment had previously collected around the roots. Another positive feedback loop was set up as coastal erosion accelerated and another coastline was actualized, one much closer to New Orleans (Penland et al. 2005). The other famous positive feedback loop with the river, the dead zone in the Gulf of Mexico from fertilizer runoff, did not play a role in Katrina's impact, at least to my knowledge, but we can fit it into our story after we discuss another element, the sun (Ferber 2004).

The Sun

The sun figures in our story in many ways, in evaporation, wind production, and bioenergy. All energy available to organisms is solar energy mediated by carbon. Photosynthesis forms carbohydrates out of water and carbon dioxide, releasing oxygen and trapping solar energy in the chemical bonds of the complex molecules. Animal metabolism burns this fuel, combining oxygen with the carbohydrates and releasing the energy plus water and carbon dioxide. It is a little more complicated than that, as nitrogen mediated by microbes in and around plant roots plays a role (and producing concentrated nitrogen fertilizers takes a lot of petroleum or carbon-stored solar energy, and they run off down the Mississippi, producing algae explosions that suck the oxygen out of the Gulf and kill the local sea fauna, creating the dead zone), but it is basically pretty simple: solar energy becomes organically accessible energy through the mediation of carbon.

The most efficient form of organically accessible carbon-mediated solar energy is sugar cane. Cane production under European supervision was shifted from the Atlantic islands to the Caribbean throughout the sixteenth to the eighteenth centuries using slave labor: at first the native Caribs, then the Irish (Cromwell, in the midst of the Wars of the Three Kingdoms, intensified the shipping of thousands of enslaved Irish to Barbados), and then the Africans. Sugar consumption in Europe worked its way down the class stratifications, displacing other forms of bioenergy, some of which came mixed with protein and vitamins (Mintz 1985). In so doing, it played a key role in a positive feedback loop described by Marx in the primitive accumulation chapter of *Capital*, for a good percentage of modern state revenue came from consumption taxes that, together with national debt, funded the military branches of the colonial enterprise. The fact that increased sugar consumption played a role in the decreasing height of British Army recruits from 1780 to 1850 (Blackburn 1997, 561) was offset by various differentials: increased mechanization and internal complexity of the armed forces for one thing (they call the Queen's Guards the Beefeaters for a reason). Here we see another multiplicity: the differential elements are carbon-mediated solar energy and human muscle power, the relations are muscular hypertrophy/atrophy/dystrophy, and the singularities are turning points intersecting genetic potentials scattered in the population.

So the sun helps explain how Africans came to the Caribbean and to Louisiana. To see the ecosocial context of this forced migration, we need to talk about yet another multiplicity in which solar energy is the key, the heat-exchange system of the planet. The elements here are sun and water and air, the relations are heating and cooling, and the singularities are the thresholds for ice ages, grand and small, as well as smaller but meteorologically interesting events, such as the Atlantic Multidecadal Oscillation, or AMO (Goldberg et al. 2001), which competes with global warming as an account for the increased frequency of high-intensity Atlantic hurricanes in the post-1990 era (Webster et al. 2005; Knutson et al. 1998). In this exchange system, we find ocean currents, including the Gulf Stream (whose heat-carrying capacity and climatological effects help explain how Northern Europe can carry the density of population it has had over the past few millennia by affecting the types of carbon-mediated solar energy it can cultivate in producing bioenergy via agriculture) and the North Equatorial Current, which along with the trade winds helped Europeans travel from the coast of Africa to the Americas. (A shorter ocean and wind-current loop system just off the coast of Africa might explain why it seems African sailors rarely went too far offshore, for it was enough for their navigational purposes up and down the western coast of Africa. It should be admitted that historical research into the exploits of early African sailors has not been pursued with nearly the same enthusiasm as with early European sailors, the Vikings in particular.)

The Wind and the Sea

Now that we have talked about the global heat-exchange system, we are in a position to address the meteorological part of our analysis. The trade winds that blow northeast to southwest off the coast of Africa tend to converge at certain points, triggering singularities and forming turbulences associated with the instability and displacement of these winds in the movement north and south of the Intertropical Convergence Zone, or ITCZ. With the proper ocean temperatures (above 80 degrees) and wind speeds, we can get tropical waves, groups of thunderstorms. At other singular points of wind speed and water temperatures, a cyclonic heat engine will be actualized forming a hurricane. Ocean water evaporates and rises, releasing energy as it condenses aloft, powering winds and forming bands of thunderstorms. In effect, part of the ocean rises into the air and falls back as rain, while part of the ocean is pushed along by the storm's winds, the "storm surge."[4]

While most hurricanes form off the West African coast, Katrina formed to the east of the Bahamas. Crossing Florida, it hit upon the Gulf loop current, a deep warm-water current that flows to the west through the Yucatáan channel, then north through the Gulf until it exits to the east through the Florida channel to join the Gulf Stream. In its current configuration, the loop current brought Katrina not only a vector, aiming it at New Orleans, but also huge amounts of energy, for it conserved the energy contribution of the evaporation rate of the 90-degree surface water, as the deep water churned to the surface by the passage of the hurricane was not as cold as it would have been for a hurricane not following the vector of the loop current.[5] As it happens, a late singularity in metrological conditions caused Katrina to swerve a bit and pass to the east of New Orleans, thus sparing the city the worst winds, but devastating Slidell and the Mississippi coast (Travis 2005; van Heerden 2007).

Katrina hit the eroded Louisiana coast, the hurricane's still-strong winds pushing its storm surge into Lake Ponchatrain and destroying some of the flood walls and levees along New Orleans's canals. Since a hurricane loses three to eight inches of storm surge for every mile of barrier islands and coastal wetlands it crosses, the Louisiana coastline of one hundred years ago would have weakened Katrina enough that the current lake and canal levees of New Orleans would have held.[6] The eroded coastline let the storm surge through, and the faulty levees collapsed rather than being over-topped. The city was flooded, as predicted (Bourne 2004; Fischetti 2001; LSU Hurricane Center 2004).

The People of New Orleans

At this point, we have to discuss the man-made disaster. We begin by moving back in time to discuss the history of Africans in colonial Louisiana.

Africans in Colonial Louisiana

By meshing the multiplicities of the global heat-exchange system and the organically accessible solar energy system, we see the actualization we call the Atlantic slave trade. The differential elements here are human muscle power and production processes, or more precisely, the amount of force against the precision of direction of that force (skill).

The Atlantic slave trade was internally complex. The eighteenth-century trade to French Louisiana, which was virtually complete by 1731, actualized the multiplicity that linked the European appreciation of real and imagined differences between Wolof and Bambara slaves, as well as Portuguese competition for slaves in Africa and competition from buyers in the French West Indies. The resumption of slave trade to Louisiana under Spanish rule, which began in 1766, is even more complex, as the trade was no longer almost exclusively from Senegal, but included slaves from central

Africa (Hall 1992). In some cases, the Atlantic slave trade tapped into the well-established trans-Saharan slave trade and took the skilled bodies of captive African peasants;[7] after transporting them across the ocean, they were deskilled or proletarianized and set to work in industrial agricultural practice on Caribbean plantations (industry can occur in plantations as well as factories) (Mintz 1985, 51–57).

I say "in some cases" because not all Africans were subjected to deskilling: the vernacular Creole architecture of Louisiana, for instance, is directly traceable to the work of skilled African slave architects who used Senegambian practices to build homes from native cypress—beginning the deforestation whose effects on coastal erosion we noted in the section titled "The Land and the River." Among other transplanted economic skills, the origins of rice cultivation in the Americas should be noted as being the result of skilled African agriculturalists (Carney 2002). In fact, proletarianization as part of industrial production on large plantations was the (highly profitable) exception to the rule, as many Africans worked at a wide range of skilled tasks.[8] (All this talk of skills and deskilling refers to the strictly political-economic concept of proletarianization, and thus it has no bearing on the creativity, resistance, and resilience of African-American culture both during and after the period of slavery. This resistance, often armed and violent, began, of course, with revolts in the slave depots of Africa, continued on the ships of the slave trade, and persisted on the American mainland [Hall 1992; Berlin 2004].)

As this system developed, the French colony of Saint Domingue became one of the most profitable—if not the single most profitable—agricultural complexes in the world, growing sugar and coffee (James 1989; Blackburn 1997). (It will not be our focus, but we could tell another story about how coffee and sugar go together, as well as how tea and sugar go together, and how that difference between French and English tastes ties into the fact that the English beat the French out of India. We could then note how the importance of India allowed the English to get out of the slave business in the nineteenth century. Why bother with slaves in the Atlantic when the future of the Empire lies in Asia? Before we even mention the Opium Wars, we can see a complex system of long-distance trade in stimulants that is quite literally political physiology.)[9]

To return to our focus, at some point in the late eighteenth century the Saint Domingue system passed a threshold: too fast a rise in the importation rate of "fresh" or "unseasoned" Africans, plus a feverish step-up in production, plus the singularities called Boukman and Toussaint led to a revolt in 1791. As the years of revolutionary war went on, quite of a few of the *gens libres de couleur* fled Saint Domingue for Louisiana, a Spanish colony, with a heavy French heritage, and they brought with them their African slaves.

This immigration accounts for the great social difference between light-skinned and dark-skinned African-Americans in New Orleans and Louisiana. Ignorance of this difference contributes to the mistake of calling the light-skinned Ray Nagin "a black mayor," a term that belongs to the binary racial classification of most of the United States but which has no traction in the trinary system of New Orleans, which includes a Creole, or mulatto, term. I'm not saying Nagin belongs to traditional high Creole society, just that his light skin allows him to play the traditional Creole role of mediation between the "blacks," or dark "Africans," and the whites. "Mediation" is a polite word: the free people of color of New Orleans reprised their role in Saint Domingue and became the hunters of escaped African slaves. The way the New Orleans Police Department took up that disciplinary function is another story that needs to be told.

Commercialized sugar production in Louisiana did not begin until 1795, as under French rule it was suppressed by the French metropolitan government to avoid competition with Saint Domingue, and under Spanish rule the cultivation was never very extensive (Rodrigue 2001, 11; Berlin 2004, 146). Louisiana was never a very prosperous or well-managed colony under French rule. Shaken to its roots by the Natchez Rebellion of 1729, Louisiana languished in the middle of the eighteenth century, only beginning to revive in the 1770s under Spanish rule (Hall 1992, chapter 4; Berlin 2004, 42–43, 88). It is only after the Haitian revolution had begun that sugar production began in earnest in Louisiana, sparked by an influx of refugee planters and using the skills and labor power of "seasoned" or "creolized" slaves from Saint Domingue. After the transfer of the vast Louisiana Territory to the United States in 1803, sugar production boomed (Rodrigue 2001, 11; Berlin 2004, 148).

The motivation for Napoleon's sale of Louisiana is generally attributed to his realization that Saint Domingue was lost to him, despite Jefferson's offer to help supply Leclerc's expeditionary force in its attempt to reinstall slavery there (Wills 2003, 42–43; and Blackburn 1988, 283), and thus that Louisiana's putative role as food supply for the much more profitable Caribbean island was mooted. The question of Napoleon's designs for a North American extension of his empire, with Louisiana as its base, is much more difficult to answer. At the same time that Jefferson bought Louisiana, he signed on with the British in attempting to suppress the Atlantic slave trade. Where would the slaves for Louisiana's sugar plantations—and the slaves for the cotton plantations of the Deep South, now made possible by the cotton gin—come from? Why, from Jefferson's home state of Virginia, among other sources for the internal slave trade.[10]

Here we find yet another multiplicity, in which physiology and psychology intersect work and climate, thus determining the reproduction rates for African slaves: negative in most parts of the Americas, but positive in the Chesapeake region. Sugar production in the Caribbean meant overwork: dawn to dusk during planting, around-the-clock during harvest and processing of the cane, and yearlong because the tropical climate allowed multiple growing seasons per year. Such overwork, along with the additional factors of bad nutrition, heat, disease, and torture, explains the life expectancy of merely seven years after arrival in the Caribbean; this means a slave owner's punitive sale of slaves to the Caribbean had a clear punitive intent, as clear as if he had killed the slave outright (Mintz 1985, 49–51; for mortality rates, see Blackburn 1997, 339). This short life expectancy necessitated a constant importation of fresh slaves to make up for the low birthrates and high infant mortality rates—children died from disease and from the infanticide slaves practiced sometimes to spare their children (James 1989, 16). The reproduction rate of the slave population was positive in the Chesapeake region because of the multiplicity governing tobacco production, linking the energy expenditure of the workers (linked to the singularities of the tobacco plant: its size, the angles of its stems and leaves, and so on) and the relatively moderate climate, which allowed the winter as a period of recuperation and eliminated the threat of tropical disease (Blackburn 1997, 459, 465–67).

So, the ancestors of the current African-American population of Louisiana came from the Caribbean, directly from Africa (mostly from Senegal), and from the northern states. One of the things the Caribbean arrivals brought with them was revolution—the hope of it among the slaves and the fear of it among the whites. After the 1729 Natchez Rebellion, the most famous episode in Louisiana colonial history is the 1795 Pointe Coupee slave revolt. Hall tells the fascinating story of how this Jacobin-inspired multiracial class revolt happened at the most radical point of the French Revolution, when the National Assembly had recognized the fait accompli of the Saint Domingue revolt by abolishing colonial slavery, and when Republican troops fought all the royal powers of Europe, including the Spanish, who ruled Louisiana at the time. A conspiracy that included

many revolutionary poor whites, the revolt was to be aimed at the proper-
tied interests rather than at "whites," but it subsequently became mytholo-
gized as a race war of black against white. Unleashing a wave of racialized
oppression of blacks, the Pointe Coupee conspiracy became the bogey that
put the fear of a racially motivated slave revolt directly into the culture and
thus into the bodies politic of white Louisianans (Hall 1992, chapter 11).
As children, scared and titillated with tales of the savage reprisals for slavery that were supposedly ready to be exacted by rebellious black savages,
with murder, looting, and rape prominent among them, whites have a fear
or even panic threshold established for them, triggered at the thought or
sight of crowds of blacks without sufficient armed guards around them.
This bit of political physiology will play a role in the Katrina aftermath as
well, exacerbated no doubt by the securitarian phobias of post-9/11 America (Fine and Turner 2001).

Political Affective Cognition: Race Perception and Fear

Race is immediately perceived, an example of what I call political cognition.
The famous self-other contact of some phenomenological description is abstract. No one has ever immediately seen an "other." To see how the problematic of the other is an abstract philosopher's problem, let us consider Eleanor Rosch's research into categorization, which forms an important part
of one of the founding texts of the embodied-embedded mind or situated
cognition school. Rosch proposes a basic level of perception/action/lin-
guistic naming in a hierarchy of abstraction (Rosch 1978). This basic level
is, in her example, "chair" rather than "furniture" or "Queen Anne." In the
same article Rosch proposes a prototype theory for internal category structure: rather than an ideal exemplar, we have concrete prototypes by which
we judge whether objects belong to a category by seeing how close or how
far an object is to our prototype, not whether or not it satisfies a list of necessary and sufficient conditions that we carry around with us.

If we adopt Rosch's model, in concrete social perception we are never
faced with the Husserlian problem "is this just a thing or is it an alter ego?"
that we resolve by distinguishing between things and subjects. Rather, we
are always confronted with other people at basic-level social categories
appropriate to our culture: for us today, the famous age, size, gender, race,
and class system. (Here it is important to say that racialized perception need
not entail racism, nor should gendered perception entail sexism, and so on.
Nor need it entail a belief in race as a natural kind. Nor need we deny that
people often make mistaken racial attributions.) So, we never see another

subject; instead, we see, for example, a middle-aged, small, neat, fit, professional black woman (Condoleeza Rice, let us say), or an elderly, patrician, tall white man (George H. W. Bush, let us say). I maintain that our political cognition habits in our bodies politic is such that no one has ever *perceived* a "subject" or an "other": we can posit such a creature, but that's a refined political act of overcoming our immediate categorization process, by which we perceive racialized and gendered persons to construct an abstraction we can call a nongendered and nonracialized member of an intersubjective community or humanity or some such. While this might be a worthy ethical ideal for which we can strive, it is not what we perceive at first glance.

But we do not just engage in political cognition, so we must also think political affect: in particular, the racialized fear that the perception of blacks, especially many blacks together, evokes in many American whites. To understand my speculation here, we first need to examine the current neuroscience on the distinction between anxiety and fear, a distinction well-known to philosophers familiar with the existential and phenomenological treatments by Kierkegaard and Heidegger.

Joseph LeDoux (1996) is the leading researcher on fear; in his work he cites Arne Öhman (1992) as one of the leading researchers looking at anxiety; he highlights the close connection of anxiety and fear. For Öhman, anxiety is "unresolved fear," a state provoked by frustration of avoidance behaviors evoked by fear. "Anxiety" is, of course, a generic term that can manifest itself in a variety of ways. The *Diagnostic and Statistical Manual of Mental Disorders* lists a full range of anxiety disorders: panic, phobias, post-traumatic stress disorder (PTSD), obsessive-compulsive disorder (OCD), and generalized anxiety (cited at LeDoux 1996, 229). LeDoux cites Öhman 1992 to the effect that panic, phobic fear, and PTSD reflect "activation of one and the same underlying anxiety response," and he goes on to claim in his own voice that "generalized anxiety most likely involves the same underlying brain system (at least partly) as the other anxiety disorders" (1996, 230). Generalized anxiety is such that it appears even when the fear trigger is not present. In psychophysiological terms, anxiety is heightened readiness for emergency action; in anxiety, chemical releases result in lower thresholds for action, or what is technically known as reflex potentiation (LeDoux 1996, 149). In anxiety, you are so jumpy that any little thing sets you off (LeDoux 1996 cites Davis 1992, 289, for anxiety as hyperarousal). In complexity theory terms, you are in a sensitive zone in which small, internal fluctuations or external events—which normally would be accounted for by homeostatic mechanisms keeping the organism in its everyday state—will instead trigger activation of an emergency reaction pattern.

On the other hand, with fear, a particular object has already triggered such a pattern, and you are then focused on dealing with that particular object or situation. Fear is affective cognition par excellence. Quick reading by the amygdala of sensory inputs primes the system and directs attention even before cognitive appraisals can begin. But once the appraisal kicks in, the cortical pathways can heighten or dampen the initial response. The triggering of an emergency pattern by the recognition of a fearful object will release endorphins, as you might need the analgesic effect to act in the emergency. Thus, as horror movie directors, Homeland Security officials, and political leaders know full well, fear is a relief compared to anxiety: "Better the devil you know than the devil you don't." The physiological basis of fear relief is that in stressful situations, endorphins are released to provide pain relief, a phenomenon called stress-related analgesia.[11] There is a threshold effect here. Repeated exposure to stress, or a single stressful event of sufficient magnitude, can set endorphin release thresholds very high. This is presumably one of the bases for thrill-seeking behavior. Traumatized people can have their endorphin release thresholds set so high by previous events that it is only in situations that evoke high-intensity reactions that endorphins are released to serve as pain relief: this is known as trauma addiction (Bloom 1999; Van der Kolk and Greenberg 1987).

I am going to speculate here, but I think it is grounded speculation. I propose that many people in Louisiana—after years of neoliberal economics that produced insecurity about employment and health care, added to relentless neoconservative anxiety production with terror alert levels and so on—were traumatized to a small degree by everyday life. Adding the natural destruction of Katrina to the mix stretched them to the limit. One could then say it is even more astonishing that the immediate response to Katrina of the vast majority of Louisianans was not racial fear, but solidarity. It was left to the government to engage in that fear. To see how this most shameful episode unfolded is the last part of our dramatization.

Hobbes and the People of New Orleans

The government reaction, at local, state, and national levels, needs to be seen in historical context. Louisiana was a slave state, and it is now ranked the forty-ninth poorest state in the nation on many measures. This is not to imply that slavery's economic and political impact was limited to the South. For just a sample of the political importance, beyond the infamous "three-fifths clause" of the U.S. Constitution, consider that ten of the pre–Civil War presidents of the United States were slaveholders and two postwar presidents had been slaveholders—a ratio that means that to date, one-quarter of the presidents in U.S. history were slaveholders (Wills 2003, 7). The role of slavery in the global and national economies outside the slave zones, especially as it impacted the capital formation of the Industrial Revolution, was also profound (Blackburn 1997; Bailey 1998).

Thirty-five percent of Louisiana's population is African-American, as opposed to 13 percent nationwide. This figure is higher in cities: the American pattern is of mostly black cities surrounded by mostly white suburbs.[12] The pattern of white flight, sparked by post–World War II suburbanization, is another multiplicity, as racial, income, and wealth population differentials cross automobile ownership rates. This was demonstrated in New Orleans, a city with a 67 percent African-American population and a 28 percent poverty rate (the national average is 12.7 percent); a large percentage of that population did not have cars, and they tended to reside in the lowest-lying areas (Hartman and Squires 2006, 3; Colten 2004). While 80 percent of the city evacuated, those who stayed behind—or were left behind—tended to be black.[13] But not all: the French Quarter, 95 percent white and located on the natural levee where Bienville started the city, and Uptown, along the same levee westward along the river, both had many whites who stayed behind.

While the startling images of the Superdome and the Convention Center dominated media coverage, one of the most important untold stories unfolded along the geographical and social differential in which money stays on high ground in New Orleans. In Uptown, the private security companies (Blackwater USA), with their M-16s and their retired Special Ops forces, their helicopters and their guard dogs, created an enclave of the protected who avoided media attention, except for the ever-vigilant *Wall Street Journal*, which reported the plans of those civic leaders to effect "demographic" changes in the city to be rebuilt (Scahill 2005, 2007; Cooper 2005). It was hoped that these plans would have been made easier by the neoliberal principles that were to have guided the federal reconstruction effort.[14]

But let us talk now about the famous sites, the Superdome and the Convention Center. The name of Hobbes sprang from the keyboards of the commentators as they heard the breathlessly reported rumors of murder, looting, and rapes and the repeated twenty-second loops of "looters" (you must recognize them by now: the woman holding up the Pampers to shield her face from the cameras, the teenage boy skipping through the puddles with his shopping cart). A state of nature, they wrote, a war of all against all, they assured us (Lowry 2005; Ash 2005; Will 2005). But what were the contents of those rumors? A "revolt" at the Orleans Parish Prison.[15] Children gang-raped and thrown, throats slit, into the freezer at the Convention Center. Snipers shooting at rescue helicopters. A lockdown of downtown after a riot in Baton Rouge following the arrival of refugees.

All these rumors were unfounded, and their similarity to rumors in panics about slave revolt cannot be ignored.[16] The production of exaggerated rumors in crisis situations is well documented; the classic in the field, *The Psychology of Rumor*, was produced in response to rumor production in America during World War II (Allport and Postman 1947). We also know of the role of rumor and wild exaggeration in triggering and intensifying race riots in twentieth-century America (Fine and Turner 2001, 42–51). While rumor production with racial ramifications was inevitable in a flooded New Orleans, what is notable is the lack of skepticism exhibited by media personnel and government officials. The complex feedback loops should be noted here, for much of the media hype came *after* Mayor Nagin and his police chief, Eddie Compass, relayed some of the most virulent of the rumors. It might be that Nagin and Compass felt that reports of mass mayhem would speed state and federal response.[17] If this was their intention, they badly miscalculated, for instead of speeding response, their reports of "tourists" being "preyed upon" ("tourist" is of course New Orleans code for "white") exceeded the fear thresholds instilled by, among other historical factors, the imagined horrors of slave revolt, with its racial revenge to be visited on whites by blacks.

Racialized fears thus have to be counted among the factors that delayed the response until Friday of hurricane week, when there was sufficient militarization of the response effort to begin "combat operations," to take back the "Little Somalia" New Orleans was fearfully imagined to have become, and even to put down an "insurgency," that most loaded of Iraq-era terms! (Chenelly 2005; see also Tierney and Bevc 2007). The militarization of the relief effort was applauded by George W. Bush in his address to the nation from New Orleans: "It is now clear that a challenge on this scale requires greater federal authority and a broader role for the armed forces—the institution of our government most capable of massive logistical operations on a moment's notice."[18] He was able to recommend the use of the army for domestic law enforcement, something the classical liberal tradition (now represented by the "paleoconservatives" in the United States) has always abhorred because of its worrying totalitarian/fascist resonances, because of the erosion of the difference between the National Guard, supposedly mostly for domestic use but now heavily deployed in Iraq, and the regular army.

We will have to await the results of patient historical work to know what "really happened" in New Orleans, though we can say that some works already provide a good start (Brinkley 2007; van Heerden 2007). We can say now with confidence, by comparing eyewitness testimony and taking into account the widely documented production of rumor and exaggeration in crisis situations, is that at most, a few score gang members were at the two sites engaging in predatory behavior. But we have to balance these stories against the small number of bodies found at the two sites. According to the *New York Times* report cited previously, "State officials have said that 10 people died at the Superdome and 24 died around the convention center—4 inside and 20 nearby. While autopsies have not been completed, so far only one person appears to have died from gunshot wounds at each facility." While rumors of rapes abounded, police active in the Superdome found little to back them up. Again according to the *New York Times:* "During six days when the Superdome was used as a shelter, the head of the New Orleans Police Department's sex crimes unit, Lieutenant David Benelli, said he and his officers lived inside the dome and ran down every rumor of rape or atrocity. In the end, they made two arrests for attempted sexual assault, and concluded that the other attacks had not happened."

It is true that the NOPD is, by general acclaim, among the worst police department in the country, including many within its ranks who are underpaid, undertrained, overly corrupt, homicidal, and fratricidal. And the Nagin–Compass team would have been motivated to cover up violence at the Convention Center and Superdome so they could claim that guarding the French Quarter antique shops instead of the people in the shelters did not really hurt anyone. Still, to propose a conspiratorial cover-up here is more than far-fetched, since many government agencies, not just the NOPD, would have to have been involved. What were far-fetched in the first place were the rumors of mass rape and carnage.

At the most, we should have had stories of a few groups of ten to fifteen young men who hunted other gang members, robbed people, perhaps raped people. What can we say about this predation? The first thing is that it does not indicate a "reversion" to a "state of nature"; gang members prey on people in these ways in every city of the country and most cities of human history. Gang predation is not some "natural" state into which societies "fall" but a social process that is part and parcel of civilization as we have known it. All the way back to Achilles and the Myrmidons, and well before that, young men have formed roving predatory gangs that prey on urban populations. The relation of such gang-formation processes to urban population density forms another multiplicity to be explored; in New Orleans, gang formation tends to follow the pattern of housing projects. The few reported murders during the Katrina aftermath can be related most plausibly either to spontaneous fights or to gang members running into each other off their favored territories. Encounters during such episodes of deterritorialization would presumably carry with them high probabilities of violence.

The following eyewitness testimony shows that not all gangs were predatory. Denise Moore related the following on the *This American Life* radio program (Moore 2005):

[Interviewer: Tell me about the men roaming with guns.] They were securing the area. Criminals, these guys were criminals. They were. Y'know? But somehow these guys got together and figured out who had guns and decided they were going to make sure that no women were getting raped. Because we did hear about the women getting raped in the Superdome. That nobody was hurting babies. They were the ones getting juice for the babies. . . . They were the ones fanning the old people. Because that's what moved the guys, the gangster guys, the most, the plight of the old people. . . ."
[Concerning the looting of the Rite-Aid at St. Charles and Napoleon.] They were taking juice for the babies, water, beer for the older people [chuckles], food. Raincoats so they could all be seen by each other and stuff. . . . I thought it was pretty cool and very well organized. [Interviewer: Like Robin Hood?] Exactly like Robin Hood. And that's why I got so mad, because they're calling *these* guys animals? *These* guys? That's what got me mad. Because I know what they did. You're calling *these* people animals? Y'know? C'mon. I saw what they did, and I was really touched by it and I liked the way they were organized about it, and that they were thoughtful about it. Because they had family they couldn't find too. Y'know? And that they would put themselves out like that on other people's behalf. I never had a high opinion of thugs myself, but I tell you one thing, I'll never look at them the same way again.

But while the predatory gangs, as opposed to the protective gangs, had an especially concentrated population on which to prey, and a police force weakened by desertion and dispersed by the mayor to restore "law and order" (guard the antique shops and restaurants of the French Quarter, the big hotels and Uptown residences being sufficiently guarded by their private security forces), we cannot forget the massive solidarity shown by the people of New Orleans. Why was it that the name of Hobbes came flying off the keyboards of our pundits, and not Rousseau or even Locke? Why the focus on the predation, which occurs everywhere, though admittedly with less intensity because of lower prey population density? What about the solidarity on display?

Do not get me wrong here. Hobbes is a brilliant philosopher, a great philosopher. His ruthless materialism far outstrips the limited minds of the current crop of Hobbes-mongers, with their credulity for outrageous rumor and their clutched pearls over the lapse in civil authority. Hobbes is crystal clear that while the sovereign has no obligation to the people, the people in turn have no obligation to a failed sovereign. The people constantly judge their sovereign's actions, and when the sovereign's power fails, then civil law lapses and the laws of nature are the only ones in operation. We can read this in several of the most prominent and important parts of *Leviathan* (Hobbes 2004). For instance, in chapter 17, "Of the Causes, Generation, and Definition of a Common-Wealth," we find the following: "If there be no Power erected, or not great enough for our security; every man will, and may lawfully [by the "laws of nature" of course] rely on his own strength and art, for caution against all other men." In chapter 21, "Of the Liberty of Subjects," we read: "The Obligation of Subjects to the Sovereign, is understood to last as long, and no longer, than the power lasteth, by which he is able to protect them. For the right men have by Nature to protect themselves, when no one else can protect them, can by no Covenant be relinquished." Finally, in chapter 27, "Of Crimes, Excuses, and Extenuations," the following rings out as clear as a bell: "That when the Sovereign Power ceaseth, Crime also ceaseth; for where there is no such Power, there is no protection to be had from the Law; and therefore every one may protect himself by his own power." Thus Lowry is so far from understanding Hobbes that what he will see as the "massive lawlessness" of New Orleans, the taking of goods when sovereign power has failed, is completely and utterly obedient to the law of nature.

Despite Hobbes's brilliance, the anthropological worth of his state of nature thought experiment is next to nothing, for the atomization he predicts in a crisis situation[19] is belied by the massive evidence of spontaneous group formation: with family kernels, of course, but also by neighborhood and also, notably, simply by civic and human affiliation. ("My people" is how the heroic teenager Jabbar Gibson described the group of neighbors and strangers he gathered on his commandeered bus [Bryant and Garza

2005].) The stories of New Orleans we tell do not always have to focus on the every man for himself fantasy of the Hobbes-mongers, or on the panicky rumors with their echoes of the fear of slave revolt, but they should also be the stories of the thousands and thousands and thousands of brave and loving people of New Orleans who refused to leave their old, their sick, their young, their helpless, and who walked miles through the floods to safety, pushing wheelchairs and floating the sick on "looted" air mattresses.[20] Yes, we saw images of helpless poor people waiting to be rescued at the Superdome and the Convention Center, but we should never forget that they rescued themselves prior to that, through heroic solidarity, through what we cannot be afraid to call "love" in the sense of *philia*, which was for Aristotle the emotional bond revealing the political nature of humanity.

How can we give a rigorous differential materialist reading of this *philia*, this solidarity, a reading in accord with the study of bodies politic? After all, we should not want to be mere Rousseau-mongers in response to the Hobbes-mongers. The question is that of the emergence of human groups. Emergence is the (diachronic) construction of functional structures in complex systems that achieve a (synchronic) focus of systematic behavior as they constrain the behavior of individual components. Theories of social emergence compete with methodological individualism, which denies that social phenomena are anything but the aggregation of individual behaviors. It is important to note that methodological individualism is far more than a theory: it is the guiding principle behind the active construction of the atomizing practices whose results are described as natural by Hobbes and his followers (Schwartz, Schuldenfrei, and Lacey 1979).

To piece together the multiplicity behind social group emergence we could begin by tracking the development of infantile face-recognition and emotional sensitivity, which inscribe brain patterns as they develop in feedback loops with caregivers.[21] Here we see that sociality is inscribed in our very bodies as the actualization of the set of linked rates of change and their singularities lying between the reciprocally determined ideal elements of infant and caregiver. (Since such caregivers are enmeshed in a historically mediated web of social relations, we should not fall for any sort of familialism in thinking these terms.) Such early bonding is a repetition of bondings that stretch back throughout human and primate history (de Waal 1996; Joyce 2007). As would be expected with complex systems in populations, not all bondings "take," of course, either from caregiver absence or neglect or from difficulties on the side of the infant. Later appearing trauma can also interrupt or destroy previously established bondings. Nonetheless, many bondings do take, and the neurological basis of these bondings, as with all brain activity, is found first in resonant cell assemblies, which form out of a chaotic firing background in a modular but decentralized network, as we argue in chapters 1 and 2. On the scale of the civic body politic, we can call empathy "solidarity."[22]

Not all group formation is of the sort we are looking for in explaining the solidarity in New Orleans. We have to distinguish between the passive affects of subjected groups and the active affects of group subjects. Subjected groups are swept into a homogeneous mass whose unity is imposed by a transcendent signifier, like a flag. Being taken up out of yourself to join a larger unit can be a hugely powerful emotional experience. We can even call it erotic if we remember that this notion of eros is wider than that of sexual union. The symbol of a subjected group is a trigger that evokes that feeling of transport into a larger whole. The rage felt when the signifier is disrespected is directly related to the joy in erotic transport into the group, and that joy is inversely related to the pain felt in being subjected to atomizing practices: the sort of everyday isolation and its concomitant feeling of powerlessness that is well-attested to in America. Imagine, then, the power of the emotions we call patriotism: the larger and more powerful the political unit you belong to, and the weaker and more isolated you feel on your own, the stronger the emotional surge, the more sacred the symbols. We can then say that the keepers of those symbols have a vested interest in increasing your pain in isolation in order to increase the power they get from controlling the keys to your joy in union. So an empire of isolated and powerless citizens would be a powerful and dangerous beast indeed!

On the other hand, we have to think of the joy of the active group subject, the immanently self-organized spontaneous group formation we saw in New Orleans and elsewhere. That solidarity was demonstrated not just among the people of New Orleans but among many of the people of Louisiana too. Alongside the brave men and women of the Coast Guard and the Louisiana Department of Wildlife and Fisheries, let us not forget the hundreds of volunteer rescuers who came to New Orleans in their trucks and their boats, pulled somehow by that solidarity to rescue strangers. These rescuers, though able to work the first few days on their own, were eventually refused entry to the area by the Federal Emergency Management Agency, which gave us the worst of all possible governmental responses: not only did they not do it themselves, they also refused to get out of the way and let the volunteers do the work (Brinkley 2007; van Heerden 2007; Tierney and Bevc 2007). This was done for two reasons: (1) the securitarian/racist panic triggered by thousands of blacks gathered together without enough police; and (2) because the current officeholders, at least at the federal level, wanted government to fail.

Here we see some of the political consequences of the neoliberal denial of the very truth of solidarity (and hence the neoconservative response of government as an expression of solidarity) and consequent production of atomized behavior (and hence government as a transcendent source of order against anarchy). You can do the inverse—strain solidarity and increase atomization—via scarcity in some situations; in others, you can increase solidarity via scarcity. Scarcity is an intensifier of underlying processes, a catalyst. And scarcity is produced, let us not forget, according to a multiplicity whose elements are rich and poor people, "good" and "bad" neighborhoods. Scarcity is produced so that poverty is actualized along the social-geographical differential relation of access to goods, a differential enforced by the police at the singularities of entry points to privileged neighborhoods and bridges to cities across the river. During the post-Katrina weakening of the police presence, we saw four types of "looting" actualized from this multiplicity: (1) getting necessities of life—food, water, medicine, diapers; (2) taking of nonnecessities for future use or resale (one of the things our Hobbes-mongers underplay is that along with the tolerated looting of type 1, type 2 cannot be condemned, for there is no crime in the state of nature, only private judgment as to what is necessary to secure the future); (3) revenge against the rich (you've taunted me with your fancy goods my whole life, so I'll wreck them so you won't have them either); (4) nihilistic rage (you've left me to die, so fuck you, I'm burning it all down).[23]

The political lesson is not that we need order from above to prevent the anarchy that is supposedly close by, but that the solidarity that holds almost all of us together, the civic and human bonds that led all those thousands to stick together and led those hundreds of volunteers to head to New Orleans, needs support only from a government that—instead of being systematically dismantled and artificially rendered inadequate so it can be, in the now horribly ironic words of the right-wing activist Grover Norquist, "drowned in a bathtub"—needs to be recalled to its proper function as the organized expression of that solidarity.

Conclusion

IS THERE A POLITICAL PHILOSOPHY implied in my theoretical work and in my treatment of the case studies? In its nominal content, we find liberal republicanism balancing individual rights and the common good, the two extremes we investigated in the Schiavo and Katrina cases, respectively. My claim to originality would be grounding those concepts in terms of affective cognition as the sense-making of bodies politic rather than in a rational cognitive subject as the political subject. Following up on our theory of political physiology, there is no single political subject, no single conceptual ground of politics. Rather, there is a naturalized politics in which government as the organized expression of the means to achieve the common good is grounded in empathic solidarity, and individual rights are grounded in singular affect.

Political physiology can also help us with a third element of political theory, after those of individual rights and the common good: sovereignty. It bears repeating that the ability of the "forces of order" to kill in a planned, systematic manner is the key to sovereignty conceived as the monopoly on the legitimate use of violence in a territory. The violence that forms an essential part of political practice must be thought of in its relation to de-subjectivizing practices that enable the controlled and targeted triggering of hunting agents or the implantation of reflexes or quasi-reflexive time-pressured decisions. In other words, we have to consider the techniques by which protoempathic identification and its inhibition on violence are overcome, as chapter 6 attempts to show. In this regard, we can also note that the ancient and modern social and corporeal techniques that manipulate the political physiology of the act of killing—colloquially speaking, the ways people psych themselves up for violence—cannot be contained in traditional military structures. In order, then, to understand terrorism as freelance political violence, we must have a clear understanding of the intersection of political rhetoric, affective neuroscience, and the act of killing.

Such rethinking of political theory in terms of affective cognition in a social context allows us to consider some of the direct political applications of our study. The intersection of politics and affect occurs every day: dramatically, in terror alerts and moral panics, and prosaically, when American electoral campaigns use functional MRI technology to produce brain scans for the study of cognitive and affective responses to political advertising (Tierney 2004; Cacioppo and Visser 2003; Raichle 2003). A philosophical study examining the intersection of politics and affect is thus an important addition to civic literacy, as a citizenry that is unaware of the way political rhetoric uses unconscious emotional valuing processes deeply rooted in brain and body risks validating the ancient antidemocratic canard about the emotional instability of "the people."

Whatever its political applications, this is ultimately a philosophy book. Turning to the current philosophical landscape, we should note that although emotion has become a topic of some interest to philosophers lately, almost all of that philosophical interest has shown an individualist orientation (with the exception of Griffiths and Scarantino 2009), so the recourse of political physiology to the concepts of emergence and complexity theory lets us think of *collective* emotions. We should note here that Griffiths and Scarantino are ontologically modest when it comes to collective emotion, while Deleuze and Guattari are more ontologically bold in their notion of haecceity, which includes affect in a singular temporal-spatial-social event (Deleuze and Guattari 1987, 260–65). On the other hand, all the work in political science that uses computer programming to model social interaction ("cellular automata" [Sawyer 2001]) uses rationalist presuppositions about human behavior, so we need affective neuroscience to let us think of collective *emotions*. In other words, what we need is a way to think of humans as collective and emotional as well as individual and rational. This is what I have done in *Political Affect*.

The study of political physiology benefits both political philosophy and cognitive science by placing affective neuroscience, which deals with component processes below the level of the subject, in a fully developed political context that eschews individualism by recognizing emergent social groups above the subject and heterogeneous assemblages that are alongside the subject. Political philosophy benefits from rethinking the social context of affect, since social commands, symbols, slogans, and images result in the conditioning of conscious subjective actions through unconscious valuing, as when we respond to social situations with decisions mediated by fear, anger, anxiety, and sadness. But at other times, the presence of socially constituted commands, symbols, slogans, and images can trigger behavior that eludes conscious control, as in de-subjectivizing panics and rages, where the conscious subject is bypassed in favor of an immediate link between a social trigger and a somatic mechanism (Grossman 1996; Griffiths 1997; LeDoux 1996; Niehoff 1999; Panksepp 1998). Since the negative affects of panic and rage—and the milder forms of fear, anger, anxiety, and sadness—are among the emotions most susceptible to political manipulation, the need for political philosophy to study political affect is evident. Not all affects are negative, however; therefore, we need to rethink political philosophy's focus on the rational subject not just in panic and rage but also in love and empathy, what Aristotle would call *philia*.

Just as political philosophy benefits from rethinking the positive as well as the negative affects, cognitive science must appreciate negative affects as well as the positive cognitive aspects of culture. Not all cultural forms empower subjects by storing heuristics for cognition; depending on the developmental path laid down for those in a particular social group (for example, one's race and gender), culture can be inhibiting or downright damaging, for it can engender negative affective patterns, thresholds, and triggers just as it denies or awards access to heuristic resources. The study of political physiology, by incorporating the results of affective neuroscience in a political framework, renews political philosophy by removing its exclusive focus on the rational cognitive subject, just as it helps cognitive science by removing the naively positive view of culture entailed by its individualism.

A further benefit of our study of political physiology is its being based in a conceptual field in which naturalizing includes room for a collective politics while difference becomes naturalized. Here, once again, the work of Deleuze is important. In *A Thousand Plateaus* Deleuze and Guattari propose that natural processes tend toward two poles of emergent systems: either stratification (centralized, hierarchical systems of homogeneous parts) or networking (heterogeneous components working together in de-centered networks). They thus provide a political physics (Protevi 2001) that, via the notions of stratification and networking, naturalizes the notions of servitude and freedom.

The move to a political physics that grounds the freedom of democratic collectivity in a natural process of networking is an important one; while some naturalizers like myself seek to naturalize social cooperation by showing how it is engendered and reproduced in the reciprocal causality of emergent social groups, others are apolitical, and still others propose an individualist (or at best family-based) politics. The most extreme rely on reductionist ultra-Darwinist presuppositions; they posit "selfish genes" or "replicators" inhabiting organisms or "vehicles" and undertaking reproductive strategies to increase their share in a population gene frequency market (Dawkins 2006). When coupled with the worst excesses of evolutionary psychology (which reduces complex social phenomena to such genetic maneuvering), the result is almost always an authoritarian/sexist politics tending toward the political affect of servitude grounded in a political physics of stratification (Arnhart 1994a, 1994b).

On the other hand, some philosophers reject political physics altogether because of their commitment to an antirealist epistemology (Braver 2007). They would diagnose political commitments in scientific discourse, but they would restrict this to the level of images and metaphors, denying the possibility of an ontology that could show social cooperation to be grounded in a real natural process of networking (concretized as *philia*, as political solidarity). While they acknowledge the differential aspect of networking, they restrict this to sign networks, which sociolinguistically construct reality for us. Thus, the best they can do is unravel the way in which, for them, some signifier chains pretend to capture scientifically the reality of the natural process of networking—even when they are sympathetic to the democratic collective politics grounded therein.

If we are to escape such "signifier enthusiasm" (Deleuze and Guattari 1987, 66) and maintain a naturalist orientation, we will have to engage the question of human nature. What does political physiology say about human nature? First, that there is one. For many years, a large part of the left adopted social constructivism to fight the good fight against racist and sexist constructions of human nature. But they threw the baby out with the bathwater by banning any discussion of human nature. We cannot escape a new serious and important discussion on human nature, and we better join it with our eyes peeled for racist and sexist assumptions, hence with an appropriately high barrier to admitting human nature discourse (Selinger forthcoming). Second, we should join the discussion not simply on the defensive, but welcoming it as a good thing. While many leftists have dallied with social constructivism, the right has continued to put forth its version of human nature: the individualist, competitive, utility-maximizing rational agent. In doing so, they often deny they have a metaphysics: they accuse the left of metaphysics in promoting collectivism, but they deny their own individualist metaphysics as well as their own actions in creating the set of social conditions that make people act as if they were individual utility maximizers. We need to insist on the political economy of consciousness, for much of sociopolitical practice tries to render irrelevant the effects of subjective agency by rendering behavior predictable, either in mass—by neoliberal economic practices that seek to produce the conditions that will, in turn, produce "rational" (predictable) behavior—or by discipline for individuals and small groups (Schwartz, Schuldenfrei, and Lacey 1979; Satz and Frerejohn 1994; Murphy 1996; Bonta and Protevi 2004; Klein 2007).

Two lines of attack present themselves. First, the metaphysics of rational agency is bad, a substantialist/essentialist line of thought. We do not have a nature; we develop one, predictably and reliably, from multiple developmental factors (there is no gene-centrism in political physiology). Second, the exclusive focus on the individualist/competitive content of the right-wing view of human nature is false: human nature is equally—nay, perhaps predominantly—prosocial. There are sociopaths, of course, but this only defeats the claim that human nature includes a widespread prosocial tendency if you have an essentialist view of nature: as if, in identifying human nature, we were isolating a finite set of necessary and sufficient characteristics for belonging to the human species and claiming that prosociality belongs on that list. The counterexample of sociopaths would defeat such a claim—if it were advanced in an essentialist manner. But we have to see nature as statistical, as the dominant cluster of the distribution of traits in a population, as we are taught by Darwin and population thinking. We might even think of nature as that which occurs "for the most part," as Aristotle puts it (*Physics* 2.8.198b35), if we can remove the teleology and just retain the truth of the observation: at any one time, species traits clump together.

We have to insist on the following: the prosocial character of human nature is revealed by the widespread capacity for protoempathic identification. There is now a large contemporary literature on empathy, some of which we discussed in chapter 1. Based in mother-child primate relations, protoempathic identification has been extended in human evolution to kin and then to in-group and finally to all other humans and, often, to other animals. We see here an occasion for the rehabilitation of the theory of moral sentiments proposed by Adam Smith and David Hume (de Waal 2006), not to mention the need to recognize the role of cooperation in nature (Kropotkin 2007; Gould 1988). The primate basis of prosociality,

Frans de Waal argues, is extended to include a sense of fairness, reciprocity, and harmonizing: "In stressing kindness, our moral systems are enforcing what is already part of our heritage. They are not turning human behavior around, only underlining preexisting capacities" (2006, 181). The challenge we face is to extend the range of prosocial impulses from the ingroup, protect them from the negative emotions, and build on them to genuine altruism, that is, acting for the sake of the other, not just feeling what the other feels (Joyce 2007). All this is not to deny the selfish nature of the basic emotions of rage and fear. The key to a fruitful left approach to political physiology is studying how such selfish, negative emotions are manipulated or, more positively, how a social order is constructed to minimize them and to maximize positive affects (Singer 1999; Gatens and Lloyd 1999).

As good Deleuzians, we cannot rest with moral language for that is too close to the application of fixed standards ("the judgment of God"). In response to the proposal that we model our moral sense on a Chomskyan language acquisition module (Hauser 2006), we have to take up Deleuze and Guattari's critique of Chomsky. In other words, we have to see the relation of the virtual and the actual as the continuous variation of variables (Deleuze and Guattari 1987, 92–110). This means that problems are fluid and complex: our moves change the conditions for future moves, often in ways we cannot predict. The interactivity of moves and problems means that no one solution exhausts a problematic field; thus, we cannot bracket pragmatics or the study of concrete action and its relation to the conditions of future action.

The upshot of a Deleuzian pragmatics approach to living through problems is that in perceiving what is right about a situation, we have to rely upon our radicalization of Noë's virtuality of perception, as we have sketched it in chapter 2. Thus, as much as any natural environment (much more so, in fact), the social field is virtual, and moral perception is the resolution of a dynamic field of potentials for practical action. That is why we cannot be content with posing moral questions, as with the famous trolley problems, for morality is not about arriving at a set of answers, or even studying the process by which answers to set questions are arrived at, but about moving from the concrete situations we find ourselves in and posing a virtual problem with a range of solutions, the actualization of which will change the conditions for future actualizations (Williams 2005, 129–51). We have to recall that a problem in the Deleuzian sense means a temporarily linked set of heterogeneous Ideas or multiplicities, a constellation in which some stand out from background, though in principle all multiplicities are connected.

This is why case studies have to be part of our methodological tool kit in studying political physiology: in them we see the coming together of a problematic field linking all multiplicities from a certain perspective, which makes some stand out. With case studies we come to realize that facing the concrete situation individuates while depersonalizing; we lose our habits to gain our singularity. And it is only in living our singularities, in feeling at the intense turning points of our lives the multiplicities crossing between us and linking us, that we can feel the empathy, the love and solidarity, the eros and *philia*, by which we best live as imbrications of the social and the somatic.

Notes

1. Above, Below, and Alongside the Subject

1. For our purposes here, we can define representations as either discrete symbols, as in classical computationalism, or network properties, as in connectionism. See Wheeler 2005 for an excellent discussion of the differences between these approaches.

2. The following extremely condensed introduction misses many important nuances. Many more developed treatments are available. At book length, there is Kaplan and Glass 1995. A noteworthy recent philosophical work is Strevens 2003. At essay length, there is Dyke 2006. Bonta and Protevi 2004 provides a primer on complexity theory as well as fairly extensive references. An excellent popular work is Cohen and Stewart 1994.

3. This notion of complexity theory as the study of emergent simplicity is expressed in the title of an excellent popularization, Cohen and Stewart's *The Collapse of Chaos* (1994).

4. Some simple mechanical systems produce nice attractors without recourse to negative feedback mechanisms. Chuck Dyke used the example of Duffing's mechanical oscillator to make this point to me in personal correspondence.

5. Not all transformation points in systems have singularities in their model, as this paragraph states. The important idea to take away from this section is that the structures of state spaces have the potential to provide a new understanding of the way systems work by suggesting a kind of causality different from linear chains of efficient causality. We can use a nontechnical vocabulary to express this new conceptuality: patterns, thresholds, triggers, sensitive zones, and so on. I will retain the singularity terminology, though, because (1) singularities do appear in the models of some systems, and (2) Deleuze uses the term (not always in a technically precise manner) to mean that which determines the internal structure of a state space, that is, the layout of the attractors. (I'd like to thank Chuck Dyke and Alistair Welchman for advice on this issue.)

6. For a treatment of human cognitive development that stresses the emergence (and later dissolution) of attractors (representing cognitive structures or "modules")

in the relation of the infant and its surrounding cultural scaffolding, see Griffiths and Stotz 2000. The breakdown in old coping habits that is the precondition for this rearrangement of attractors representing affective cognition patterns is called "unlearning" in Freeman 2000a and 2000b. In chapter 5 we will consider such unlearning in relation to Deleuze and Guattari's notion of the "Body without Organs."

7. For an excellent popular science overview of the concept of emergence and many applications, see Cohen and Stewart 1994. Specialized studies for emergence in specific scientific fields are Hütteman and Terzidis 2000 for physics; Luigi-Luis 2002 for chemistry; Shanks and Joplin 1999 and Boogerd et al. 2005 for biochemistry; and Sawyer 2001 for sociology.

8. As we will see in chapters 3 and 4, we focus on Deleuze and Guattari's notion of the organism as a patterned body politic rather than as a purely biological notion. Regarding the latter—which is not completely irrelevant to our investigation—see West-Eberhard 2003: "The emergent qualities of different levels of organization are one reason why biology needs to be studied at different levels, and why molecular biology, cell biology, or genetics alone cannot solve all the important questions of evolutionary biology" (61).

9. In recent and noteworthy attempts, McDonough 2002 provides a taxonomy of twenty-seven (!) concepts of emergence; Pihlstrom 1999 provides an excellent overview of the field and a pragmatist defense of emergence, while Schröder 1998 confines emergence to an epistemic category and Spurrett 2000 claims Bhaskar fails in his case for "strong emergence." We should note that worrying about the concept of emergence is something of a philosopher's obsession; many scientists just get down to the practice of studying cases of emergence without worrying about precisely defining its concept. Chuck Dyke, who is a philosophical expert on complexity theory and emergence (Dyke 1988, 1989, 1990, 2006), put it like this in personal correspondence with me: "The trick is to know where to look and what to look for [in searching for scientific work on emergence]. You don't look for cases that make a big deal about 'emergence' with fanfares and flags, but cases where emergence is taken for granted and used without fuss." Dyke goes on to recommend Abrahamson and Weis 1997 as an example of such a low-key work with emergence.

10. Their teamwork in producing *Anti-Oedipus, Kafka, A Thousand Plateaus,* and *What Is Philosophy?* is itself an example of emergence. Readers unfamiliar with Deleuze and Guattari may wish to consult the early parts of chapter 3 for orienting remarks concerning their relation to other strands of contemporary French philosophy.

11. Manuel DeLanda insists on not admitting to his social ontology any individuals unless one can show a concrete morphogenetic process for that individual (see DeLanda 1997, 2006).

12. For a methodological essay on this issue in "social neuroscience" (hence, close to our concerns with affective cognition in bodies politic), see Bernston and Cacioppo 2004. In emotion theory, see Lewis 2005. In neuroscience, see Freeman

2000a and 2000b and Thompson and Varela 2001. For a sustained philosophical treatment, see Thompson 2007.

13. See chapter 3 for references to work on Aristotle's biology, including the issues we briefly touch on here, namely, feminine teratology and patriarchal semenology.

14. We must be careful in calling bodies politic, as parts of transversally emergent assemblages, "cyborgs" because of the notion of disembodied information that is part of the history of that term, as shown in Hayles 1999. Bodies politic regulate concrete flows of matter and energy, not simply "information."

15. See also Massumi 1992 in this regard, although he focuses on Deleuze and Guattari. The question of Deleuze's materialism and/or realism—or the relation of philosophy and science in his thought (queen, handmaiden, or something else entirely)—is extremely complex. I will defer this issue to another context, though the confrontation with the position established in Williams 2003—that mathematics and science are for Deleuze mere illustrations of a fundamentally philosophic stance—would be essential to any such endeavor.

16. We must be careful with "incarnation" to avoid any Platonist overtones. The virtual is not the Realm of Platonic Ideas; it is in mutual presupposition with the actual rather than existing on a higher plane of reality. An actualization can change the virtual conditions for further actualizations.

17. DeLanda 2002 points out the importance for Deleuze of the work of Albert Lautman concerning this point (31).

18. The rules that codify games, that police their borders, are always retrospective with regard to concrete experimentation. "What *was* that? Was it a new move in the sport, or does it create a new sport?" Massumi 2002 (71–80) helped me think through these issues.

19. Varela, Lachaux, Rodriguez, and Martinerie 2001 is a review article covering one hundred or so studies of the 1990s that used nonlinear dynamics for modeling brain function. Many problems concerning the analytic philosophy questions of epistemological versus ontological emergence, synchronic versus diachronic emergence, mereological supervenience, and so forth could be raised. We should at least recognize, however, that bona fide continental philosophers such as Deleuze and Guattari afford us a starting point in tackling questions that have arisen independently in analytic philosophy. This seems to me to be an excellent opportunity for dialogue.

20. Silberstein and McGeever 1999 and Thompson and Varela 2001 show how thinking in terms of complex systems studied by means of nonlinear dynamics changes the terms of the classic debate summarized by McDonough 2002, which remains burdened with an impoverished view of matter. Goldstein 1999 also provides a sympathetic account of emergence in terms of complexity theory. I deal with hylomorphism extensively in Protevi 2001.

21. DeLanda 2002 attempts to outflank the entire reductionism question by pro-

posing a Deleuzian epistemology that redefines science from the search for laws in nature to the search for topological regularities in scientific fields, or as he puts it, the distribution of singular and ordinary points in a problem (127–28).

22. DeLanda 2002, 80, 110, 126 (where quasi-causes are said to replace final causes), and 160 (where he provides a list of Deleuzian terms for this concept, including "dark precursor" from *Difference and Repetition* and "line of flight" from *A Thousand Plateaus*). See also Juarrero 1999 for the need to reform the notion of formal and final cause (127, 143).

23. This Spinozist/Nietzschean trope is taken up in a social-psychological vein by Haidt 2001.

24. I explore the threefold "sense of sense" in Protevi 1994 and 1998.

25. For a developmental systems theory (DST) approach to the biological roots of cognition, see Griffiths and Stotz 2000. For a dynamical systems approach, see Christensen and Hooker 2001. On the notion of sense-making, several references are available here. Varela 1991 points to what he calls the "surplus of signification" opened by the sense-making of the bacterium: "There is no food significance in sucrose except when a bacterium swims upgradient" (87). Jonas 2003 notes that "the organic even in its lowest forms prefigures mind, and . . . mind even on its highest reaches remains part of the organic" (1). To my pleasant surprise, I found after writing these sections that Thompson 2007 similarly upholds the "strong continuity" thesis of life and cognition laid out here. Thompson's treatment is extensive and will be an important work in cognitive science for years to come. For a precise statement of the strong continuity thesis, which poses the difference between a Cartesian and an Aristotelian notion of consciousness as well as making an exciting appeal to self-organization theories, see Wheeler 1997.

26. Personal communication from John C. Larkin, Louisiana State University.

27. This article is of particular interest to us for its use of dynamical systems concepts such as "attractor."

28. The ontogeny of emotional phenotypes, to use the terms of Parkinson, Fischer, and Manstead 2005. For an overview of this important work, see Griffiths and Scarantino 2009. For more on emotional development, see Stern 1985 and Bräten 1998.

29. Important works in affective neuroscience regarding the basic emotions are Damasio 1994, 1999, 2003; LeDoux 1996; and Panksepp 1998. For philosophical discussions, see Griffiths 1997 and Prinz 2004. For an explication of "affect programs," see Griffiths 1997.

30. Ekman 1992 is a classic statement of the universalist position, and Averill 1982 is a classic statement of social constructivism. A major component of social constructivism is the idea that a neutral bodily "arousal" must be coupled with a judgment of a state of affairs to count as a specific kind of emotion (Averill 1982, 20). This idea would seem to be defeated by research on dedicated neural circuits for basic emotions (Panksepp 1998); according to this line of thought, there is no such

thing as a neutral arousal in need of further interpretation, but only already specified neural, physiological, and behavioral response patterns.

31. We can note here that Colombetti and Thompson 2007 criticize Lewis for still maintaining a separation of somatic and cognitive aspects of emotion as separate phases nonetheless linked in an ongoing process; their enactive approach favors a more intimate relation in which cognition/appraisal does not merely interact with the somatic but is constituted thereby. Colombetti and Thompson write: "Lewis' model . . . allows for considerable overlap among the processes subserving appraisal and emotion. Nevertheless, emotion constituents (arousal, action tendencies, and feelings) and appraisal constituents (perception, attention, and evaluation) remain conceptually distinct at the psychological level and subserved by distinct subsystems at the neural level. [This] . . . leaves less room for a concept of *embodied appraisal*" (2007, 54; italics in original). Although I favor Colombetti and Thompson's approach, we need not settle this rather technical dispute here as we seek merely to provide an overview of a rapidly developing field.

32. Damasio's view is not without its critics, who reject the somatic theory as based in what they see as an outmoded James-Lange tradition. Even among those sympathetic to the somatic theory, controversies remain concerning the precise role of cortical versus midbrain and brainstem structures in generating basic emotions. Some of the debates within the field are accessibly summarized in Watt 2000 and Panksepp 2003 (on Damasio 1999 and 2003, respectively). For a philosophical defense of the somatic theory, see Prinz 2004.

33. Paul Griffiths claims that the wide range of phenomena covered by the vernacular term "emotion" renders it in need of different types of theory. His phrase is that "emotion is not a natural kind" (1997, 2004). For Griffiths, Damasio is best seen here as describing a wide range of "felt affective states" as the domain of affective neuroscience, of which emotion proper is only one part (2004, 243).

34. Social emotions can be naturalized by providing evolutionary explanations for their selection and inheritance, but this need not entail the gene-centered notions of evolution, the massive modularity of mind, or the adaptationism favored by contemporary evolutionary psychology. See Griffiths 2003 on "Machiavellian emotions." As Griffiths 2006 might put it, to be naturalizers, we must have an evolutionary psychology, but that need not resemble what is now known as an "uppercase" Evolutionary Psychology. (For a sane and balanced overview of the controversies surrounding evolutionary psychology in general, see Laland and Brown 2002; for a rip-roaring attack on it, see Rose and Rose 2000. For an article-length overview, see Griffiths 2006.) To have a "lowercase" evolutionary psychology, we need a notion of multiple levels of selection in which evolved primate social cognitive (Dunbar 1998; Adolphs 2002) and emotional (de Waal 1996; Panksepp 1998) capacities are sustained and amplified in natural selection working in and on human culture (Jonathan Turner 2000; Richerson and Boyd 2005, 196ff.). With DST in mind, I want to say that as useful as Richerson and Boyd 2005 is in discussing cultural evolution

(for instance, they show that the notion of "meme" doesn't hold), I don't buy their metaphor of gene-environment "interaction" in which genes are "recipes" for development (9). I would also claim that their notion of culture as transmission of "information," which is further specified as a "mental state" (5), underplays the complex notion of corporeal patterns, thresholds, and triggers I stress in discussing bodies politic.

35. Shaun Gallagher will say that the details of Damasio's proposal "either inflate the body to the level of ideas in a phenomenologically untenable way, or reduce it to neuronal processes" (2005, 135). But if we take into account Colombetti and Thompson's reminder that as-if loops require constant somatic updating and hence are not mere neurocentric representations (2007, 59), we can retain the "somatic marker" hypothesis.

36. That Hutchins defines cognition in terms of representations need not trouble us. Most proponents of the embodied-embedded school (Clark and Wheeler, for sure, but also Thompson) maintain a role for representations in some cognitive acts. They simply displace it from the center of cognition, making it a special case, called for only in certain circumstances.

37. Pierre Bourdieu's notion of *habitus* would be an alternate vocabulary to our Deleuze-inspired work in "bodies politic" (see note 39). See also Shusterman 2008 for recent work on "body consciousness" that refers to Bourdieu.

38. For Merleau-Ponty, the body is an active subject whose practical abilities allow objects to appear as correlates of possible actions. For an early and noteworthy feminist critique see Butler 1989. The resonances—backward to Bergson, and forward to Gibson and the "enactive" school—are noteworthy; Young's critique of Merleau-Ponty's unconscious adoption of a masculine body-subject could in principle be extended to these other figures. See Shusterman 2008 for recent work in this area.

39. Dyke 1999 shows the convergence of Bourdieu's thought and dynamical systems thought. I prefer Deleuze and Guattari to Bourdieu because they place the production of bodies politic within a full-fledged and wide-ranging naturalism.

40. His investigation of "techniques of the self" is not an accommodation by the later Foucault to liberal regimes, as if the individual were a refuge from the totalizing power Foucault supposedly theorized in his middle period. Individualizing subjectivities is just the mode of biopower in our world: you direct yourself to find your best use of personal (and that means genetic and organic) capital. Think how often we are enjoined by television commercials to "ask your doctor if X is right for you." I have greatly benefited from reading Nealon 2008 in thinking about these points.

2. Bodies Politic

1. We can also mention in this context the field of social neuroscience. While there are some differences of emphasis between my approach and that of social

neuroscience (I would probably emphasize the intermeshing of developmental processes with differing timescales rather than the interaction of social and biological levels as does social neuroscience), the resonances are far stronger than the dissonances. For methodological issues, see Bernston and Cacioppo 2004; for specific issues of interest to political affect, see in particular Meaney 2004 on the effects of maternal care on gene expression and phenotype development in mammals, and Adolphs 2004 on emotion and social cognition.

2. As I argue in note 34 to chapter 1, we have to think of evolutionary psychology in the context of the developmental systems theory, that is, in a framework in which social evolution works alongside genetic and epigenetic factors. Thus, in evaluating current research in evolutionary psychology, which offers a variety of hypotheses about the type of cognitive module said to be responsible for racialized perception, we have to consider current social factors in the development of such modules. In this context, we need not decide between the competitor theories—or even enter into the many controversies about the notion of massive cognitive modularity—but we can note the difference between those that posit some sort of essentializing process, whether directed to natural or social kinds, and those that propose a module for identifying social coalitions. The arguments are summarized in Cosmides, Tooby, and Kurzban 2003. Of particular interest in the works treated therein is Hirschfeld 1996. See also Phelps and Thomas 2003 for an argument for caution regarding overestimation of neurological findings regarding racial perception.

3. This is not to deny that some philosophers of the embodied mind orientation, such as Shaun Gallagher, Daniel Hutto, Mathew Ratcliffe and others, are investigating the field of social cognition. However, such interest rarely includes an overt connection with political categories.

4. The term "economic" derives etymologically from the law *(nomos)* of the household *(oikos)*. Ever since the era of Mary Wollstonecraft, such politicization of the structures of "private life" or "the domestic sphere" is the common conceptual foundation of feminism, antiracism, and other social movements.

5. During the first drafting of this chapter, in July 2006, the state of Israel was engaged in military combat with a nonstate actor, Hezbollah, a group whose political wing forms part of the government of a state, Lebanon, but whose military wing is separate from the Lebanese armed forces. Is it a war when one of the parties is a nonstate actor? Is it, instead, a police action? There is no settled terminology here. The Israel versus Hezbollah action is an example of fourth-generation warfare (4GW) across a state border, in contrast to the more typical cases of 4GW, which operate within a state, as in Iraq. 4GW analyses typically stress the decentralized or distributed cognitive elements at work, as in the following example: "The central secret to Hezbollah's success is that it trained its (global) guerrillas to make decisions autonomously (classic 4GW), at the group level. In every area—from firing rockets to defending prepared positions to media routing around jamming/disruption—we have examples of Hezbollah teams deciding, adapting, innovating, and collaborat-

ing without reference to any central authority. The result of this decentralization is that Hezbollah's aggregate decision cycles are faster and qualitatively better than those of their Israeli counterparts" (Robb 2006). Other works have examined the affective components of 4GW, as in Cole 2003, which includes an analysis of the use of religious documents in the emotional preparations of the September 11, 2001, hijackers.

6. "Place themselves" should be seen in terms of Foucault's "techniques of the self," just as "are placed" should be seen in terms of the therapeutic intervention he analyzed under the rubric of "normalization." For recent work on Foucault and corporeal techniques, see Nealon 2008 and Shusterman 2008.

7. There are important issues surrounding the debates on the group mind (Wilson 2004) that we cannot enter here. Suffice it to say that the exact details involved in a precise notion of a group decision-making process are complex and controversial. I think it reasonable to say that our folk psychology of groups includes something like the claims I make here. An even larger project would involve articulating these debates with the Deleuzoguattarian notions of the subjected group and the group subject (Deleuze and Guattari 1984).

8. There are very complex issues here surrounding the work of Talcott Parsons and Niklas Luhmann that are beyond our ability to address in this context.

9. Two points need to be made here. (1) For some thinkers, "affect" and "emotion" are used interchangeably, and each has both physiological and psychological, or objective and subjective, aspects. (2) Readers of Deleuze know that he does not oppose the use of the terms "objective" and "subjective" as I do here. I do so only as a first approximation. I will explain how my notion of political affect as the sense-making of the body politic fits Deleuze's threefold ontology of virtual/intensive/actual as well as being grounded in biological capacities of sense-making. Neither the Deleuzian nor the biological elements here can be parsed using an objective versus subjective scheme.

10. We part company with Damasio 1999 and 2003 in that we don't assume social dynamics are always homeostatic, that is, the restoration of a set point for a totality. Rather, social dynamics most often maintain a state of nonequilibrium, moving among tendencies of growing cohesion and growing dissension.

11. State armies engaged in urban counterinsurgency warfare sometimes utilize such classic 4GW tactics (see Weizman 2007).

12. This notion of affect has obvious parallels with the Heideggerian notion of attunement *(Befindlichkeit)*. For a treatment of embodied-embedded cognition with reference to Heidegger and to Hubert Dreyfus's Heideggerian critiques of the primacy of representation, see Wheeler 2005. See also Noë 2004 for a notion of enactive perception, which ties perception to embodied skills for practical interaction with objects.

13. See especially Deleuze 1988 and Deleuze and Guattari 1987. For this notion of learning as finding out what the mixtures of bodies brings about, see the descrip-

tion of infant orality in Rochat 2001: "Beyond the erotic motivation and the pleasure associated with food, oral contacts provide infants with opportunities to learn about themselves" (54).

14. This is, of course, a speculative reconstruction in terms of political affect. For an excellent treatment of the Spinozist basis of the theory of political affect, see Gatens and Lloyd 1999. For a sober historical account of the Nuremberg rallies, providing names, dates, and statistics, see Burden 1967. On the physiological front, Berghaus 1996 remarks on the neurophysiological effects of ritual dancing and drumming (44), while Thamer 1996 mentions the "euphoria" and "general enthusiasm" under the rubric of "The Management of the Irrational." Sargant 1957 briefly mentions the "rhythmic chanting, torchlight processions, and the like," as well as the "states of hysterical suggestibility" generated at the rallies (137), practices shared with tribal initiation ceremonies and religious revivals. Different techniques achieve the same ends in police interrogation and the eliciting of confessions, according to Sargant. For more on ecstatic trances and group formation by means of dancing, see McNeil 1995. Freeman 2000a and 2000b mention dancing and "unlearning." For an analysis of rave culture in these terms, see Sylvan 2005, which also contains a wonderful collection of first-person testimonials.

15. Technically speaking, Noë 2004 is ambivalent as to the partner to movement in this differential relation. At times he says that "sensations" (200) or "sensory stimulation" vary with movement (66), and at other times it is the "perceptual relation to the object" that varies (200). Clark 2006 interrogates this point.

16. Again, an alternate vocabulary for the embodied social skills that make possible the sense-making of bodies politic would be Bourdieu's notions of habitus enabling negotiation of a field on the basis of symbolic capital.

17. Dreyfus 1991 and 1992 are important sources for this argument against rules. Dreyfus often cites Bourdieu as making the same point.

3. The Organism in Aristotle and Kant

1. The status of the organism is a perennial topic in bio-philosophy. Is it an emergent, integrative whole constituting a necessarily central focus of biology, or can it somehow be bracketed in favor of "mechanical" factors (which would now be located in the molecular operations of DNA)? For a historical survey, see Grene and Depew 2005. A good introduction to contemporary issues is Sterelny and Griffiths 1999.

2. *Autarcheia* resolves into *autos* (self) and *archē* (foundation, principle, directing force), whence "foundational principled self-direction."

3. For an early and prescient analysis of the extension of the notion of human capital to the genetic endowment of individuals, see Foucault 2004 (221–44). Foucault's analyses are picked up in Thompson 2004. The commonly repeated sociobiologistic understanding of returns on investment in a genetic stock market can be criticized not merely for its genetic reductionism but also for its naïveté in political

economy. To understand how the stock market really works—largely as a mechanism for speculation in liquid ownership shares rather than as a means of efficiently allocating resources for production—see Henwood 1997.

4. It should be clear from chapter 1 that I want developmental systems theory, not evolutionary psychology (as in Arnhart 1994a and 1994b), to be the theoretical underpinning for my attempt to think of Aristotle's political physiology.

5. In this section I take up analyses set forth in Protevi 1994. Although in neither work do I address all the specialist issues raised by my remarks—each sentence I write, as in all writings on Aristotle, could be nuanced, contextualized, and contested—I do try to mark major controversies. A more complete list of the secondary sources that guide my reading of Aristotle can be found in Protevi 1994, but I acknowledge here once again the profound insight of Kosman 1969, a simply beautiful piece of philosophical scholarship.

6. Citations from Aristotle are from the Oxford Classical Text editions. Barnes 1984 is the standard English-language edition.

7. In keeping with the theme of this chapter, we focus on the human organism and its relation to divine erotic provocation. For an article proposing that divine teleology (which cannot be seen as demiurgic) reaches through the totality of sublunar nature, see Kahn 1985. For an article positing that divinely inspired natural teleology is anthropocentric (that is, that man is the [only] beneficiary of natural striving after divine perfection), see Sedley 1991.

8. For a brief, clear, and nontechnical treatment of the biopsychological in Aristotle, see Robinson 1989.

9. For an interesting treatment of cognition and affect in Aristotle in relation to contemporary affective neuroscience, which criticizes the cognition-first theory of emotion as well as the role functionalism of thinkers trying to articulate Arisotle's philosophy of mind, see Kafetsios and LaRock 2005. For a critique of functionalism from a neo-Aristotelian perspective, taking on board Kauffman's ideas about self-organization, see Wheeler 1997.

10. Freeman 2000b offers an account of neurodynamics we can adapt to the interpretation of *akrasia.* For Freeman, the difference between rational and emotional behaviors must be seen in terms of rationality as "the constraint of high-intensity chaotic activity of components of the forebrain by the cooperative dynamics of consciousness," while emotionality involves "the escape of subsystems owing to an excess of chaotic fluctuations in states of strong arousal." (I take these formulations from the abstract of the Web version of this essay.)

11. Scholarship on Kant's bio-philosophical thought has lagged behind that on Aristotle, but it has shown signs of picking up in the last ten years. As late as 1992, *The Cambridge Companion to Kant* did not include a chapter on the critique of teleological judgment (Guyer 1992). Recent works concerning Kant and bio-philosophy include the useful overview that comprises chapter 4 of Grene and Depew 2005. For attempts to articulate Kant and contemporary biology, see Van de Vijver, Van

Speyboeck, and Vandevyvere 2003; Van de Vijver et al. 2005; and Weber and Varela 2002. For philosophical evaluations of Kant's arguments, see Aquila 1991; Ginsborg 2001, 2004; and Guyer 1991, 2001.

12. I cite the *Akademie* edition pages for Kant quotations, with paragraphs first, then pages. I will use Werner Pluhar's translation of the *Critique of Judgment* (Kant 1987), which puts the AA pagination in the margins, and Lewis White Beck's translation of the *Critique of Practical Reason* (Kant 1956), which puts the AA pagination in brackets in the text as well as in the running heads at the top of the page.

13. In the cognitive, theoretically knowing body, understanding is to order the manifold of sensation, mediated by forms of intuition and the schematism of the transcendental imagination. Here the constitution of an object would entail the organization of a body that could be experienced as self-identical and recognized as the same. The self-constitution of a cognitive subject capable of such object-constitution would be a similar forceful organization. Kant is clear on the coercion of imagination by understanding in cognition: "When the imagination is used for cognition, then it is under the constraint *[Zwange]* of the understanding" (Kant 1987, 316).

14. In morality, Kant writes, reason exercises its *Gewalt* (here equally well translated by "force," "violence," or "authority" in addition to Pluhar's choice of "dominance") over sensibility (Kant 1987, 269; see also 271, where "human nature" can only harmonize with the good "through the *Gewalt* that reason exercises over sensibility").

15. Compare the *Critique of Practical Reason*, where "pleasure always affects one and the same life-force *[Lebenskraft]* which is manifested in the faculty of desire" (Kant 1956, 23). For an extended treatment of life in the *Critique of Judgment*, see chapter 5 of Makkreel 1990.

16. Guyer notes that Kant's treatment of the sublime is "unstable," sometimes positing a single complex emotion and at other times a series of emotions (Guyer 1996, 204). We need not settle this issue here.

17. In *Critique of Judgment* ¶66, Kant interprets organization of the organism in terms of banishment of chance and the gratuitous.

18. For a challenging article relating affective neuroscience to Kant's deontological ethics, see Greene 2008.

4. The Anorganic Body in Deleuze and Guattari

1. From time to time, they do use the term in a purely biological sense (1984, 144; 1987, 54); it is the contrast with the Body without Organs (BwO) that brings out the political sense.

2. The founding work in examining Deleuze's bio-philosophy is Ansell Pearson 1999. Also of interest are Hansen 2000; DeLanda 1997, 2002; Parisi 2004; Braidotti 2002, 2006; and Toscano 2006.

3. For a reading of Artaud in terms of his "nerves" as collective emotions relating the somatic and the social, see Brown 2005.

4. For influential readings of *Anti-Oedipus*, see Massumi 1992 and Holland 1999.

5. For a fascinating account of infant development that seeks to coordinate intersubjective psychoanalysis and developmental psychology, see Stern 1985. Stern rejects the fusion model, tracing the development from the "emergent self" (corresponding to early stages of the body schema) through the "core self," the "subjective self," and the "verbal self." It is only in the later stages that the processes of Oedipalization that Deleuze and Guattari denounce take place.

6. Judge Schreber is the paradigm case of schizophrenic paranoia and divine contact for Deleuze and Guattari. Schreber was a German judge whose mental illness nonetheless allowed him to write extensive memoirs and whose social standing attracted the attention of Freud to his case (see Schreber 2000). Deleuze and Guattari make two points in analyzing Freud's treatment of Schreber. First, his father really did strap him into corrective orthopedic machines, although Freud evinces no interest in this real history. This is characteristic, Deleuze and Guattari think, of psychoanalysis's willingness to wash its hands of real social injustice. Second, Freud's treatment completely rejects the social/cosmic dimensions of Schreber's delirium and forces his libidinal investments into an Oedipal triangle.

7. To anticipate our discussion of *A Thousand Plateaus*, the BwO here is the "full" BwO, the body without any regulated flows. *A Thousand Plateaus* will give a positive valence to what it calls the full BwO; the catatonic body is there called an "empty" BwO.

8. See Damasio 1994 (165–201) for an extended discussion of somatic markers, particularly 180–83 for the role of somatic mapping in the prefrontal cortex. Damasio cites work in mirror neurons located in the cortex as possibly involved in as-if loops or "internal simulation" (1999, 281).

9. DeLanda corrects the imprecise linking of "sedimentation" and "folding" by claiming that it is geologically more correct to have "cementation" as the second articulation, with folding occurring at a different spatial scale (1997, 290n82).

10. Stern also rejects the notion of superseded stages of development (1985).

11. We should note that West-Eberhard claims that viability constraints allow more developmental plasticity than is usually acknowledged. See her discussion of "cohesiveness" (2003, 8–10).

5. Terri Schiavo

1. For a discussion of this reading of the Constitution, contrasting it to the view of a "Constitution of detail" with a limited number of "enumerated rights," see Dworkin 1988, and with regard to privacy rights concerning the right to die, Dworkin 1993. A particularly succinct encapsulation of that view, from an important dissent to which we will return, is that of Justice Harlan in *Poe v. Ullman*, 367 U.S. 497 (1961): we must approach the Constitution "not in a literalistic way, as if we had a

tax statute before us, but as the basic charter of our society, setting out in spare but meaningful terms the principles of government" (367 U.S. at 540).

2. The Schiavo case was not a (jurisprudential) event in the full Deleuzian sense, or at least it was only an ordinary event, not an "emission of singularities," that is, the establishment of a precedent. It may turn out to be an event in some other (cultural, political) sense, if it results in changes in state laws regulating end-of-life issues.

3. The right to privacy is established in the tradition of modern decisions on substantive due process, beginning with Justice Harlan's dissent in *Poe v. Ullman*, 367 U.S. 497 (1961) and whose main decisions include *Griswold v. Connecticut*, 381 U.S. 479 (1965) and *Roe v. Wade*, 410 U.S. 113 (1973). Later important decisions concerning the right to privacy include *Planned Parenthood of Southeastern Pennsylvania v. Casey*, 505 U.S. 833 (1992), which reaffirmed its relevance to abortion, and *Washington v. Glucksberg*, 521 U.S. 702 (1997), which defeated a claimed right to assisted suicide.

4. We should also recall that Agamben clearly shows that Deleuze's notion of "a life" is not comparable to the Aristotelian notion of "nutritive life" that allows for the attribution of life to a subject and that would thus be congruent with the isolation of bare life upon which can be made the series of distinctions sought by bio-politics. See Agamben's essay "Absolute Immanence," where he comments on Deleuze 2003 (Agamben 1999b, 232–33). We should note that *Homo Sacer* conducts its analyses of current medical technology in the chapter on "politicizing death" in terms of coma, not PVS, and further, as if the bare life in question was located in a zone of indistinction between human and animal: "The comatose person has been defined as an intermediary being between man and an animal" (Agamben 1997, 165), when precisely what is in question in PVS is the relation of human and "vegetative" life, or in my terms, the relations among personality, person, and organic system, when all three are seen as complex material systems.

5. For a reading of this decision, see Cornell 2005. Cornell also criticizes Rawls et al. 1997, which also supports assisted suicide, for relying on the active/passive distinction rather than on intention relative to hastening death.

6. For those of you who have heard the abuse meme circulating as a possible explanation of the collapse, you should know that the homicide police called by the paramedics as a matter of course when an apparently healthy young woman collapses suddenly at home found no sign of struggle in the apartment or sign of trauma on Terri Schiavo's neck or face. Of course you cannot conclude conclusively from a negative, so the abuse meme can live on, though probably in a more hostile overall environment, as its plausibility is damaged. It can thus be reproduced o˘ in the most favorable environments, the brains and blogs of the American far wing. Given the fact that it has lived this long, even in the face of the police, well as the utter implausibility of supposing that an allegedly abusive M

avo would then turn around and give Terri Schiavo's doctors a million dollars' worth of motivation to discover that abuse, we can conclude that those environments are quite forgiving indeed to that meme.

7. For overviews and critiques of theory of mind accounts, see Gallagher 2005; Hutto 2008; and Ratcliffe 2007.

8. Note the way Cheshire tries to sneak in the potential for pleasure on the part of Terri Schiavo at the end of his affidavit (Cheshire 2005).

9. We should note the manner of Deleuze's death here. Braidotti 2006 has insightful comments on his suicide in terms of affect and affirmation (233–34).

10. As we have seen in chapter 1, to avoid a dualism that comes from so sharply confining mind to humanity that other organisms are comparable to mechanical devices, we must adopt the strong continuity thesis on biological cognition. As we recall, the point is not to ascribe mind as self-consciousness to organisms but to think of biological cognition as sense-making in its threefold nature: (1) sensibility (ability to sense/perceive difference in the environment); (2) signification (the ability to "meaningfully" distinguish what is good for the organism from what is bad for it); and (3) directionality or orientating itself in the environment with regard to its judgment as to what is good and bad for it.

11. Noting, of course, the overuse of antibiotics, which has bred superbacteria.

12. Foucault 1994: "Death is therefore multiple, and dispersed in time . . . long after the death of the individual, miniscule, partial deaths continue to dissociate the islets of life that still subsist" (141).

13. The notion of xenotransplantation will need to be thought of in this register, as well as the nontransplantability of the brain, which establishes brain death as the threshold beyond which organ harvesting is allowed. On these points, see Agamben's relatively rushed analyses in *Homo Sacer* (1997, 160–65). Agamben earlier discusses Aristotelian potentiality, but in the context of sovereign power, not organismic unity (1997, 44–48); as I have argued, the two are indissociable.

14. The home plays a particularly important role in American jurisprudence on privacy, starting with Bill of Rights strictures against forced quartering of soldiers and against unreasonable searches.

6. The Columbine High School Massacre

1. *Advocate* (Baton Rouge, Louisiana), April 21, 2004. An Ascension Parish grand jury declined to indict the two, citing insufficient evidence.

2. While many researchers list anger as a basic emotion, Panksepp 1998 lists rage as one of his basic emotions (see chart at Jonathan Turner 2000, 68–69).

3. Studies on electrical stimulation of the brains (ESB) in rats have shown male competition for access to sexual resources as a possible third type of brain circuit (94).

4. The connection of such rage blackouts and the legal category of temporary

insanity is an important question we cannot entertain here. Averill 1982 offers a useful treatment of some of the legal history and issues in the insanity and temporary insanity categories. The burgeoning field of legal neuroscience will be increasingly important in this area. See Marcus 2002 for an introduction to the field of general neuroethics; for a widely cited article in legal neuroscience, see Greene and Cohen 2004.

5. Homologies are organs in different species united by common descent. Analogies are organs in different species united by similar function. Panksepp 1998 (17) has a brief discussion.

6. In some territorial mammal species, such as lions, a newly victorious alpha male will try to kill the offspring of his defeated adversary. My point concerns the display and submission behavior among animals of the same generation, hence of roughly the same size, in one-on-one combat. The well-known phenomena of chimpanzee wars and murders always involve ambushes in which at least two but often seven or eight chimpanzees will attack a single, isolated victim (see de Waal 1996, 38). Insect warfare seems too far removed from our concerns to be interesting, unless we attain an extremely high level of abstraction concerning mass society. The Western cultural figuring of Asian societies as anthills or insect colonies, however, deserves attention.

7. See Damasio 1994 (165–201) for an extended discussion of somatic markers, particularly 180–83 for the role of somatic mapping in the prefrontal cortex. Damasio cites work in mirror neurons located in the cortex as possibly involved in as-if loops or "internal simulation" (1999, 281). See also Colombetti and Thompson 2007 (59–60) for an important clarification: the somatic marker provoked by a neural as-if body loop is not a disembodied representation but a felt quality continuously maintained and updated with bodily information, specifically with the full range of biochemical activity that cannot be simulated in a neural as-if loop.

8. As the anonymous reviewer of a version of this argument reminded me, the standard evolutionary explanation for the adoption of signaling rather than fighting among nonhuman animal conspecifics does not involve empathetic identification but rather an instinctually embedded cost-benefit analysis. For example, the risk of harm from a fight outweighs the benefits of mating, so that it is better to accept defeat and wait to find another opportunity later.

9. These phenomena suggest that political physiology as the imbrication of social and somatic can shed light on pornography and thanatography (the bodily reaction to images of violence). I hope to treat their intersection in the Abu Ghraib scandal as well as in the current wave of torture porn films (the *Saw* and *Hostel* series in particular, but let's not forget Mel Gibson's *The Passion of the Christ*) in a follow-up book with the working title "Extreme Philosophy." In doing so, I will continue the line of investigation Susan Hurley began in her work on media violence (2004).

10. See Niehoff 1999 (75), citing Archer 1988 on "protective aggression"; on the release of norepinephrine in attack situations (127); and for a summary of Gray

1977, which postulates a behavioral inhibition system tied to physiological arousal (130).

11. See LeDoux 1996 for the role of the amygdala in the unconscious and non-verbal "emotional memory system" (200–203); see Bloom 1999 for clinical problems in treating people burdened with nonverbally stored traumatic memories.

12. As we recall, a singularity is a critical point in a system's structure and history in which a change of behavior patterns is possible. Singularities in social systems are such that a vague suggestion from a monarch ("Will no one rid me of this meddlesome priest?") will preserve "plausible deniability" while at the same time being as effective as a direct command from a superior closer in rank to the killer.

13. The long-distance killing by the Allies in the European theater of World War II was no less effective than that of the Pacific theater, even though the race hatred directed at the Germans was nowhere near as intense as that directed at the Japanese (Dower 1987).

14. This is, by the way, an excellent example of the Deleuzian distaste for essentialism: you're never going to be able to come up with a set of necessary and sufficient conditions to define "courage"; much better to investigate the morphogenesis of warrior and soldierly bodies and see if there are any common structures to those production processes. We must ask how the warrior and the soldier are different actualizations of the virtual multiplicity linking political physiology and geopolitics.

15. See Grossman 1996 (180–85) for military use of psychopaths, where he unfortunately relates psychopathology to a "genetic predisposition." For a nonreductionist biological account of psychopaths as individuals with low-intensity set points, that is, high thresholds for reward and punishment, see Niehoff 1999 (129 and 181), and also on psychopathology and "kindling" (need for greater and greater stimulus) (166). We could hypothesize that in addition to their "stimulus hunger," there is some malfunction in the mirror neurons of true cold-blooded killers: they just do not identify with the victim.

16. We are dealing with very complex matters here regarding post-traumatic stress disorder (PTSD) in the current Iraq campaign (Hoge et al. 2004). Anecdotal evidence relayed to the author in personal communication by Lieutenant Colonel Pete Kilner of West Point suggests that officers who had talked and thought about the aftereffects of killing had less guilt than did enlisted men and women who had no such preparation.

17. Here we see that the "extended mind" hypothesis need not always be happy-go-lucky technophilia. Not that all such treatments descend to that level, but there is at least a trend in that direction in the literature.

7. Hurricane Katrina

1. An evocative portrayal of the Mississippi can be found in Barry 1998. A number of quite small river drainage systems in Texas and Alabama empty di-

rectly into the Gulf of Mexico, but the quantities here are negligible compared to the Mississippi.

2. For details on the historical geography of New Orleans, see Colten 2004. Colten reports that by 1727 the French in New Orleans had added a four-foot-high bulwark (19), by 1763 levees reached fifty miles upriver (20), and by 1812 the year of Louisiana statehood, levees reached to Baton Rouge on the east bank (21).

3. See also Martin and Zajac 2005. The Corps' claim that the levees were in good condition but were simply "overtopped" has been debunked by other reviews (Grunwald and Glasser 2005; van Heerden 2007).

4. The pressure surge accompanying a hurricane, as water rises due to low air pressure, is quite small in comparison to the wind-driven storm surge.

5. An excellent primer on hurricane formation can be found on NASA's Web site, http://earthobservatory.nasa.gov/Library/Hurricanes/printall.php.

6. General Carl Strock of the Army Corps of Engineers claims that coastal erosion did not play a role in the storm surge of Hurricane Katrina because the storm bypassed the barrier islands south and west of the city (U.S. Army Corps of Engineers 2005). This claim is criticized in van Heerden 2007.

7. The cognitive decision-making powers of peasant societies are sometimes decentralized and hidden in ritual. For an analysis of Balinese peasant society along these lines—and the superiority of these practices to centralized and bureaucratized decision making—see Lansing 1991 and 2006.

8. According to Fogel and Engerman 1974: "While the great majority of slaves were agricultural laborers, it is not true that these agriculturalists [were proletarianized. Most were] slaves engaged in the full range of agricultural activities. These included the planting, raising, and harvesting of virtually every type of crop, as well as animal husbandry, dairying, land improvement, use and maintenance of equipment and machinery, and the construction of buildings" (41).

9. On sugar and tea, see Mintz 1985; on coffee and other stimulants in European modernity, see Schivelbusch 1993; on coffee and tea as sources of caffeine, see Weinberg and Bealer 2002. On the Opium Wars, see Fay 1998.

10. For a refreshingly critical overall look at Jefferson, see Wills 2003; on Jefferson's sales of slaves, 121. On the magnitude of the internal slave trade, see Berlin 2004. "Driven by the cotton and sugar revolutions in the southern interior, the massive deportation [a "Second Middle Passage"] displaced more than a million men and women, dwarfing the transatlantic slave trade that had carried Africans to the mainland" (161).

11. "Endorphins" is shorthand for a variety of neuropeptides that allow for stress-induced analgesia. For general overviews of this phenomenon, see Bloom 1999; LeDoux 1996, 132; or Niehoff 1999, 146–47.

12. The infamous Gretna bridge incident, where police blocked passage of refugees from Katrina coming out of New Orleans, is a singularity that marks a thresh-

old along a racial differential: New Orleans is 66 percent black, Gretna is 33 percent black. For immediate reporting, see Johnson 2005; for a considered view, see Brinkley 2007.

13. Some of those who stayed behind were "essential personnel" for city government and private business; these people were required by their employers to stay. Those dependent on these essential personnel also tended to stay.

14. As reported in the *Wall Street Journal*, September 15, 2005, B1: "Congressional Republicans, backed by the White House, say they are using relief measures for the hurricane-ravaged Gulf coast to achieve a broad range of conservative economic and social policies, both in the storm zone and beyond. Some new measures are already taking shape. In the past week, the Bush administration has suspended some union-friendly rules that require federal contractors pay prevailing wages, moved to ease tariffs on Canadian lumber, and allowed more foreign sugar imports to calm rising sugar prices. Just yesterday, it waived some affirmative-action rules for employers with federal contracts in the Gulf region." Six weeks later, Bush was forced to restore the prevailing wage features of the Davis-Bacon Act, but congressional testimony in 2007 to the House Domestic Policy Subcommittee spoke of a "'wild, wild West' environment in New Orleans that has subjected the workforce to hazardous working conditions and wage theft" (Kucinich 2007).

15. The most likely origin of the riot rumor is that panicked prisoners, locked in their cells and abandoned by guards fleeing the building, were making noise to be rescued, per Human Rights Watch 2005.

16. The following articles debunked the carnage myths within a week to a month afterward: Younge 2005; CNN 2005; Thevenot and Russell 2005; and Dwyer and Drew 2005. For critical reflection on such disaster myths, see Tierney, Bevc, and Kuligowski 2006.

17. This interpretation has been offered by my colleague Alexandre Leupin. It should be noted that any surprise at "black" government officials repeating racialized rumors relies on the faulty assumption of a binary racial system in New Orleans and, furthermore, overlooks the taking up by the NOPD of the traditional role of free people of color in maintaining slave order.

18. Bush 2005. This is not the time to enter the details of the controversy surrounding the possible or threatened invocation of the Insurrection Act as it would affect relations between state and federal officials concerning the federalization of military operations versus the maintenance of state control over the Louisiana National Guard. For brief discussions, see Brinkley 2007 (569) and Tierney and Bevc 2007 (44–45).

19. Hobbes will acknowledge the possibility of temporary alliances in the state of nature, as in this passage from *Leviathan*, chapter 13, "On the Natural Condition of Mankind," where he writes: "If one plant, sow, build, or possesse a convenient Seat, others may probably be expected to come prepared with forces united." So, while people can form temporary alliances in the state of nature, they won't be able to form

durable political units if these fall short of the absolute sovereign. Timescales are the key here: the longer the state of nature goes on (and Hobbes is as equally concerned with competition for honor in the state of nature as he is with competition for material goods), the more the atomizing forces take hold.

20. For testimonies about volunteer rescue efforts, see van Heerden 2007 and Brinkley 2007. For a sociological take that confirms that such prosocial behavior is the norm in disasters and catastrophes, see Rodriguez, Trainor, and Quarantelli 2006.

21. See Hendriks-Jansen 1996 (252–77) for a fascinating discussion of caretaker-infant interaction, with extensive citations of the relevant literature. See also Schore 1994.

22. For social solidarity through entrainment, see McNeill 1995. See also Freeman 2000a and 2000b. For a general treatment of entrainment, see Strogatz 2003.

23. Reports of defecation on the floor of looted shops as a sign of social revenge need to be thought of as well (Brinkley 2007, 506). This practice is apparently not uncommon in burglaries of homes of wealthy people (Friedmaan 1968). For a comparison of pre- and post-Katrina crime rates in New Orleans, with attention paid to the impoverishment of the population following deindustrialization and the subsequent shift to poor-paying service work, see Frailing and Harper 2007.

Bibliography

Abrahamson, Warren, and Arthur Weis. 1997. *Evolutionary Ecology across Three Trophic Levels.* Princeton, N.J.: Princeton University Press.

Ackrill, J. L. 1999. "Aristotle on Eudaimonia." In *Aristotle's "Ethics,"* edited by Nancy Sherman. New York: Rowman and Littlefield.

Adolphs, Ralph. 2002. "Social Cognition and the Human Brain." In *Foundations in Social Neuroscience,* edited by John Cacioppo et al. Cambridge, Mass.: MIT Press.

————. 2004. "Emotion, Social Cognition, and the Human Brain." In *Essays in Social Neuroscience,* edited by John Cacioppo and Gary Bernston. Cambridge, Mass.: MIT Press.

Agamben, Giorgio. 1997. *Homo Sacer: Sovereign Power and Bare Life.* Translated by Daniel Heller-Roazen. Stanford, Calif.: Stanford University Press.

————. 1999a. *Remnants of Auschwitz: The Witness and the Archive.* Translated by Daniel Heller-Roazen. New York: Zone Books.

————. 1999b. *Potentialities.* Translated by Daniel Heller-Roazen. Stanford, Calif.: Stanford University Press.

————. 2004. *The Open: Man and Animal.* Translated by Kevin Attell. Stanford, Calif.: Stanford University Press.

————. 2005. *State of Exception.* Translated by Kevin Attell. Chicago: University of Chicago Press.

Allport, Gordon, and Leo Postman. 1947. *The Psychology of Rumor.* New York: Henry Holt.

American Civil Liberties Union (ACLU). 2006. FBI Document claimed via Freedom of Information Act. http://action.aclu.org/torturefoia/released/022306/2600.pdf.

Andrews, K., L. Murphy, R. Munday, et al. 1996. "Misdiagnosis of the Vegetative State: Retrospective Study in Rehabilitation Unit." *British Medical Journal* 313: 13–16.

Ansell Pearson, Keith. 1999. *Germinal Life: The Difference and Repetition of Deleuze.* London: Routledge.

Aquila, Richard. 1991. "Unity of Organism, Unity of Thought, and the Unity of the Critique of Judgment." *Southern Journal of Philosophy* 30:139–55.

Archer, John. 1988. *The Behavioral Biology of Aggression.* Cambridge: Cambridge University Press.

Arendt, Hannah. 1998. *The Human Condition.* Chicago: University of Chicago Press.

Arnhart, Larry. 1994a. "The Darwinian Biology of Aristotle's Political Animals." *American Journal of Political Science* 38, no. 2:464–85.

———. 1994b. "A Sociobiological Defense of Aristotle's Sexual Politics." *International Political Science Review* 15, no. 4:389–415.

Arquilla, John, and David Ronfeldt. 2000. *Swarming and the Future of Conflict.* Santa Monica, Calif.: RAND Corporation.

Ash, Timothy Garton. 2005. "Just Below the Surface." *Guardian Weekly,* September 9.

Averill, James R. 1982. *Anger and Aggression: An Essay on Emotion.* New York: Springer.

Bailey, Ronald. 1998. " 'Those Valuable People, the Africans': The Economic Impact of the Slave(ry) Trade on Textile Industrialization in New England." In *The Meaning of Slavery in the North,* edited by D. Roediger and M. H. Blatt. New York: Garland.

Bargh, John, and Tanya Chartrand. 1999. "The Unbearable Automaticity of Being." *American Psychologist* 54:462–79.

Barnes, Jonathan, ed. 1984. *The Complete Works of Aristotle.* Princeton, N.J.: Princeton University Press.

Barry, John. 1998. *Rising Tide: The Great Mississippi Flood of 1927 and How It Changed America.* New York: Simon and Schuster.

Bartky, Sandra. 1988. "Foucault, Femininity, and the Modernization of Patriarchal Power." In *Feminism and Foucault: Paths of Resistance,* edited by Lee Quinby and Irene Diamond. Boston: Northeastern University Press.

Baugh, Bruce. 2003. *French Hegel: From Surrealism to Postmodernism.* New York: Routledge.

Berghaus, Günther. 1996. "The Ritual Core of Fascist Theatre." In *Fascism and Theatre: Comparative Studies on the Aesthetics and Politics of Performance in Europe, 1925–1945,* edited by Günther Berghaus. Providence, R.I.: Berghahn Books.

Berlin, Ira. 2004. *Generations of Captivity: A History of African-American Slaves.* Cambridge, Mass.: Harvard University Press, Belknap Press.

Bernston, Gary, and John Cacioppo. 2004. "Multilevel Analyses and Reductionism: Why Social Psychologists Should Care about Neuroscience and Vice Versa." In *Essays in Social Neuroscience,* edited by John Cacioppo and Gary Bernston. Cambridge, Mass.: MIT Press.

Beyerstein, Lindsay. 2005. "Local cops thwart tube-rape conspiracy." *Majikthise,* March 26. http://majikthise.typepad.com/majikthise_/2005/03/local_cops_thwa.html.

Blackburn, Robin. 1988. *The Overthrow of Colonial Slavery: 1776–1848.* London: Verso.

———. 1997. *The Making of New World Slavery.* London: Verso.

Blair, James, Derek Mitchell, and Karina Blair. 2005. *The Psychopath: Emotion and the Brain.* Oxford: Blackwell.

Bloom, Sandra. 1999. Trauma Theory Abbreviated. http://www.sanctuaryweb .com.

Bonta, Mark, and John Protevi. 2004. *Deleuze and Geophilosophy.* Edinburgh: Edinburgh University Press.

Boogerd, F. C., F. J. Bruggeman, R. C. Richardson, A. Stephan, and H. V. Westerhoff. 2005. "Emergence and Its Place in Nature: A Case Study of Biochemical Networks." *Synthese* 145:131–64.

Bordo, Susan. 1993. "Anorexia Nervosa: Psychopathology as the Crystallization of Culture." In *Unbearable Weight: Feminism, Western Culture, and the Body.* Berkeley: University of California Press.

Bourne, Joel. 2000. "Louisiana's Vanishing Wetlands: Going, Going . . ." *Science* 289 (September 15): 1860–63.

———. 2004. "Gone with the Water." *National Geographic* (October).

Bradshaw, David. 2001. "A New Look at the Prime Mover." *Journal of the History of Philosophy* 39, no. 1:1–22.

Braidotti, Rosi. 2002. *Metamorphoses: Towards a Materialist Theory of Becoming.* Cambridge, England: Polity Press.

———. 2006. *Transpositions: On Nomadic Ethics.* Cambridge, England: Polity Press.

Bräten, Stein, ed. 1998. *Intersubjective Communication and Emotion in Early Ontogeny.* New York: Cambridge University Press.

Braver, Lee. 2007. *A Thing of This World: A History of Continental Anti-Realism.* Evanston, Ill.: Northwestern University Press.

Brinkley, Douglas. 2007. *The Great Deluge: Hurricane Katrina, New Orleans, and the Mississippi Gulf Coast.* New York: Harper Perennial.

British Broadcasting Company. 2006. "British Army Discipline and Capital Punishment 1914." http://www.bbc.co.uk/dna/h2g2/A944363.

Brown, Drew. 2006. "FBI Memos Reveal Allegations of Abusive Interrogation Techniques." Knight-Ridder Washington Bureau, February 23. http://www.realcities .com/mld/krwashington/13945827.htm.

Brown, Steven. 2005. "Collective Emotions: Artaud's Nerves." *Culture and Organization* 11, no. 4 (December): 235–47.

Brown, Wendy. 2006. "American Nightmare: Neoliberalism, Neoconservatism, and De-democratization." *Political Theory* 34, no. 6:690–714.

Bryant, Salatheia, and Cynthia Leonor Garza. 2005. "School Bus Commandeered by Renegade Refugees First to Arrive at Astrodome." *Houston Chronicle,* September 1.

Burden, Hamilton. 1967. *The Nuremberg Party Rallies: 1923–1939.* New York: Praeger.

Burke, Carol. 2004. *Camp All-American, Hanoi Jane, and the High-and-Tight: Gender, Folklore, and Changing Military Culture.* Boston: Beacon Press.

Burnyeat, Miles. 1980. "Aristotle on Learning to Be Good." In *Essays on Aristotle's Ethics*, edited by Amélie Oksenberg Rorty. Berkeley: University of California Press.

Bush, George W. 2005. "President Discusses Hurricane Relief in Address to Nation." White House press release, September 15.

Butler, Judith. 1989. "Sexual Ideology and Phenomenological Description: A Feminist Critique of Merleau-Ponty's *Phenomenology of Perception.*" In *The Thinking Muse: Feminism and Modern French Philosophy*, edited by Jeffner Allen and Iris Marion Young. Bloomington: Indiana University Press.

Cacioppo, John, and Penny Visser. 2003. "Political Psychology and Social Neuroscience: Strange Bedfellows or Comrades in Arms?" *Political Psychology* 24, no. 4: 647–56.

Canetti, Elias. 1984. *Crowds and Power.* Translated by Carol Stewart. New York: Farrar, Straus, and Giroux.

Carney, Judith. 2002. *Black Rice: The African Origins of Rice Cultivation in the Americas.* Cambridge, Mass.: Harvard University Press.

Chalmers, David. 1995. "Facing Up to the Problem of Consciousness." *Journal of Consciousness Studies* 2, no. 3:200–219.

Chenelly, Joseph. 2005. "Troops Begin Combat Operations in New Orleans." *Army Times*, September 2.

Chernin, Kim. 1994. *The Obsession: Reflections on the Tyranny of Slenderness.* New York: Perennial.

Cheshire, William. 2005. Report to the Florida Department of Children and Families, March 23. http://www.dcf.state.fl.us/news/affidavit.pdf.

Christensen, Wayne, and Cliff Hooker. 2001. "Self-directed Agents." In "Contemporary Naturalist Theories of Evolution and Intentionality," edited by J. MacIntosh, special supplementary volume, *Canadian Journal of Philosophy* 31.

Clark, Andy. 1997. *Being There: Putting Brain, Body and World Together Again.* Cambridge, Mass.: MIT Press.

———. 2003. *Natural-Born Cyborgs: Minds, Technologies, and the Future of Human Intelligence.* New York: Oxford University Press.

———. 2006. "Vision as Dance? Three Challenges for Sensorimotor Contingency Theory." *Psyche.* http://psyche.cs.monash.edu.au/.

CNN. 2005. "Police Reject 'Vicious Rumors' of Dead Children; No Confirmed Sexual Assaults." September 9, 1:02 p.m. http://www.cnn.com/2005/US/09/07/news.update/index.html.

Cohen, Jack, and Ian Stewart, 1994. *The Collapse of Chaos.* New York: Penguin.

Cole, Juan. 2003. "Al-Qaeda's Doomsday Document and Psychological Manipulation." http://www.juancole.com/essays/qaeda.htm.

Colombetti, Giovanna, and Evan Thompson. 2007. "The Feeling Body: Toward an Enactive Approach to Emotion." In *Developmental Aspects of Embodiment and Con-*

sciousness (Jean Piaget Symposia), edited by Willis F. Overton, Ulrich Mueller, and Judith Newman, 45–68. Hillsdale, N.J.: Lawrence Erlbaum.

Colten, Craig. 2004. *An Unnatural Metropolis: Wresting New Orleans from Nature.* Baton Rouge: Louisiana State University Press.

Cooper, Christopher. 2005. "Old line families escape the worst; plot the future; Mr. O'Dwyer, at his mansion, enjoys highball with ice; meeting with the mayor." *Wall Street Journal,* September 8.

Cornell, Drucilla. 2005. "Who Bears the Right to Die?" *Graduate Faculty Philosophy Journal* 26, no. 1:173–88.

Correll, J., G. Urland, and T. Ito. 2006. "Event-Related Potentials and the Decision to Shoot: The Role of Threat Perception and Cognitive Control." *Journal of Experimental Social Psychology* 42:120–28.

Cosmides, Leda, John Tooby, and Robert Kurzban. 2003. "Perceptions of Race." *Trends in Cognitive Sciences* 7, no. 4 (April): 173–79.

Cullen, Dave. 1999. "Inside the Columbine High Investigation." http://www.salon.com (September 23).

———. 2004. "The Depressive and the Psychopath." http://Slate.msn.com/id/2099203 (April 20).

Damasio, Antonio. 1994. *Descartes' Error.* New York: Avon.

———. 1999. *The Feeling of What Happens.* New York: Harcourt.

———. 2003. *Looking for Spinoza.* New York: Harcourt.

Davis, M. 1992. "The Role of the Amygdala in Fear-Potentiated Startle: Implications for Animal Models of Anxiety." *Trends in Pharmacological Science* 13:35–41.

Dawkins, Richard. 2006. *The Selfish Gene.* 3rd ed. New York: Oxford University Press.

Decety, Jean, and Claus Lamm. 2006. "Human Empathy through the Lens of Social Neuroscience." *Scientific World Journal* 6:1146–63.

DeLanda, Manuel. 1991. *War in the Age of Intelligent Machines.* New York: Zone Books.

———. 1997. *A Thousand Years of Nonlinear History.* New York: Zone Books.

———. 2002. *Intensive Science and Virtual Philosophy.* London: Continuum.

———. 2006. *A New Philosophy of Society: Assemblage Theory and Social Complexity.* London: Continuum.

Deleuze, Gilles. 1968. *Différence et répétition.* Paris: Presses Universitaires de France.

———. 1969. *Logique du sens.* Paris: Minuit.

———. 1983. *Nietzsche and Philosophy.* Translated by Hugh Tomlinson. New York: Columbia University Press.

———. 1988. *Spinoza: Practical Philosophy.* Translated by Robert Hurley. San Francisco: City Lights.

———. 1990a. *Logic of Sense.* Translated by Mark Lester, with Charles Stivale. New York: Columbia University Press.

————. 1990b. *Pourparlers*. Paris: Minuit.

————. 1994. *Difference and Repetition*. Translated by Paul Patton. New York: Columbia University Press.

————. 1995. *Negotiations*. Translated by Martin Joughin. New York: Columbia University Press.

————. 2004. "The Method of Dramatization." Translated by Michael Taormina. In *Desert Islands and Other Texts*, edited by David Lapoujade. New York: Semiotexte.

Deleuze, Gilles, and Félix Guattari. 1972. *L'Anti-Oedipe*. Paris: Minuit.

————. 1980. *Mille Plateaux*. Paris: Minuit.

————. 1984. *Anti-Oedipus*. Translated by Robert Hurley, Mark Seem, and Helen R. Lane. Minneapolis: University of Minnesota Press.

————. 1987. *A Thousand Plateaus*. Translated by Brian Massumi. Minneapolis: University of Minnesota Press.

de Waal, Frans. 1996. *Good Natured: The Origins of Right and Wrong in Humans and Other Animals*. Cambridge, Mass.: Harvard University Press.

————. 2006. *Primates and Philosophers*. Princeton, N.J.: Princeton University Press.

Dower, John. 1987. *War without Mercy*. New York: Pantheon.

Dreyfus, Hubert. 1991. *Being-in-the-World: A Commentary on Heidegger's Being and Time, Division I*. Cambridge, Mass.: MIT Press.

————. 1992 [1972]. *What Computers Still Can't Do: A Critique of Artificial Reason*. Cambridge, Mass.: MIT Press.

Dunbar, Robin. 1998. "The Social Brain Hypothesis." *Evolutionary Anthropology* 6:178–90.

Dworkin, Ronald. 1988. *Law's Empire*. Cambridge, Mass.: Belknap Press, Harvard University Press.

————. 1993. *Life's Dominion*. New York: Knopf.

Dwyer, Jim, and Christopher Drew. 2005. "Fear Exceeded Crime's Reality in New Orleans." *New York Times*, September 29.

Dyke, Chuck. 1988. "Cities as Dissipative Systems." In *Entropy, Information and Evolution*, edited by Bruce Weber, David Depew, and James Smith. Cambridge, Mass.: MIT Press.

————. 1989. *The Evolutionary Dynamics of Complex Systems: A Study in Biosocial Complexity*. Oxford: Oxford University Press.

————. 1990. "Strange Attraction, Curious Liaison: Clio Meets Chaos." *Philosophical Forum* 21, no. 4 (Summer): 369–92.

————. 1999. "Bourdieuean Dynamics." In *Bourdieu: A Critical Reader*, edited by Richard Shusterman. Oxford: Basil Blackwell.

————. 2006. "Primer: On Thinking Dynamically about the Human Ecological Condition." In *How Nature Speaks: The Dynamics of the Human Ecological System*, edited by Yrjö Haila and Chuck Dyke. Durham, N.C.: Duke University Press.

Ehrenreich, Barbara. 1997. *Blood Rites*. New York: Henry Holt.

Ekman, Paul. 1992. "An Argument for Basic Emotions." *Cognition and Emotion* 6:169–200.

Fabing, Howard. 1956. "On Going Berserk: A Neurochemical Inquiry." *American Journal of Psychiatry* 113 (November): 409–15.

Fausto-Sterling, Anne. 2000. *Sexing the Body: Gender Politics and the Construction of Sexuality.* New York: Basic Books.

Fay, Peter Ward. 1998. *The Opium War, 1840–1842: Barbarians in the Celestial Empire in the Early Part of the Nineteenth Century and the War by Which They Forced Her Gates Ajar.* Chapel Hill: University of North Carolina Press.

Ferber, Dan. 2004. "Dead Zone Fix Is Not a Dead Issue." *Science* 305 (September 10): 1557.

Fine, Gary, and Patricia Turner. 2001. *Whispers on the Color Line.* Berkeley: University of California Press.

Fischetti, Mark. 2001. "Drowning New Orleans." *Scientific American* 285, no. 4 (October): 76–86.

Fitzpatrick, Kevin. 2005. "Bare Sovereignty: *Homo Sacer* and the Insistence of Law." In *Politics, Metaphysics and Death: Essays on Giorgio Agamben's "Homo Sacer,"* edited by Andrew Norris. Durham, N.C.: Duke University Press.

Fletcher, J. D. 1999. "Using Networked Simulation to Assess Problem Solving by Tactical Teams." *Computers in Human Behavior* 15:375–402.

Fogel, William, and Stanley Engerman. 1974. *Time on the Cross: The Economics of American Negro Slavery.* New York: Norton.

Fonstad, Mark, and W. Andrew Marcus. 2003. "Self-Organized Criticality in Riverbank Systems." *Annals of the Association of American Geographers* 93, no. 2: 281–96.

Foucault, Michel. 1972. *The Archaeology of Knowledge and the Discourse on Language.* Translated by A. M. Sheridan Smith. New York: Pantheon.

———. 1977. *Discipline and Punish: The Birth of the Prison.* Translated by Alan Sheridan. New York: Vintage.

———. 1978. *The History of Sexuality.* Vol. 1, *An Introduction.* Translated by Robert Hurley. New York: Pantheon.

———. 1994. *The Birth of the Clinic.* Translated by A. M. Sheridan Smith. New York: Vintage.

———. 2003. *"Society Must Be Defended": Lectures at the Collège de France, 1975–76.* Translated by David Macey. New York: Picador.

———. 2004. *Naissance de la biopolitique.* Paris: Seuil.

Frailing, Kelly, and Dee Wood Harper. 2007. "Crime and Hurricanes in New Orleans." In *The Sociology of Katrina: Perspectives on a Modern Catastrophe,* edited by David Brunsma, David Overfelt, and J. Steven Picou. New York: Rowman and Littlefield.

Freeman, Walter J. 2000a. *How Brains Make Up Their Minds.* New York: Columbia University Press.

———. 2000b. "Emotion Is Essential to All Intentional Behaviors." In *Emotion, Development and Self-Organization: Dynamic Systems Approaches to Emotional Development*, edited by Marc Lewis and Isabela Granic. New York: Cambridge University Press.

Friedmaan, Albert. 1968. "The Scatological Rites of Burglars." *Western Folklore 27*, no. 3 (July): 171–79.

Furley, David J. 1980. "Self-Movers." In *Essays on Aristotle's Ethics*, edited by Amélie Oksenberg Rorty. Berkeley: University of California Press.

Gallagher, Shaun. 2005. *How the Body Shapes the Mind*. New York: Oxford University Press.

Gallese, Vittorio. 2001. "The 'Shared Manifold' Hypothesis: From Mirror Neurons to Empathy." *Journal of Consciousness Studies 8*, nos. 5–7:33–50.

Gallese, Vittorio, and Alvin Goldman. 1998. "Mirror Neurons and the Simulation Theory of Mind-Reading." *Trends in Cognitive Sciences* 2:493–501.

Gallese, Vittorio, C. Keysers, and G. Rizzolatti. 2004. "A Unifying View of the Basis of Social Cognition." *Trends in Cognitive Sciences 8*, no. 9:396–403.

Gatens, Moira, and Genevieve Lloyd. 1999. *Collective Imaginings: Spinoza, Past and Present*. New York: Routledge.

Gianino, J. T., et al. 2002. "The Minimally Conscious State: Definition and Diagnostic Criteria." *Neurology* 58:349–53.

Ginsborg, Hannah. 2001. "Kant on Understanding Organisms as Natural Purposes." In *Kant and the Sciences*, edited by Eric Watkins. Oxford: Oxford University Press.

———. 2004. "Two Kinds of Mechanical Inexplicability in Kant and Aristotle." *Journal of the History of Philosophy 42*, no. 1:33–65.

Goldberg, S. B., C. W. Landsea, A. M. Mestas-Nunez, and W. M. Gray. 2001. "The Recent Increase in Atlantic Hurricane Activity: Causes and Implications." *Science* 293 (July 20): 474–79.

Goldstein, Jeffrey. 1999. "Emergence as a Construct: History and Issues." *Emergence* 1, no. 1:49–72.

Gotthelf, Allan, ed. 1985. *Aristotle on Nature and Living Things: Philosophical and Historial Studies Presented to David M. Balme on His Seventieth Birthday*. Bristol: Bristol Classical Press.

Gotthelf, Allan, and James Lennox, eds. 1987. *Philosophical Issues in Aristotle's Biology*. Cambridge: Cambridge University Press.

Gould, Stephen Jay. 1988. "Kropotkin Was No Crackpot." *Natural History 97*, no. 7:12–18.

Gray, J. A. 1977. "Drug Effects on Fear and Frustration: Possible Limbic Site of Action of Minor Tranquilizers." In *Handbook of Psychopharmacology*, edited by L. L. Iversen, S. D. Iversen, and S. H. Snyder. Vol. 8, *Drugs, Transmitters, and Behavior*. New York: Plenum.

Greenberg, Karen, and Joshua Dratel. 2005. *The Torture Papers: The Road to Abu Ghraib*. Cambridge: Cambridge University Press.

Greene, Joshua. 2003. "From Neural 'Is' to Moral 'Ought': What Are the Moral Implications of Neuroscientific Moral Psychology?" *Nature Reviews Neuroscience* 4 (October): 847–50.

———. 2008. "The Secret Joke of Kant's Soul." In *Moral Psychology*, edited by Walter Sinnott-Armstrong. Vol. 3, *The Neuroscience of Morality: Emotion, Brain Disorders, and Development*. Cambridge, Mass.: MIT Press.

Greene, Joshua, and Jonathan Cohen. 2004. "For the Law, Neuroscience Changes Everything and Nothing." *Philosophical Transactions of the Royal Society of London* B359:1775–85.

Greene, Joshua, and Jonathan Haidt. 2002. "How (and Where) Does Moral Judgment Work?" *Trends in Cognitive Sciences* 6, no. 12:517–23.

Grene, Marjorie, and David Depew. 2005. *The Philosophy of Biology: An Episodic History*. Cambridge: Cambridge University Press.

Griffiths, Paul. 1997. *What Emotions Really Are: The Problem of Psychological Categories*. Chicago: University of Chicago Press.

———. 2003. "Basic Emotions, Complex Emotions, Machiavellian Emotions." In *Philosophy and the Emotions*, edited by Anthony Hatzimoysis. New York: Cambridge University Press.

———. 2004. "Is Emotion a Natural Kind?" In *Thinking about Feeling: Contemporary Philosophers on Emotions*, edited by Robert Solomon. New York: Oxford University Press.

———. 2006. "Evolutionary Psychology." In *The Philosophy of Science: An Encyclopedia*, edited by Sahotra Sarkar. New York: Routledge.

Griffiths, Paul, and Russell Gray. 1997. "Replicator II—Judgement Day." *Biology and Philosophy* 12:471–92.

———. 2001. "Darwinism and Developmental Systems." In *Cycles of Contingency: Developmental Systems and Evolution*, edited by Susan Oyama, Paul Griffiths, and Russell Gray. Cambridge, Mass.: MIT Press.

———. 2004. "The Developmental Systems Perspective: Organism-Environment Systems as Units of Development and Evolution." In *Phenotypic Integration: Studying the Ecology and Evolution of Complex Phenotypes*, edited by Massimo Pigliucci and Katherine Preston. New York: Oxford University Press.

———. 2005. "Discussion: Three Ways to Misunderstand Developmental Systems Theory." *Biology and Philosophy* 20:417–25.

Griffiths, Paul, and Andrea Scarantino. 2009. "Emotions in the Wild: The Situated Perspective on Emotion." In *Cambridge Handbook of Situated Cognition*, edited by Philip Robbins and Murat Aydele. Cambridge: Cambridge University Press.

Griffiths, Paul, and Karola Stotz. 2000. "How the Mind Grows: A Developmental Perspective on the Biology of Cognition." *Synthese* 122:29–51.

Grossman, Dave. 1996. *On Killing: The Psychological Cost of Learning to Kill in War and Society*. Boston: Little, Brown.

Grunwald, Michael, and Susan B. Glasser. 2005. "Experts Say Faulty Levees Caused Much of Flooding." *Washington Post,* September 21, A1.

Guyer, Paul. 1991. "Natural Ends and the End of Nature: Reply to Richard Aquila." *Southern Journal of Philosophy* 30:157–65.

———, ed. 1992. *The Cambridge Companion to Kant.* Cambridge: Cambridge University Press.

———. 1996. *Kant and the Experience of Freedom.* Cambridge: Cambridge University Press.

———. 2001. "Organisms and the Unity of Science." In *Kant and the Sciences,* edited by Eric Watkins. Oxford: Oxford University Press.

Haidt, Jonathan. 2001. "The Emotional Dog and Its Rational Tail: A Social Intuitionist Approach to Moral Judgment." *Psychological Review* 108:814–34.

Haila, Yrjö, and Chuck Dyke, eds. 2006. *How Nature Speaks: The Dynamics of the Human Ecological System.* Durham, N.C.: Duke University Press.

Hall, Gwendolyn Midlo. 1992. *Africans in Colonial Louisiana.* Baton Rouge: Louisiana State University Press.

Hansen, Mark. 2000. "Becoming as Creative Involution? Contextualizing Deleuze and Guattari's Biophilosophy." *Postmodern Culture* 11, no. 1.

Hardt, Michael. 1993. *Gilles Deleuze: An Apprenticeship in Philosophy.* Minneapolis: University of Minnesota Press.

Hardt, Michael, and Antonio Negri. 2000. *Empire.* Cambridge, Mass.: Harvard University Press.

———. 2004. *Multitude: War and Democracy in the Age of Empire.* New York: Penguin.

Harris, William. 2001. *Restraining Rage: The Ideology of Anger Control in Classical Antiquity.* Cambridge, Mass.: Harvard University Press.

Hartman, Chester, and Gregory D. Squires. 2006. "Pre-Katrina, Post-Katrina." In *There Is No Such Thing as a Natural Disaster: Race, Class, and Hurricane Katrina,* edited by Chester Hartman and Gregory D. Squires. New York: Routledge.

Hatzimoysis, Anthony, ed. 2003. *Philosophy and the Emotions.* New York: Cambridge University Press.

Hauser, Marc. 2006. *Moral Minds: How Nature Designed Our Universal Sense of Right and Wrong.* New York: HarperCollins.

Hayles, N. Katherine. 1999. *How We Became Posthuman.* Chicago: University of Chicago Press.

Hendriks-Jansen, Horst. 1996. *Catching Ourselves in the Act: Situated Activity, Interactive Emergence, Evolution, and Human Thought.* Cambridge, Mass.: MIT Press.

Henwood, Doug. 1997. *Wall Street: How It Works and for Whom.* London: Verso.

Hirschfeld, Lawrence. 1996. *Race in the Making: Cognition, Culture, and the Child's Construction of Human Kinds.* Cambridge, Mass.: MIT Press.

Hobbes, Thomas. 2004. *Leviathan.* New York: Barnes and Noble.

Hoge C., C. Castro, S. Messer, D. McGurk, D. Cotting, and R. Koffman. 2004. "Combat

Duty in Iraq and Afghanistan, Mental Health Problems, and Barriers to Care." *New England Journal of Medicine* 351:13–22.

Holland, Eugene. 1999. *Deleuze and Guattari's Anti-Oedipus: Introduction to Schizoanalysis.* New York: Routledge.

Human Rights Watch. 2005. "New Orleans: Prisoners Abandoned to Floodwaters." http://www.hrw.org/english/docs/2005/09/22/usdom11773.htm.

Hurley, Susan. 1998. *Consciousness in Action.* Cambridge, Mass.: Harvard University Press.

———. 2004. "Imitation, Media Violence, and Free Speech." *Philosophical Studies* 117, nos. 1–2:165–218.

Hutchins, Edwin. 1995. *Cognition in the Wild.* Cambridge, Mass.: MIT Press.

Hüttemann, Andreas, and Orestis Terzidis. 2000. "Emergence in Physics." *International Studies in the Philosophy of Science* 14, no. 3:267–81.

Hutto, Daniel. 2008. *Folk Psychological Narratives: The Sociocultural Basis of Understanding Reasons.* Cambridge, Mass.: MIT Press.

Jablonka, Eva, and Marion J. Lamb. 2005. *Evolution in Four Dimensions: Genetic, Epigenetic, Behavioral, and Symbolic Variation in the History of Life.* Cambridge, Mass.: MIT Press.

James, C. L. R. 1989 [1938]. *The Black Jacobins: Toussaint L'Ouverture and the San Domingo Revolution.* New York: Vintage.

Johnson, Chip. 2005. "Police Made Their Storm Misery Worse." *San Francisco Chronicle,* September 9.

Joyce, Richard. 2007. *The Evolution of Morality.* Cambridge, Mass.: MIT Press.

Juarrero, Alicia. 1999. *Dynamics in Action: Intentional Behavior as a Complex System.* Cambridge, Mass.: MIT Press.

Kafetsios, Konstantin, and Eric LaRock. 2005. "Cognition and Emotion: Aristotelian Affinities with Contemporary Emotion Research." *Theory and Psychology* 15, no. 5:639–57.

Kahn, Charles. 1985. "The Place of the Prime Mover in Aristotle's Teleology." In *Aristotle on Nature and Living Things: Philosophical and Historical Studies Presented to David M. Balme on His Seventieth Birthday,* edited by Allan Gotthelf. Bristol: Bristol Classical Press.

Kant, Immanuel. 1956. *Critique of Practical Reason.* Translated by Lewis White Beck. Indianapolis: Bobbs-Merrill.

———. 1987. *Critique of Judgement.* Translated by Werner Pluhar. Indianapolis: Hackett.

Kaplan, Daniel, and Leon Glass. 1995. *Understanding Nonlinear Dynamics.* New York: Springer.

Keller, Evelyn Fox. 1996. *Refiguring Life: Metaphors of Twentieth Century Biology.* New York: Columbia University Press.

———. 2000. *The Century of the Gene.* Cambridge, Mass.: Harvard University Press.

Kilner, Pete. 2000. "Military Leaders' Obligation to Justify Killing in War." Presentation to the Joint Services Conference on Professional Ethics. Washington, D.C., January 27–28. http://www.usafa.edu/JSCOPE00/Kilner00.html.

Kirkland, Faris. 1995. "Postcombat Reentry." In *War Psychiatry: Textbook of Military Medicine, Part I*, edited by Russ Zajtchuk. Washington, D.C.: Office of the Surgeon General.

Klein, Naomi. 2007. *The Shock Doctrine: The Rise of Disaster Capitalism*. New York: Henry Holt.

Knutson, T. R., R. E. Tuleya, and Y. Kurihara. 1998. "Simulated Increase of Hurricane Intensities in a CO_2-Warmed Climate." *Science* 279:1018–20.

Kosman, Aryeh. 1969. "Aristotle's Definition of Motion." *Phronesis* 14:40–62.

———. 1987. "Animals and Other Beings in Aristotle." In *Philosophical Issues in Aristotle's Biology*, edited by Allan Gotthelf and James Lennox. Cambridge: Cambridge University Press.

Kraut, Richard. 1989. *Aristotle on the Human Good*. Princeton, N.J.: Princeton University Press.

———. 1999. "Aristotle on the Human Good. An Overview." In *Aristotle's "Ethics,"* edited by Nancy Sherman. New York: Rowman and Littlefield.

Kropotkin, Peter. 2007. *Mutual Aid: A Factor of Evolution*. London: Dodo Press.

Kucinich, Dennis. 2007. "Two Years after Hurricane Katrina and the Administration Still Refuses to Make Gulf Coast Recovery a Priority." Press release, August 29. http://www.kucinich.house.gov.

Laland, Kevin, and Gillian Brown. 2002. *Sense and Nonsense*. Oxford: Oxford University Press.

Lane, Richard D., and Lynn Nadel, eds. 2000. *Cognitive Neuroscience of Emotion*. New York: Oxford University Press.

Lansing, Stephen. 1991. *Priests and Programmers*. Princeton, N.J.: Princeton University Press.

———. 2006. *Perfect Order: Recognizing Complexity in Bali*. Princeton, N.J.: Princeton University Press.

Laureys, Stephen, Adrian Owen, and Nicholas Schiff. 2004. "Brain Function in Coma, Vegetative State, Minimally Conscious State, Locked-in Syndrome, and Brain Death." *Lancet Neurology* 3, no. 4 (September): 537–46.

LeDoux, Joseph. 1996. *The Emotional Brain*. New York: Simon and Schuster.

Lefebvre, Alexandre. 2005. "A New Image of Law: Deleuze and Jurisprudence." *Telos* 130 (Spring): 103–26.

———. 2008. *The Image of Law: Deleuze, Bergson, Spinoza*. Stanford, Calif.: Stanford University Press.

Lennox, James. 2001. *Aristotle's Philosophy of Biology: Studies in the Origins of Life Sciences*. Cambridge: Cambridge University Press.

Lewis, Marc. 2000. "Emotional Self-Organization at Three Timescales." In *Emotion, Development and Self-Organization: Dynamic Systems Approaches to Emotional De-*

velopment, edited by Marc Lewis and Isabela Granic. New York: Cambridge University Press.

———. 2005. "Bridging Emotion Theory and Neurobiology through Dynamic Systems Modeling." *Behavioral and Brain Science* 28:169–245.

Lewontin, Richard. 2002. *The Triple Helix: Gene, Organism, and Environment*. Cambridge, Mass.: Harvard University Press.

Libet, Benjamin. 2004. *Mind Time: The Temporal Factor in Consciousness*. Cambridge, Mass.: Harvard University Press.

Lifton, Robert. 1973. *Home from the War*. New York: Simon and Schuster.

Louisiana State University (LSU) Hurricane Center. 2004. "Hurricane Pam Exercise." http://hurricane.lsu.edu/floodprediction/PAM_Exercise04/.

Lowry, Rich. 2005. "A National Disgrace." *National Review Online*, September 2.

Luigi-Luis, Peter. 2002. "Emergence in Chemistry: Chemistry as the Embodiment of Emergence." *Foundations of Chemistry* 4, no. 3:183–200.

Macedonia, M. 2002. "Games, Simulation, and the Military Education Dilemma." http://www.educause.edu/ir/library/pdf/ffpiu018.pdf.

Maibom, Heidi. 2007. "The Presence of Others." *Philosophical Studies* 132, no. 2:161–90.

Makkreel, Rudolf. 1990. *Imagination and Interpretation in Kant*. Chicago: University of Chicago Press.

Marcus, Steven, ed. 2002. *Neuroethics: Mapping the Field*. New York: Dana Press.

Marshall, S. L. A. 1978. *Men against Fire: The Problem of Battle Command*. Norman: Oklahoma University Press.

Martin, Andrew, and Andrew Zajac. 2005. "Corps Officials: Funding Levels Not to Blame for Flooding." *Chicago Tribune*, September 1.

Massumi, Brian. 1992. *A User's Guide to Capitalism and Schizophrenia: Deviations from Deleuze and Guattari*. Cambridge, Mass.: MIT Press.

———. 2002. *Parables for the Virtual: Movement, Affect, Sensation*. Durham, N.C.: Duke University Press.

Maturana, Humberto, and Francisco J. Varela. 1980. *Autopoiesis and Cognition: The Realization of the Living*. Boston: Riedel.

Mayo, Thomas. 2005. "Life-Support Stopped for 6-Month-Old in Houston." HealthLawProfBlog, March 16. http://lawprofessors.typepad.com/healthlawprof _blog/2005/03/lifesupport_sto.html.

McCarter, M. 2005. "Lights! Camera! Training!" *Military Training Technology* 10, no. 2. http://www.military-training-technology.com/article.cfm?DocID=949.

McDonough, Richard. 2002. "Emergence and Creativity: Five Degrees of Freedom." In *Creativity, Cognition and Knowledge: An Interaction*, edited by Terry Dartnell. Westport, Conn.: Praeger.

McKinnon, Susan. 2006. *Neo-liberal Genetics: The Myths and Moral Tales of Evolutionary Psychology*. Chicago: Prickly Paradigm Press.

McMahan, Jeff. 2002. *The Ethics of Killing: Problems at the Margins of Life.* New York: Oxford University Press.

McNeill, William. 1995. *Keeping Together in Time: Dance and Drill in Human History.* Cambridge, Mass.: Harvard University Press.

Meaney, Michael. 2004. "The Nature of Nurture: Maternal Effects and Chromatin Remodeling." In *Essays in Social Neuroscience,* edited by John Cacioppo and Gary Bernston. Cambridge, Mass.: MIT Press.

Mills, Catherine. 2005. "Linguistic Survival and Ethicality: Biopolitics, Subjectivation and Testimony in *Remnants of Auschwitz.*" In *Politics, Metaphysics and Death: Essays on Giorgio Agamben's "Homo Sacer,"* edited by Andrew Norris. Durham, N.C.: Duke University Press.

Mintz, Sidney. 1985. *Sweetness and Power: The Place of Sugar in Modern History.* New York: Penguin.

Moore, Denise. 2005. "After the Flood." *This American Life* (NPR radio program), September 9.

Morowitz, Harold J. 2002. *The Emergence of Everything: How the World Became Complex.* New York: Oxford University Press.

Murphy, James. 1996. "Rational Choice Theory as Social Physics." In *The Rational Choice Controversy: Economic Models of Politics Reconsidered,* edited by Jeffrey Friedman. New Haven, Conn.: Yale University Press.

Nealon, Jeff. 2008. *Foucault beyond Foucault: Power and Its Intensifications since 1984.* Stanford, Calif.: Stanford University Press.

Negri, Antonio. 1991. *The Savage Anomaly: The Power of Spinoza's Metaphysics and Politics.* Translated by Michael Hardt. Minneapolis: University of Minnesota Press.

Niehoff, Debra. 1999. *The Biology of Violence.* New York: Free Press.

Nisbett, Richard E., and Dov Cohen. 1996. *Culture of Honor: The Psychology of Violence in the South.* Boulder, Colo.: Westview Press.

Noë, Alva. 2004. *Action in Perception.* Cambridge, Mass.: MIT Press.

Norman, Richard. 1969. "Aristotle's Philosopher-God." *Phronesis* 14:63–74.

Öhman, Arne. 1992. "Fear and Anxiety as Emotional Phenomena: Clinical, Phenomenological, Evolutionary Perspectives, and Information-Processing Mechanisms." In *Handbook of the Emotions,* edited by Michael Lewis and Jeannette Haviland. New York: Guilford.

O'Sullivan, Simon. 2006. *Art Encounters: Deleuze and Guattari: Thought beyond Representation.* London: Palgrave Macmillan.

Oyama, Susan. 2000 [1985]. *The Ontogeny of Information: Developmental Systems and Evolution.* 2nd ed. Durham, N.C.: Duke University Press.

Oyama, Susan, Paul Griffiths, and Russell Gray. 2001. *Cycles of Contingency.* Cambridge, Mass.: MIT Press.

Panksepp, Jaak. 1998. *Affective Neuroscience.* New York: Oxford University Press.

———. 2003. "Damasio's Error?" *Consciousness and Emotion* 4, no. 1:111–34.

Parisi, Luciana. 2004. *Abstract Sex: Philosophy, Bio-technology, and the Mutations of Desire*. London: Continuum.

Parkinson, Brian, Agneta Fischer, and Athony Manstead. 2005. *Emotions in Social Relations: Cultural, Group and Interpersonal Processes*. New York: Psychology Press.

Patton, Paul. 2000. *Deleuze and the Political*. New York: Routledge.

Pellegrin, Pierre. 1986. *Aristotle's Classfication of Animals*. Translated by Anthony Preus. Berkeley: University of California Press.

———. 1987. "Logical Difference and Biological Difference: The Unity of Aristotle's Thought." In *Philosophical Issues in Aristotle's Biology*, edited by Allan Gotthelf and James Lennox. Cambridge: Cambridge University Press.

Penland, S., P. F. Connor, A. Beall, S. Fearnley, and S. J. Williams. 2005. "Changes in Louisiana's Shoreline, 1855–2002." *Journal of Coastal Research* 44 (Spring): 7–39.

Phelps, Elizabeth, and Laura Thomas. 2003. "Race, Behavior, and the Brain: The Role of Neuroimaging in Understanding Complex Social Behaviors." *Political Psychology* 24, no. 4 (December): 747–58.

Pihlstrom, Sami. 1999. "What Shall We Do with Emergence? A Survey of a Fundamental Issue in the Metaphysics and Epistemology of Science." *South African Journal of Philosophy* 18, no. 2 (May): 192–211.

Preus, Anthony. 1975. *Science and Philosophy in Aristotle's Biological Writings*. New York: Olms.

Prinz, Jesse. 2004. *Gut Reactions: A Perceptual Theory of Emotion*. New York: Oxford University Press.

Protevi, John. 1994. *Time and Exteriority: Aristotle, Heidegger, Derrida*. Lewisburg, Penn.: Bucknell University Press.

———. 1998. "The 'Sense' of 'Sight': Heidegger and Merleau-Ponty on the Meaning of Bodily and Existential Sight." *Research in Phenomenology* 28:211–23.

———. 1999. "*Inventio* and the Unsurpassable Metaphor: Ricoeur's Treatment of Augustine's Time Meditation." *Philosophy Today* 43, no. 1:86–94.

———. 2000. "A Problem of Pure Matter: Fascist Nihilism in *A Thousand Plateaus*." In *Nihilism Now! Monsters of Energy*, edited by Diane Morgan and Keith Ansell Pearson. London: Macmillan.

———. 2001. *Political Physics: Deleuze, Derrida and the Body Politic*. London: Athlone/Continuum.

Raichle, Marcus. 2003. "Social Neuroscience: A Role for Brain Imaging." *Political Psychology* 24, no. 4:759–64.

Ratcliffe, Matthew. 2007. *Rethinking Commonsense Psychology: A Critique of Folk Psychology, Theory of Mind, and Simulation*. London: Palgrave Macmillan.

Rawls, John, Ronald Dworlin, Thomas Nagel, Robert Nozick, Thomas Scanlon, and Judith Jarvis Thomson. 1997. "Assisted Suicide: The Philosophers' Brief." *New York Review of Books*, February 27.

Richerson, Peter, and Robert Boyd. 2005. *Not by Genes Alone: How Culture Transformed Human Evolution.* Chicago: University of Chicago Press.

Richey, Warren. 2007. "US Terror Interrogation Went Too Far, Experts Say: Reports Find That Jose Padilla's Solitary Confinement Led to Mental Problems." *Christian Science Monitor*, August 13.

Robb, John. 2006. "The Secret of Hezbollah's Success." *Global Guerrillas.* http://globalguerrillas.typepad.com/globalguerrillas/2006/07/the_secrets_of_.html (July 26).

Robert, Jason Scott, Brian K. Hall, and Wendy M. Olson. 2001. "Bridging the Gap between Developmental Systems Theory and Evolutionary Developmental Biology." *Bioessays* 23, no. 10:954–62.

Robinson, Daniel. 1989. *Aristotle's Psychology.* New York: Columbia University Press.

Rochat, Philippe. 2001. *The Infant's World.* Cambridge, Mass.: Harvard University Press.

Rodrigue, John. 2001. *Reconstruction in the Cane Fields.* Baton Rouge: Louisiana State University Press.

Rodríguez, Havidán, Joseph Trainor, and Enrico L. Quarantelli. 2006. "Rising to the Challenges of a Catastrophe: The Emergent and Prosocial Behavior Following Hurricane Katrina." *Annals of the American Academy of Political and Social Science* 604 (March): 82–101.

Rosch, Eleanor. 1978. "Principles of Categorization." In *Cognition and Categorization*, edited by Eleanor Rosch and Barbara Lloyd. Hillsdale, N.J.: Lawrence Erlbaum.

Rose, Hilary, and Steven Rose. 2000. *Alas, Poor Darwin: Arguments against Evolutionary Psychology.* New York: Harmony Books.

Rothschild, Babette, and Marjorie Reid. 2006. *Help for the Helper: The Psychophysiology of Compassion Fatigue and Vicarious Trauma.* New York: Norton.

Rudrauf, David, Antoine Lutz, Diego Cosmelli, Jean-Philippe Lachaux, and Michel Le Van Quyen. 2003. "From Autopoiesis to Neurophenomenology: Francisco Varela's Exploration of the Biophysics of Being." *Biological Research* 36, no. 1:27–65.

Sargant, William. 1957. *Battle for the Mind: A Physiology of Conversion and Brain-Washing.* New York: Doubleday.

Satz, Debra, and John Ferejohn. 1994. "Rational Choice and Social Theory." *Journal of Philosophy* 91, no. 2:71–87.

Sawyer, R. Keith. 2001. "Emergence in Sociology: Contemporary Philosophy of Mind and Some Implications for Sociological Theory." *American Journal of Sociology* 107, no. 3:551–85.

Scahill, Jeremy. 2005. "Blackwater Down." *Nation*, October 10.

———. 2007. *Blackwater: The Rise of the World's Most Powerful Mercenary Army.* New York: Nation Books.

Scarry, Elaine. 1985. *The Body in Pain: The Making and the Unmaking of the World.* New York: Oxford University Press.

Schivelbusch, Wolfgang. 1993. *Tastes of Paradise: A Social History of Spices, Stimulants, and Intoxicants.* New York: Vintage.

Schore, Allan. 1994. *Affect Regulation and the Origin of the Self: The Neurobiology of Emotional Development.* Hillsdale, N.J.: Lawrence Earlbaum.

———. 2000. "The Self-Organization of the Right Brain and the Neurobiology of Emotional Development." In *Emotion, Development and Self-Organization: Dynamic Systems Approaches to Emotional Development,* edited by Marc Lewis and Isabela Granic. New York: Cambridge University Press.

Schreber, Daniel Paul. 2000. *Memoirs of My Nervous Illness.* New York: NYRB Classics.

Schröder, Jürgen. 1998. "Emergence: Non-Deducibility or Downwards Causation?" *Philosophical Quarterly* 48, no. 193:433–52.

Schwartz, Barry, Richard Schuldenfrei, and Hugh Lacey. 1979. "Operant Psychology as Factory Psychology." *Behaviorism* 6:229–54.

Sedley, David. 1991. "Is Aristotle's Teleology Anthropocentric?" *Phronesis* 36, no. 2:179–96.

Selinger, Evan. Forthcoming. *Embodying Technoscience.* Copenhagen: VIP Press.

Shanks, Niall, and Karl Joplin. 1999. "Redundant Complexity: A Critical Analysis of Intelligent Design in Biochemistry." *Philosophy of Science* 66, no. 2:268–82.

Shay, Jonathon. 1995. *Achilles in Vietnam.* New York: Scribner.

———. 2002. *Odysseus in America.* New York: Scribner.

Shusterman, Richard. 2008. *Body Consciousness: A Philosophy of Mindfulness and Somaesthetics.* Cambridge: Cambridge University Press.

Silberstein, Michael, and John McGeever. 1999. "The Search for Ontological Emergence." *Philosophical Quarterly* 49, no. 195:182–200.

Simons, Ronald. 1996. *Boo! Culture, Experience, and the Startle Reflex.* New York: Oxford University Press.

Singer, Peter. 1999. *A Darwinian Left: Politics, Evolution, and Cooperation.* New Haven, Conn.: Yale University Press.

Singer, T., B. Seymour, J. O'Doherty, H. Kaube, R. J. Dolan, and C. Frith. 2004. "Empathy for Pain Involves the Affective but Not Sensory Components of Pain." *Science* 303 (February 20, 2004): 1157–62.

Sinnerbrink, Robert. 2005. "From *Machenschaft* to Biopolitics: A Genealogical Critique of Biopower." *Critical Horizons* 6, no. 1:239–65.

Smith, Daniel W. 1996. "Deleuze's Theory of Sensation: Overcoming the Kantian Duality." In *Deleuze: A Critical Reader,* edited by Paul Patton. Oxford: Blackwell.

———. 2003. "Deleuze and the Liberal Tradition." *Economy and Society* 32, no. 2 (May): 288–324.

Solomon, Robert, ed. 2004. *Thinking about Feeling: Contemporary Philosophers on Emotions.* New York: Oxford University Press.

Spurett, David. 2000. "Bhaskar on Open and Closed Systems." *South African Journal of Philosophy* 19, no. 3:188–209.

Sterelny, Kim, and Paul Griffiths. 1999. *Sex and Death: An Introduction to Philosophy of Biology*. Chicago: University of Chicago Press.

Stern, Daniel. 1985. *The Interpersonal World of the Infant: A View from Psychoanalysis and Developmental Psychology*. New York: Basic Books.

Strevens, Michael. 2003. *Bigger than Chaos: Understanding Complexity through Probability*. Cambridge, Mass.: Harvard University Press.

Strogatz, Steven. 2003. *Sync: How Order Emerges from Chaos in the Universe, Nature, and Everyday Life*. New York: Hyperion.

Stueber, Karsten. 2006. *Rediscovering Empathy: Agency, Folk Psychology, and the Human Sciences*. Cambridge, Mass.: MIT Press.

Sylvan, Robin. 2005. *Trance Formation: The Spiritual and Religious Dimensions of Global Rave Culture*. New York: Routledge.

Thamer, Hans-Ulrich. 1996. "The Orchestration of the National Community: The Nuremberg Part Rallies of the NSDAP." In *Fascism and Theatre: Comparative Studies on the Aesthetics and Politics of Performance in Europe, 1925–1945*, edited by Günther Berghaus. Providence, R.I.: Berghahn Books.

Thevenot, Brian, and Gordon Russell. 2005. "Reports of Anarchy at Superdome Overstated." *Seattle Times*, September 26.

Theweleit, Klaus. 1987–89. *Male Fantasies*. 2 vols. Minneapolis: University of Minnesota Press.

Thompson, Evan. 2001. "Empathy and Consciousness." *Journal of Consciousness Studies* 8, nos. 5–7:1–32.

———. 2007. *Mind in Life: Biology, Phenomenology, and the Sciences of Mind*. Cambridge, Mass.: Harvard University Press.

Thompson, Evan, and Francisco J. Varela. 2001. "Radical Embodiment: Neural Dynamics and Consciousness." *Trends in Cognitive Sciences* 5, no. 10:418–25.

Thompson, Kevin. 2004. "The Spiritual Disciplines of Biopower." *Radical Philosophy Review* 7, no. 1:59–76.

Tidwell, Mike. 2004. *Bayou Farewell: The Rich Life and Tragic Death of Louisiana's Cajun Coast*. New York: Vintage.

Tierney, John. 2004. "The 2004 Campaign: Advertising. Using M.R.I.'s to See Politics on the Brain." *New York Times*, April 20.

Tierney, Kathleen, and Christine Bevc. 2007. "Disaster as War: Militarism and the Social Construction of Disaster in New Orleans." In *The Sociology of Katrina: Perspectives on a Modern Catastrophe*, edited by David L. Brunsma, David Overfelt, and J. Steven Picou. New York: Rowman and Littlefield.

Tierney, Kathleen, Christine Bevc, and Erica Kuligowski. 2006. "Metaphors Matter: Disaster Myths, Media Frames, and Their Consequences in Hurricane Katrina." *Annals of the American Academy of Political and Social Science* 604 (March): 57–81.

Toch, Hans. 1992. *Violent Men: An Inquiry into the Psychology of Violence*. Washington, D.C.: American Psychological Association.

Toscano, Alberto. 2006. *The Theatre of Production*. London: Palgrave Macmillan.

Travis, John. 2005. "Scientist's Fears Come True as Hurricane Floods New Orleans." *Science* 309 (September 9): 1656–59.

Turner, Jonathan. 2000. *On the Origins of Human Emotions: A Sociological Inquiry into the Evolution of Human Affect*. Stanford, Calif.: Stanford University Press.

Turner, J. Scott. 2000. *The Extended Organism: The Physiology of Animal-Built Structures*. Cambridge, Mass.: Harvard University Press.

U.S. Army Corps of Engineers (USACE). 2005. Press release, September 3. http://www.usace.army.mil/PA-09-01.pdf.

Van der Kolk, Bessel. 1996. "The Body Keeps the Score: Approaches to the Psychobiology of Posttraumatic Stress Disorder." In *Traumatic Stress*, edited by Bessel Van der Kolk, Alexander McFarlane, and Lars Weisaeth. New York: Guilford.

Van der Kolk, Bessel, and Mark Greenberg. 1987. "The Psychobiology of the Trauma Response: Hyperarousal, Constriction, and Addiction to Traumatic Reexposure." In *Psychological Trauma*, edited by Bessel A. Van der Kolk. Washington, D.C.: American Psychiatric Press.

Van de Vijver, Gertrudis, Linda Van Speyboeck, and Windy Vandevyvere. 2003. "Reflecting on Complexity of Biological Systems: Kant and Beyond?" *Acta Biotheoretica* 51:101–40.

Van de Vijver, Gertrudis, Linda Van Speybroeck, Dani De Waele, Filip Kolen, and Helena De Preester. 2005. "Philosophy of Biology: Outline of a Transcendental Project." *Acta Biotheoretica* 53:57–75.

van Heerden, Ivor. 2007. *The Storm: What Went Wrong and Why during Hurricane Katrina*. New York: Penguin.

Varela, Francisco J. 1976. "Not One, Not Two." *CoEvolution Quarterly*, Fall, 62–67.

———. 1979. "Reflections on the Chilean Civil War." *Lindisfarne Letter* 8 (Winter): 13–19.

———. 1991. "Organism: A Meshwork of Selfless Selves." In *Organism and the Origins of Self*, edited by Alfred I. Tauber. The Hague: Kluwer.

———. 1995. "Resonant Cell Assemblies: A New Approach to Cognitive Functions and Neuronal Synchrony." *Biological Research* 28:81–95.

———. 1999. "The Specious Present: A Neurophenomenology of Time Consciousness." In *Naturalizing Phenomenology: Issues in Contemporary Phenomenology and Cognitive Science*, edited by Jean Petitot, Francisco J. Varela, Bernard Pachoud, and Jean-Michel Roy. Stanford, Calif.: Stanford University Press.

———. 2002. "Autopoïese et émergence." In *La Complexité, vertiges et promesses*, edited by Réda Benkirane. Paris: Le Pommier.

Varela, Francisco J., and Nathalie Depraz. 2000. "At the Source of Time: Valence and the Constitutional Dynamics of Affect." In *Ipseity and Alterity: Interdisciplinary Approaches to Intersubjectivity*, edited by S. Gallagher and S. Watson. Rouen: Publications de l'Université de Rouen.

Varela, Francisco J., F. J. Lachaux, J.-P. Rodriguez, and J. Martinerie. 2001. "The

Brainweb: Phase Synchronization and Large-Scale Integration." *Nature Reviews: Neuroscience* 2:229–39.

Varela, Francisco J., Evan Thompson, and Elizabeth Rosch. 1991. *The Embodied Mind.* Cambridge, Mass.: MIT Press.

Vogt, Erik. 2005. "S/Citing the Camp." In *Politics, Metaphysics and Death: Essays on Giorgio Agamben's "Homo Sacer,"* edited by Andrew Norris. Durham, N.C.: Duke University Press.

Watson, Justin. 2002. *The Martyrs of Columbine.* New York: Palgrave Macmillan.

Watt, Douglas. 2000. "Emotion and Consciousness: Part II. A Review of Antonio Damasio's *The Feeling of What Happens.*" *Journal of Consciousness Studies* 7, no. 3:72–84.

Weber, Andreas, and Francisco J. Varela. 2002. "Life after Kant: Natural Purposes and the Autopoietic Foundations of Biological Individuality." *Phenomenology and the Cognitive Sciences* 1, no. 2:97–125.

Webster, P. J., G. J. Holland, J. A. Curry, and H. R. Chang. 2005. "Changes in Tropical Cyclone Number, Duration, and Intensity in a Warming Environment." *Science* 309:1844–46.

Wedin, Michael. 1988. *Mind and Imagination in Aristotle.* New Haven, Conn.: Yale University Press.

Weinberg, Bennett, and Bonnie Bealer. 2002. *The World of Caffeine: The Science and Culture of the World's Most Popular Drug.* New York: Routledge.

Weizman, Eyal. 2007. *Hollow Land: Israel's Architecture of Occupation.* London: Verso.

West-Eberhard, Mary Jane. 2003. *Developmental Plasticity and Evolution.* New York: Oxford University Press.

Wheeler, Michael. 1997. "Cognition's Coming Home: The Reunion of Mind and Life." In *Proceedings of the Fourth European Conference on Artificial Life,* edited by P. Husbands and I. Harvey. Cambridge, Mass.: MIT Press.

———. 2005. *Reconstructing the Cognitive World.* Cambridge, Mass.: MIT Press.

Will, George. 2005. "Leviathan in Louisiana." *Newsweek,* September 12.

Williams, James. 2003. *Gilles Deleuze's "Difference and Repetition": A Critical Introduction and Guide.* Edinburgh: Edinburgh University Press.

———. 2005. *Understanding Poststructuralism.* Chesham, Ireland: Acumen Press.

Wills, Garry. 2003. *"Negro President": Jefferson and the Slave Power.* Boston: Houghton Mifflin.

Wilson, Robert A. 2004. *Boundaries of the Mind: The Individual in the Fragile Sciences: Cognition.* Cambridge: Cambridge University Press.

Wood, Denis. 2004. *Five Billion Years of Global Change.* New York: Guilford.

Young, Iris Marion. 2005. *On Female Body Experience: "Throwing Like a Girl" and Other Essays.* New York: Oxford University Press.

Younge, Gary. 2005. "Murder and Rape: Fact or Fiction?" *Guardian,* September 6.

Zahavi, Dan. 2005. *Subjectivity and Selfhood.* Cambridge, Mass.: MIT Press.

Publication History

Portions of chapter 1 were previously published as "Deleuze, Guattari, and Emergence," *Paragraph: A Journal of Modern Critical Theory* 29, no. 2 (July 2006): 19–39. Reprinted with permission of Edinburgh University Press.

Portions of chapters 1 and 2 were previously published as "Beyond Autopoiesis: Inflections of Emergence and Politics in the Work of Francisco Varela," in *Emergence and Embodiment: Essays in Neocybernetics,* ed. Bruce Clarke and Mark Hansen (Durham, N.C.: Duke University Press, 2008), 94–112. Copyright 2008. Reprinted with permission of Duke University Press.

Portions of chapters 3 and 4 were previously published as "The Organism as the Judgment of God: Aristotle, Kant, and Deleuze on Nature (That Is, on Biology, Theology, and Politics)," in *Deleuze and Religion,* ed. Mary Bryden (London: Routledge, 2001), 30–41. Reprinted with permission of Taylor and Francis Books.

Portions of chapter 5 were previously published as "The Terri Schiavo Case: Biopolitics and Biopower," in *Deleuze and Law: Forensic Futures,* ed. Rosi Braidotti, Claire Colebrook, and Patrick Hanafin (London: Palgrave Macmillan, 2008), 59–72. Reprinted with permission of Palgrave Macmillan.

Portions of chapter 5 were previously published as "The Schiavo Case: Deleuzean Jurisprudence, Biopower, and Privacy as Singularity," in *Deleuzean Events: Writing/ History,* ed. Hanjo Berressem (Hamburg: Lit Lektorat, 2008), 203–20. Reprinted with permission of Lit Lektorat.

Portions of chapter 6 were previously published as "Affect, Agency, and Responsibility: The Act of Killing in the Age of Cyborgs," *Phenomenology and the Cognitive Sciences* 7, no. 2 (2008): 405–13. Reprinted with the kind permission of Springer Science and Business Media.

Portions of chapter 7 were previously published as "Katrina," *Symposium: Canadian Journal of Continental Philosophy / Revue canadienne de philosophie continentale* 10, no. 1 (Spring 2006): 363–81.

Index

John Protevi is professor of French studies at Louisiana State University. His other books include *Political Physics: Deleuze, Derrida, and the Body Politic* and *Time and Exteriority: Aristotle, Heidegger, Derrida.*

10/12/12

"Imbrications" = Overlapping
like shingles, a
tiles

Producing bodies—politic for
civic action, neighborhood
involvement, ~~visga~~ street
planning, residential—neighboring
connection.

When turning to advocacy,
we claimed residents, we
claimed community, we
claimed group, we claimed
majority.

Cato's Group controversy

Purcell: You're one of
these big clothes
are, I'm a resident